THE PROBLEM OF FREEDOM IN MARXIST THOUGHT

SOVIETICA

PUBLICATIONS AND MONOGRAPHS

OF THE INSTITUTE OF EAST-EUROPEAN STUDIES

UNIVERSITY OF FRIBOURG/SWITZERLAND

Edited by

PROF. DR J. M. BOCHEŃSKI

VOLUME 32

JAMES J. O'ROURKE

THE PROBLEM OF FREEDOM
IN MARXIST THOUGHT

*An Analysis of the Treatment of Human Freedom
by Marx, Engels, Lenin
and Contemporary Soviet Philosophy*

D. REIDEL PUBLISHING COMPANY

DORDRECHT-HOLLAND / BOSTON-U.S.A.

Library of Congress Catalog Card Number 73–86095

ISBN 90 277 0383 3

Published by D. Reidel Publishing Company
P.O. Box 17, Dordrecht, Holland

Sold and distributed in the U.S.A., Canada, and Mexico
by D. Reidel Publishing Company, Inc.
306 Dartmouth Street, Boston,
Mass. 02116, U.S.A.

Printed in The Netherlands by D. Reidel, Dordrecht

to
Carol
and to
my Mother and Father

TABLE OF CONTENTS

PART II / SOVIET PHILOSOPHY

PREFACE

This study seeks to present the theory of freedom as found in one line of the Marxist tradition, that which begins with Marx and Engels and continues through Lenin to contemporary Soviet philosophy. Although the primary goal is simply to describe how freedom is conceived by the thinkers of this tradition, an attempt is also made to ascertain whether or not their views are strongly deterministic, as has often been presumed by Western commentators.

A remark is in order regarding the scope of the term 'contemporary Soviet philosophy'. The Soviet stage in Marxist philosophy stretches back to the 1917 revolution. However, for the purposes of this study only works published after 1947 were examined, and the vast majority of them date from the 1960's. Apart from the fact that most works of previous periods were not available, bibliographical indications, such as the titles of the articles in *Pod znamenem marksizma,* did not suggest that the theory of freedom was then a major concern. In fact, even after 1947 there was little development of this theme until the upsurge of works in philosophical anthropology during the last decade. On the other hand, it is not being suggested that the conception of freedom found in recent writings is representative of earlier Soviet philosophy, during the Stalinist 'dead' period or earlier. Only further research could establish that.

This work was presented as a doctoral dissertation at the University of Fribourg, Switzerland, under the direction of Professor J. M. Bocheński. The research was done at the University's Institute of East European Studies. To its director, Professor Bocheński, I owe an unpayable debt of gratitude: without his encouragement and advice, this study would not have been completed; without his own work as a model of philosophical scholarship, it would have been much more defective than it is. I would also like to thank the other members of the Institute for their many hours of good-hearted and serious discussion, so useful for the clarification of my own tasks. Finally, the greatest credit must be given to my patient and long-suffering wife, who literally saw the work through from beginning to end, encouraging the original plan, sustaining the research with constant moral support and contributing materially to its completion by typing the manuscript and correcting the proofs.

St. Anselm's College
Manchester, N.H.

CHAPTER I

INTRODUCTION

1. POINT OF DEPARTURE

It would be difficult to find a basic notion over which the East and the West appear to be more divided than that of human freedom. This point of ideological conflict has been so obvious that it has even been endorsed by the matter-of-factness of language, which has accepted the characteristic of 'freedom'[1] as a basis for classifying communist and non-communist nations: the latter being referred to collectively as the 'free world', with the implication that the former are somehow unfree. Moreover, Western commentators on communism have always sought to substantiate this usage by pointing to the totalitarian nature of the Soviet system and the anti-humanistic aspects of communist ideology. From their own side, the communists have been no less vocal in attacking the 'enslavement of man' in the capitalist system and in hailing their own political and social doctrine as the true basis for the final liberation of humanity. In short, one of the most basic and hotly argued disputes between the communist and non-communist worlds concerns the question – who is the true guardian of freedom?

It must be emphasized at the very beginning that this dispute is not the point of departure of the present work, and that it will not be our concern to establish whether the communist systems and their general ideology are inimical or favorable to the social and political freedom of man. Such a study would have to be based on broad empirical data and would necessarily have to take into account the social, historical, political and cultural factors which contributed to the formation of communism as a concrete reality. This is a task for a political scientist or sociologist, and has in fact received the attention of numerous Western scholars.[2]

Our point of departure is that vast body of theoretical doctrine which is known as Marxist–Leninist philosophy. There can be no doubt that however one may question the monolithic and homogeneous quality of Soviet thought[3], it does seek to work out a philosophical explanation to satisfy virtually every major problem raised in the history of Western philosophy. It is a system to the extent that it seeks completeness; and this system displays a unity which derives both from the closed tradition of the classics and the peculiar boundary lines dictated by the demands of political ideology. Now within the context of this body of thought, an attempt has been made to present a Marxist–Leninist solution to the problem of freedom. This has been recognized as one of the perennial problems of philosophy[4], and has been treated on a niveau which, although it does not attain that of Soviet ontology or epistemology, nevertheless exceeds that of ideology and represents genuine philosophical reflexion. It is this philosophical reflexion, and not the political and ideological pronouncements on freedom, which will be the main concern of this study.

The fact that this study will abstain from drawing any connections between the philosophy and the reality of communism will certainly disappoint those who take seriously the doctrine of the unity of theory and practice and see it embodied, in an exemplary manner, in the Soviet notion of freedom.[5] Without denying that communism is in a genuine sense a philosophy in action, let us only underline, that from a *methodological* point of view it is especially important in the treatment of the notion of freedom to separate theory and practice in a rigorous manner, for the temptation here is great to allow judgments on the political realities of communism prejudice an objective assessment of the Soviet philosophical position.

2. NATURE OF THE WORK

The following pages will present and analyze the most general, fundamental notions concerning human freedom as they were introduced by Marx and Engels, passed on by Lenin, and finally interpreted and articulated by contemporary Soviet philosophers. Thus this study is, first of all, exclusively *theoretical*. It will be concerned with the ultimate nature of human freedom, within the contexts of ontology, philosophical psychology, and moral and social philosophy. The questions to be discussed are those such as: Is freedom compatible with universal determinism? Does man have freedom of choice? What is the relation between free will and moral responsibility? These are properly philosophical questions and cannot be handled in any other discipline. Secondly, this study is *historical*. It will not attempt any systematic answers to these questions but will be concerned to present the answers which are found in the classics of Marxism–Leninism and the writings of contemporary Soviet philosophers. The criticism will be predominantly immanent. It must further be specified that although the treatment of the classics is quite extensive, due to the absence of a satisfactory secondary literature, nevertheless it assumes a secondary role, insofar as it serves principally to lay down the foundations for the subsequent presentation of the Soviet view. An exhaustive study of the notion of freedom in Marx, for example, would have to be both more detailed and broader in scope than our treatment. Thus, the present work can be regarded as a contribution to Sovietology, and insofar as it is philosophical Sovietology it falls within the *genre* of the history of contemporary philosophy.

3. PREVIOUS STUDIES

In spite of the fact that the problem of freedom and determinism is one of the most basic and inherently interesting philosophical problems, there have been no book-length studies and, to the best of the author's knowledge, not even a single article published in the West on the treatment of this problem in Soviet philosophy. This can be traced partially to the long-running neglect of anthropological questions in Soviet philosophical works themselves. Indeed, as late as 1959 a Western Sovietologist could observe that "questions dealing with the person" had not yet received in Soviet philosophy any ready-made answers, and that this problem area was one of the "empty domains" where future development was to be hoped for.[6] To a certain extent this hope has been fulfilled, for the sixties have witnessed a significant upsurge in Soviet publications on the philosophical problems of man.[7] And the notion of freedom was one of the beneficiaries of this boom.[8] Thus, the recent substantial work in this area seems to indicate an important lacuna in Western philosophical Sovietology.

On the other hand, although no separate studies have been written, one can find summary treatments and isolated remarks, first of all in works dealing with broader topics or with the entirety of Soviet philosophy.[9] Here the Soviet interpretation of the meaning of freedom is approached from a particular, limited point of view, in keeping with the scope and aim of the work as a whole. Also, with one exception,[10] the bibliographical base of these treatments is extremely narrow, principally due to the fact that these works ante-date the recent crescendo of Soviet publications on philosophical anthropology. Still, in this indirect and rather modest literature on the subject, some of the root conceptions which figure prominently in the Soviet position are explained and criticized. Secondly, if one looks beyond Sovietological literature to studies of 'Marxism–Leninism' and 'Marxism'[11], i.e. those which are based mainly on the 'classics', the literature on freedom becomes somewhat broader.[12] These works would seem to reveal indirectly the Soviet view, since Soviet philosophy is deliberately and wholeheartedly Marxist–Leninist. Yet in this connection it must be noted that there have been no studies of freedom in Engels – his position has been more or less explicitly identified with that of Marx[13] – or in Lenin; and in certain ways these thinkers are more important for Soviet philosophy than is Marx. Finally, there are of course numerous studies which touch on the 'Marxian' notion of freedom, especially as it is found in the *Frühschriften*. It has been assumed – by extrapolating from the political realities – that Marx's early humanist ideas have not been taken over by the Soviets[14], and thus that the new Marxology is not directly relevant to the understanding of the Soviet theory.[15] This assumption will be examined below. Here let it only be remarked that this Marxological literature does not intend to reveal the Soviet position.

4. PRELIMINARY SURVEY OF THE PROBLEMS

Now one of the most striking features of this secondary literature, with the exception of Marxology, is its consistently critical attitude. For one reason or another, the Marxist–Leninist view is taken to task, and the total picture which emerges is decidedly negative. That is, it is asserted that human freedom is denied or explained away, or that the deterministic principles of Marxist–Leninist philosophy effectively exclude the possibility of freedom, and therefore that in the debate between freedom and determinism, Marxist–Leninists clearly belong to the determinist[16] camp.

It will be helpful, in providing a first orientation in some of the problems which must be discussed in a presentation of the Marxist–Leninist theory of freedom, to restate briefly some of these criticisms. To determine whether they are correct will be one of the partial aims of our later investigations.

(a) Perhaps the most frequently voiced objection to Marxism is that which points to the incompatibility of freedom and *historical determinism*. In the Marxist view history is governed by laws in much the same way as are natural phenomena; or at least there is a close analogy between the two. Further, it is even maintained by Marxists that knowledge of these laws enables one to predict future events. Now – the objection runs – if history is a determined, law-bound process, then what significance can possibly be ascribed to the human will?[17] The actions of men can no longer be regarded as issuing from free decisions of the will; if they are law-bound, then they are mere links in the total causal process of history. Consequently, the affirmation of historical laws directly rules out the possibility of human freedom.

A closely related objection focuses on Marxist *economic determinism*. This doctrine allegedly asserts "that all human conduct is determined by economic processes, by the class structure of society".[18] It is further pointed out that according to the Marxist view the real motives of an individual's actions are not known to him. Although he thinks that he is deciding on a particular course of action because it is right, this is an illusion. In fact, "all his decisions are determined by class interest".[19] Such a conception, which might be called 'psycho-economic determinism', clearly explains away the reality of free choice in much the same manner as does Freud's theory of the unconscious motivation of psychic acts.[20]

(b) The ontology of Marxism–Leninism is dialectical *materialism*. This means that it sees the unity of the world in its materiality. Everything real is either matter or a form of the existence of matter. Nothing else exists – especially not an autonomous spiritual order. Now Western critics have maintained that such an ontological materialism rules out freedom.[21] What lies behind this critique is the view that while all material phenomena are connected with one another in unambiguous and fully determined relations, in the realm of the human spirit there is an openness, a relative indeterminacy within whose limits the person can function as the source of his own decisions and actions. Without this autonomy – exactly what the Marxists allegedly deny – freedom seems to be excluded.

(c) Turning from one basic constituent of Marxism–Leninism, its materialism, to the other basic constituent, its *dialectics* of being, we find in the Western literature an even more severe critique of its conse- quences for personal freedom. It centers around the "dialectical theory of the individual"[22]. According to this theory, which is seen to be basi- cally of Hegelian derivation, the individual has reality only insofar as he exists within the whole *(das Ganze)* or the 'universal'. That is, indivi- dual being has merely a relative status; its existence is equivalent to its integration in a larger entity which alone really exists. Consequently, the person, who falls under the category 'individual', has no autonomous being; he is not a subsistent subject but a mere moment in the structure of a larger whole. Now it is pointed out by the critics that this larger whole which really exists is, in Marxist theory, the society, or humanity. Thus the individual person is totally integrated, ontologically, into society; he has reality only insofar as he is a "concrete appearance *(Erscheinung)* of the social universal *(Sozial-Allgemeinen)*".[23] Expressed in slightly different terms, this socio-ontological theory upholds a total identity of individual and society, and reserves substantiality only for the latter.[24]

It is obvious that this position is in fact the most radical denial of personal freedom. If the individual has no substantiality, if he has no autonomy of being, it is senseless to inquire further whether some of his activities, e.g., his decisions, can be free, for this would presume his reality as a subject. But for the Marxist–Leninist – so the critique runs – only the society or humanity as a whole is a real subject and can function as the bearer of freedom.[25]

(d) If the previous three critiques have sought to show that freedom is incompatible with the principles of Marxism–Leninism – its historical and economic determinism, its materialism, and its dialectics – a fourth critique claims that the Marxist–Leninists' own explanation of freedom is itself a rejection of the true meaning of the word. It is pointed out that Engels accepted as valid the Hegelian thesis that freedom is "insight into necessity", and further that Plekhanov's interpretation of this thesis more or less expresses the prevailing Soviet view.[26] Now according to this famous Russian Marxist, man is free when he becomes conscious of the necessity of his actions. The free man is the one who in seeing his lack of free will, realizes the "subjective and objective impossibility of acting differently"[27] than he is acting, and at the same time regards this action as desirable. Thereby, the dualism of subject and object is overcome in the Hegelian sense, that "freedom is this, to wish nothing but oneself".[28] In human consciousness, there occurs a total identification with necessity, so that one can say both that "freedom has grown out of necessity" and that necessity has been "transformed into freedom".[29] With regard to the historical context, the Plekhanovite view explains man's acts as necessary links in the chain of historical events; the person is 'free' precisely to the extent that he realizes the inescapable necessity of his own historical role.

Now this view has been taken to task on several accounts: (1) that it places freedom in the understanding, while in reality freedom is a property of the will;[30] (2) that it assumes an infinite being, "in whom there is no place for a restriction by an object standing outside of and over against it"[31], and that to speak of freedom as "conscious necessity" in relation to finite beings means nothing else than an "actual denial of individual freedom";[32] (3) finally, that it is clearly fatalistic.[33] These critical observations are meant to apply both to Plekhanov and to contemporary Soviet philosophers, whose positions are seen as identical.[34]

(e) As a final point, it can simply be observed that almost every commentator on Soviet Marxism–Leninism asserts that freedom of choice is simply denied by Soviet philosophers.[35]

This manifold critique, which is found scattered in the Western literature on Marxism–Leninism, shows that there is not one but several dilemmas of freedom and determinism which arise within this system. There is a whole nest of problems which spring from the principles of dialectical and historical materialism, and it will be necessary to treat each one in its turn.

5. AIM AND GENERAL OUTLINE

The primary purpose of this study will be to present the understanding of freedom in the Marxist tradition from the early Marx to contemporary Soviet philosophers. That is, the primary concern will be to describe

how they understand human freedom in its various forms and connections. A secondary aim will be to ascertain whether or not these views
are decidedly deterministic, in the manner in which it is understood
and criticized by Western commentators, as presented in the previous
section.

It will be necessary first to examine the classics – Marx, Engels and
Lenin – because the Soviets depend heavily on them in working out
their own theory of freedom, more so than in other areas of philosophy.
This will constitute Part I. Part II will begin with an examination of
some general principles of the Soviet conception of man which are
important for an understanding of human freedom, and then proceed
to a treatment of the doctrine of freedom, both in its general principles
and specific forms. A conclusion will summarize and evaluate some
of the results.

PART I

THE CLASSICS

CHAPTER II

MARX

The notion of freedom plays a central role in the thought of Karl Marx. Although Marx does not offer us many explicit descriptions of what he means by 'freedom' – partially because he grew weary of hearing social reformers ineffectually parade it about – there is no doubt that his notion of freedom often figures significantly in the background which gives meaning to his more specific and immediate concerns. It is for him one of those fundamental categories which are constantly assumed, and often seem nearly too obvious to be explained. For example, one can easily forget that the ultimate meaning of history is not the mere development of socio-economic forms culminating in a communist system, but rather the progressive liberation of mankind. Similarly, the notion of freedom lurks behind the critique of religion and the whole description of the forms of economic alienation. Further, as will be seen presently, the theme of the freedom of man has a pervasiveness and extent in the long development of his thought which marks it as one of those basic themes providing continuity to his work. He articulated certain basic principles of his understanding of freedom even before working out the critique of alienation, and he saw fit to reiterate these principles, though in a different perspective, as late as the third, posthumously published volume of *Capital*.

It is well-known that Marx's thought undergoes a very profound evolution. What must not be forgotten is that this is an evolution in *genre* of thought and prevailing subject matter rather than a reversal of positions. Beginning with philosophical analysis, he turns to social theory and finally to economics, intermittently devoting his efforts to political journalism. And even this shift of interest is not totally exclusive: one can find social theory in his philosophical works, economics in his political journalism, and, most important for us, philosophical remarks and assumptions in all of them. It is mainly within Marx's very early period, where he is engaged in separating himself from the philosophical teaching of Hegel which he had once enthusiastically embraced, that his 'development' means the rejection of previously held convictions. Here Marx turns against his patrimony, gradually and selectively criticizing those Hegelian principles that did not accord with his emerging social humanism.

This holds equally well for the development of his theory of freedom. In those early works preceding the *Economic and Philosophical Manuscripts,* there is an evident chronological progress of the rejection and acceptance of certain positions. But the total conception which emerges at the end of this period remains relevant for the rest of his work. It is not later rejected, but merely allowed to fall into the background. From that point on, Marx moves on to different themes and endeavors without actually contradicting his previous work; he simply abandons it. First there is the discussion of freedom within the context of the theory of alienation. This discussion is found predominantly in the *Economic and Philosophical Manuscripts;* but one finds the basic points repeated in the *German Ideology* and even, with different clothing, in *Capital.* In a similar way, the problematic of the relation between human freedom and the forms and movement of history is not restricted to any one work, or at some point rejected by Marx. One can only say that it is one of the basic themes of Marx's thought.

For this reason, the present chapter can adopt neither a purely chronological nor a strictly thematic plan. The very first works (up to 1843) will be presented in the order in which Marx wrote them, to show the emergence of a Marxian theory of freedom over against the Hegelian philosophy of spirit. Here some of Marx's basic notions relevant to his understanding of freedom will be brought to light. Following will be two 'thematic' sections: the first will deal with freedom and alienation, Marx's analysis of man's loss of freedom and the presentation of an ideal in whose realization this loss will be recouped; the second section will be devoted to the structure of the historical process and man's relation to it, examining two inter-related aspects – the sense in which history is a continual liberation of mankind, and the emphasis on history's 'determination' of human actions. In the final section, after a summary of the results of the first three sections, there will be an examination of two particular notions to which Marx only very seldom addressed himself but which greatly interest scholars concerned with his philosophical anthropology, namely the ontological autonomy of the person and the notion of free will. In conclusion, an attempt will be made to judge how well Marx stands up to the charges of determinism presented in the introduction.

1. THE EMERGENCE OF MARX'S THEORY OF FREEDOM FROM THE 'PHILOSOPHY OF SPIRIT'

The Hegelian philosphy was the theoretical frame of reference within which the young Marx formulated his thought.[1] At first an avowed disciple of Hegel, he only gradually separated himself from Hegel's views. This is particularly evident in the discussion of freedom found in the earliest writings, those which pre-date the *Economic and Philosophical Manuscripts*. Here we can see Marx operating with Hegelian categories, but progressively altering their sense and finally explicitly rejecting some of the basic Hegelian notions.

The early writings are not only important as a stage in Marx's intellectual development. They also contain key ideas which Marx never abandons, and since their mode of expression is much more philosophical than the later writings (and it is accepted here as legitimate to seek a philosophical doctrine in Marx[2]) they are of indispensable value for comprehending the whole of Marx's philosophy of man. This applies with even stronger justification to his conception of human freedom. It is no exaggeration to say that a neglect of these writings renders nearly impossible a correct understanding of Marx's total view.[3]

We will consider the works in their chronological order, beginning with the doctoral dissertation and closing with the essay 'On the Jewish Question', in an attempt to single out the ideas expressed therein which are relevant to the notion of freedom.

1.1. *Freedom as the Principle of the Epicurean Philosophy*

In his doctoral dissertation, completed in *1841* and entitled *On the Difference Between the Democritean and Epicurean Philosophies of Nature,* Marx argues from a Hegelian point of view for the philosophical pre-eminence of the Epicurean physics over that of Democritus. While the latter leaves unresolved several contradictory aspects of the atoms, the former transcends these contradictions speculatively, bringing them together in a higher synthesis. More precisely, this speculative advance is accomplished by conceiving the atoms as possessing freedom of self-consciousness. This, in Marx's opinion, is the leading principle of the Epicurean philosophy: "It is not gastrology…, but the absoluteness and freedom of self-consciousness which is the principle of the Epicurean philosophy."[4]

Marx applauds Epicurus's introduction of the principle of freedom to explain the deflection of atoms; if they fell only in a straight line or varied only as a result of a collision with each other, they would not be genuine 'atoms', i.e. autonomous, absolute first principles.[5] However, what is more important to Marx is that Epicurus subordinates his natural philosophy to a moral conception of man. He points out that the real goal of the Epicurean natural philosophy is not the establishment of scientific knowledge but "the *atarxia* of self-consciousness".[6] Anything which could disturb the autonomous, self-contained development of the human spirit towards this ideal must be rejected, including both physical laws and the so-called divine heavenly bodies.[7] In fact, man's autonomy is conceived in such a radical fashion that there can be "nothing good which lies outside of him; the only good which he has in relation to the world is the negative movement, to be free from it".[8]

Now although Marx himself does not endorse the Epicurean position *en bloc*[9], it is clear from the text that he is in genuine sympathy with its leading principles, especially those which seem to be compatible with the Hegelian philosophy of spirit. One of these is the rejection of any scientific, physical determinism. To consider spirit as subject to the laws of physical motion would be to deny its proper character. Spirit is autonomous *(selbständig)* in relation to nature.[10] Further, Marx underlines the fact that freedom is an essential trait of spirit, for spiritual being is able to develop according to its own inner law rather than in response to some extrinsic force. That is, spirit is free not only in the negative sense, from nature, but also in the positive sense that it has the power to realize its own inner entelechy. In these conceptions Marx stands with Hegel and comments favorably on Epicurus. But in one point, his admiration for Epicurus actually outweighs his allegiance to Hegel. He rejects any absolute, divine or earthly, which might jeopardize the independence of man: "The maxim of Promytheus, 'In a word, I hate each and every god', is its [philosophy's] own maxim, its own motto against all heavenly and earthly gods which do not recognize human self-consciousness as the highest deity. There should be none other beside it"[11]. Hegel's absolute, especially in its theological sense, is deposed, and humanity is set up as the supreme subject. Spirit is specified as *human* spirit, as the self-consciousness of mankind.[12] And therewith the meaning of freedom also changes; it now carries the specification of being *human* freedom. There is no indication that Marx had individual freedom in mind. To that extent he is still thinking in Hegelian categories; the subject is supra-individual, the whole of humanity. But that he revises Hegel in the interests of the supremity and autonomy of man is clear. Human freedom is the highest goal, and this consists in the autonomous realization of man's self-consciousness.

1.2. *The Spheres of Human Freedom*

In the first years of Marx's public life as an author, he takes the opportunity of restating and developing these early ideas in a sort of political-philosophical journalism. The articles written chiefly for the *Rhenische Zeitung* during 1842–1843 deal with various social and political issues, such as the freedom of the press and the relation of the state to its citizens. But Marx's general philosophical position is clearly in the forefront, and much that was merely implicit in the dissertation is here explicitly stated.

In these articles Marx shows himself enamoured of the idea of freedom. Indeed, his romanticist ebullience is so concentrated that one wonders whether there is for him any other positive value. Freedom is, first, the generic *essence* of all spiritual being.[13] All aspects of spirit, including law, ethics, the state, and the press, have freedom as their essence. Further, their realization of freedom is the measure of their *goodness*.[14] A good state, law or ethics is one which is a rational realization of freedom. Marx is thereby saying two things. Spiritual being is essentially free because its basic characteristic is its ability to determine the direction of its own development, unlike material being whose movement is always determined *ab alio*. And spiritual being only attains its proper good when this freedom becomes a reality, when its actual existence corresponds to its 'essence' or 'concept'.[15]

Now Marx follows Hegel in distinguishing essentially different spheres of *Geist*. And since each one of these has its own proper inborn laws, each is characterized by a different species of freedom.[16] That is, each can follow its own proper law in a way characteristic to its own life. To make any one particular species of freedom the norm for a different sphere is a violation and 'intolerance' of the necessarily pluralistic nature of freedom.[17] The freedom of the *press* is not to be justified on the basis of freedom of competition – this would be merely to replace one heteronomy, censorship, by another, the rules of economic life – but on the very nature of what a press is, the intellectual expression of human spirit.[18] Censorship is not just a modification but a total annihilation of its basic function. Similarly, *morality* "recognizes only its own universal and rational religion".[19] Kant, Fichte and Spinoza were right in rejecting positive religion's claims on moral man, because while morality is based on the autonomy of the human spirit, religion is based on its heteronomy. Finally, the *state* should also be a rational realization of freedom.[20] Displaying his early adhesion to liberal political theory, Marx considers the state as a free association of individuals[21], which embodies the general will of the people.[22] Further, a special status is due to the state, because it is the great organism within which the other spheres of spirit find their realization. And there should be – at least in theory – no tension between individual rights and state power, since in obeying its rationally constructed laws the citizen is actually only following the natural laws of his own reason.[23]

It is important to note that although Marx emphasizes the autonomy which the spheres of spiritual reality individually possess, this does not mean that they constitute some sort of objective being, separate from man. They are no more than types of human spirit, because, to repeat, spirit is necessarily human. The state, press and morality are forms of the realization of human freedom. Marx states that neither animals nor gods could create a free press, for to be a 'product of freedom' means precisely to be a human product.[24]

Further, not only does the notion of freedom include that of man, but man himself is defined by his freedom; freedom is man's essential defining property.[25] For example, it is the characteristic which distinguishes the work of a man from that of a beaver; although in both cases a similar result may be achieved, their activity is essentially different – the human effort is carried out freely.[26] In a passage which reminds one of Sartre, Marx says that the loss of freedom is the real mortal danger for man, since in losing freedom man actually loses himself.[27]

However, Marx is certainly not suggesting a theory of absolute freedom. It is man's mode of existence, his way of realizing himself which is free. He does not create his own essence or the rules for realizing its potentialities. These are given. Numerous passages suggest that Marx holds, at this stage of his development, a kind of natural law theory of man and human morality.[28] There is a human essence and a fundamental character to the various spheres of his activity. Man attains his good only by realizing his humanity according to the laws embodied therein. Here lies both his proper good and his radical autonomy. The inborn laws of his nature do not unfold and realize themselves automatically; this is an ethical process, and not merely an ontological one, for man can actually fail to realize his nature. Marx, as a critic of his times, deplored in particular two external forms of this ethical failure: the existence of autocratic government and the prevalence of positive religion. Both represent the submission of man to forces which lie outside of him; the absolute ruler stands above the will of the people just as religious values transcend man's natural existence. Thus the principle of heteronomy replaces the principle of freedom, for man is, in this situation, not all that his nature would allow him to be.

1.3. *The Human Individual as Subject*

The philosophical anthropology which Marx was developing, more or less as a humanistic revision of Hegelian philosophy, entered a brand new stage with his *Critique of the Hegelian Philosophy of State,* written in the summer of 1843. Under the influence of Feuerbach, whose *Essence of Christianity* appeared in 1841, Marx subjected Hegel's political doctrine to a biting critique, which touched not only Hegel's conception of the state but also the basic principles of his metaphysics. In particular, Marx rejects both the ontological idealism and the monism of Hegel.

First of all, Marx repudiates the Hegelian view that the family and civil society are a result of the dialectical unfolding of objective spirit, particularly as it is found incorporated in the state.[29] For Marx this is a reversal of the real state of affairs. It is not objective spirit, the 'idea' as it is found in its immediate stage in the state, which is the basic reality, but rather the family and civil society.[30] Empirical reality is primary, ideal reality secondary. Thus the state is not a precondition for the family, but vice versa. This critique of Hegel enunciates a basic Marxian thesis which is never to be surrendered: the foundation of all human thought, history and institutions is the daily concrete existence of empirical human beings. There is nothing that is more fundamental.

The obvious implication for the conception of freedom is that freedom can no longer be sought in the self-realization of the 'human spirit' alone. It must also exist as an element of the every-day conditions of concrete human society. Marx does not specify which aspect of that every-day existence is the *most* fundamental; he will later say it is man's productive life. But it is made explicit that, in opposition to Hegel, real empirical men possess more than just 'formal' freedom.[31]

A second important aspect of Marx's critique of Hegel is his rejection of monism. Not only is it true that empirical reality has precedence over ideal reality, but on the empirical level the last and final ground of being is a plurality of individual substances. In a clearly Aristotelian vein, Marx objects that Hegel hypostasizes predicates instead of attributing them to subjects, whose existence they share. In Marx's view, "the existence of the predicates is the subject".[32] Further, there is a plurality of these subjects, for a predicate never exhausts its possible modes of existence in a single thing.[33] With this position Marx radically overthrows the Hegelian ontological scheme: while for Hegel individual being is just a dialectical moment of a larger whole and is thereby deprived of ontological autonomy, for Marx it is the "real *ens (ὑποχείμενον, subject)*".[34]

This affirmation of the primacy of the category of substance is meant to apply above all to human beings. Individual persons are the basis of all social and political reality; they are its *supposita (Träger)*.[35] The state is ontologically dependent on individuals both for its origin[36] and its formal existence,[37] as well as in its functioning. State functions are "no more than modes of existence and modes of operation of the social qualities of men".[38] The individual citizens are the true agents, the driving forces which move the state forward. They are not its by-products but its prime movers.

It is important to take full notice of Marx's substantialist reaction to Hegel's collectivist ontology, for the very charges he levels against his idealist mentor are laid at his own door by contemporary critics.[39]

To what extent Marx was able to hold on to the position unequivocally asserted in the work discussed here can only be decided after his later works have been examined. Let it only be said that this is a crucial point in the evaluation of the Marxist theory of freedom. If man has no autonomy of being then he cannot be the subject of freedom. Unless, as Marx says, the individual is conceived as the real subject, all qualities must be attributed to something else, some 'mystical entity'. Freedom ceases to be a quality of persons and becomes a quality of society or the state. And that is to say that personal freedom does not exist.

1.4. *The Liberal Ideal of Freedom and the Social Nature of Man*

Now it cannot be assumed that this ontological individualism implied for Marx an ethical individualism. Only a few months after completing the critique of Hegel, Marx launched an open attack in *Zur Judenfrage* on the tradition of liberal democracy of sanctifying the egoistic tendencies of the private individuals composing civil society. In particular – and what is interesting for our investigation – this took the form of a critique of the liberal ideal of freedom.[40]

In the liberal conception, freedom consists in the maximum absence of restraints on the actions of individuals. It affirms the principle that an individual ought to be able to do as he pleases in the course of his own private pursuit of happiness, so long as his actions do not conflict with the similar pursuit of his neighbors.[41] Laws become merely a set of rules indicating the boundaries within which a man must contain his activities.[42] Inside of these boundaries, he, as an individual, is absolutely free from the interference of other men and institutions.

Marx vehemently rejected this conception, not because – as for Hegel – individual freedom has no reality except as a part of the whole, but because the liberal view mistook the negative tendencies of man, his egoism, for his true essence. Man is not correctly defined as *homo lupus,* in the Hobbesian tradition. This definition characterizes only the negative relation of men to one another, which does not serve to distinguish men from animals. It is rather men's positive relation to each other which is characteristically human. The *differentia specifica* is their *social* character. Thus the liberal conception of freedom went wrong because it was based on a false anthropology, one in which men were conceived as isolated monads.[43] In fact, it is of man's very nature to live together, to *co*-operate. Therein lies the double meaning of the term 'species-being' *(Gattungswesen)*: (1) there is an essence possessed by all members of the human species, and (2) the proper feature of this essence is precisely the fact that men relate themselves positively to the other members of the species. It might be underlined here that when Marx defines man as a social being, this does not imply that the individual is ontologically subordinate to society. The process by which man becomes a species-being is *founded upon* his concrete individuality: "Only when the real, individual man has taken back into himself the abstract citizen and as an individual, in his empirical life, his individual work and his individual relationships, has become a *species-being, ...*, only then is human emancipation achieved".[44]

Marx had pointed out earlier that freedom consists in the ability to follow the inborn laws of one's own nature, rather than to be determined by external factors.[45] Now this principle is applied, in view of the specification of what man's nature is. Since man is essentially a social being, he achieves his freedom by positively affirming and developing his concrete social relations. i.e., in the family, the community, the state, etc. Social action is the proper sphere of realization of human freedom.[46]

1.5. *Summary*

During this early period of his thought, ending at the close of 1843 before he moved to Paris, Marx developed a point of view which is significant as his first formulation of a philosophical conception of freedom. It will be helpful to present a more synoptic picture of this position by summing up the main points.

Although Marx gradually detached himself from the Hegelian philosophy, he never escaped totally from his master's influence. He inherited and retained certain basic principles, of which the following are relevant to the notion of freedom: (1) The world is constituted of a spectrum of different species of things, made different by their inherent essences – if you will, their 'inborn laws'. (2) There can be (and almost always is) a disparity between what a being is essentially and what it is actually. Its existence can fail to measure up to its concept; that is, it can be undeveloped, unfulfilled. (3) The mode of realization of a being's essence is itself peculiar to that type of being. There is a characteristically different type of vital activity for each type. (4) Freedom is the mark of that mode of realization which is self-realization. It is not a being's static isolation from other things but its dynamic autonomy, its ability to chart its own path toward the actualization of its inner potencies.

Taking these principles and more or less explicitly retaining them throughout these years, Marx added his own specifications, in the form of a critique of the philosophy of spirit: (5) In the *Dissertation* and the articles in the *Rheinische Zeitung*, he rejected Hegel's absolutism (in both its theological and its cosmological sense): *Man*, and not God or The Whole, is the sole bearer of freedom. Freedom is a distinguishing characteristic of man's mode of activity – to act freely means to act in a human manner. (6) The *Critique of the Hegelian Philosophy of State* rejects the supra-individualism and idealism of Hegel: The subject of freedom is not human history or the state, but the *concrete individual*. And (7) the sphere in which freedom is attained is man's *every-day existence* – his work, his personal relationships, etc. Consicousness and self-consciousness are merely pre-conditions for freedom; they are not, as in Hegel, its preferred sphere of realization. (8) Finally, in the writings of the second half of 1843, Marx identifies the proper and supreme form of human life as man's social existence, instead of his theoretical self-consciousness: The subject of freedom is man as a *social* being, in the sense that his proper activity is to relate himself positively to the other members of his species. Consequently, freedom can finally be described as the self-realization of man as a species-being, insofar as he consciously fulfills his own social nature by treating his fellow men in his daily existence as ends in themselves. One becomes free, not through isolation from other persons in self-centered activity, but, paradoxically, to the extent that one transcends his egoism and makes other human beings the motivating purpose of his actions.

2. FREEDOM AND ALIENATION

When Marx first elaborated his basic ideas concerning the nature of freedom, as just presented, he had not yet come into his own as an original thinker. There was very little which subsequent commentators would have been able to term 'Marxism'. If he had not gone on to give these ideas an interpretation which was new and characteristically his own, this would have been merely the work of a young Hegelian or a radical Feuerbachian. Marx emerged as a thinker in his own right, and gave a precision to his notion of freedom which stamped it as his own, in his critique of the basic concepts of political economy. In the *Economic and Philosophical Manuscripts* he introduced the thesis that the economic life is decisive for man's entire mode of existence. The other aspects, including the political and the religious, are only of secondary importance. Further, he felt that in the capitalist system of production this economic life took such a form, that far from being a result of human self-development, it deprived men of their very humanity, thereby representing a radical loss of freedom. Marx's theory of alienated labor is an explanation of the causes and forms of this loss of freedom.

Since Marx considered freedom and alienation as correlative, though opposing, notions, it will be necessary to examine the latter concept in some detail. As will be shown, this is important also for another reason: Marx believed that the elimination of alienation would lead to the establishment of a society of free men. Freedom and alienation are not only logical but also historical negations of each other.

In order to show that the condition of alienation is in fact a frustation of man's nature, an attempt will first be made to indicate what that human nature is for Marx. Then the various forms of alienation will be described. And finally, attention will be turned to the theory of communism, as the state of affairs in which alienation will allegedly be overcome and the realm of freedom established.

2.1. *Man as a Productive Being*

As we have seen, for Marx freedom involves man's self-realization. By this term is meant not some arbitrary determination by the subject, but the actualization of what he is potentially according to his human nature. Thus it is appropriate to enquire briefly into what Marx understands this nature to be.

That Marx actually does continue to affirm the universality of a nature in all men has been disputed, particularly on the basis of the sixth thesis on Feuerbach.[47] This text will be examined in detail below. For the moment let us only note: (1) that Marx explicitly spoke of such a nature, using the terms 'human nature', 'human essence' and 'species-being', in his early works such as the *Manuscripts*[48] and occasionally in his later writings such as *Capital*[49]; (2) that both he and Engels singled out characteristic human properties, faculties and activities which distinguish man in general from all other living beings; and (3) that a basic distinction is either asserted or implied throughout his whole work between the actual condition of man and that which would be worthy of and thus correspond to his true nature.[50] Such evidence seems sufficient for assuming that Marx continued to believe that there is some kind of general human nature.

Now how does Marx conceive this human nature? What is man? Departing from tradition, Marx avoids defining man by his consciousness or rationality.[51] These are passive traits. What is more basic is his activity, his particular type of active interchange with nature and society.[52] Taking a cue from Hegel's *Phenomenology,* Marx insists that the relationship between subject and object obtaining during the operation of *all* human faculties is a creative process, the object being transformed into an 'object for man' and the subject into an 'objective being'.[53] This is what Marx terms 'praxis' or more simply 'productive activity'. In the *German Ideology* the crucial importance of productive activity is emphasized: "The way in which men produce their means of subsistence... is a definite form of activity of these individuals, a definite form of expressing their life, a definite *mode of life* on their part. As individuals express their life, so they are. What they are, therefore, coincides with their production...".[54]

Of course, the form of productive activity with which Marx is mostly occupied is economic production: Men "begin to distinguish themselves from animals" when they produce their material means of life[55]; Franklin is praised for defining man as a tool-making animal[56], etc. However, it is important to remember that productivity is seen by Marx as a general human trait, characterizing economic, social, artistic, and even scientific activity. He clearly regarded the latter as properly human activities. They actually have priority over economic labor, which was to assume less and less importance with the progress of technology. Thus, it is not correct to state the Marxian view of man in the alleged genus-species definition, 'Man is a working animal'. Labor is exclusively human, but it is not the only form of properly human activity.

It is difficult to specify further the structure of this productive activity, in its generic sense. However, certain features seem to stand out: (1) It is a bi-polar relation in which each of the poles is involved essentially, and not just accidentally. In Bradleyan terms, it is an internal relation. (2) On one side, this involves a transformation of the object. The young Marx speaks of "the becoming of nature for man"[57], the later Marx of the transformation of natural raw material into a form useful for man's life.[58] But not only physical nature is transformed; society also can be transformed by human activity. Unlike animal activity, human production is universal; the entire universe falls under its transforming power.[59] (3) On the other side, the subject becomes objectivized through the process. Man is produced[60]. His nature changes in the sense that it becomes real for the first time.[61] It emerges into the objective world. (4) Productive activity is social activity; it always involves, either directly or indirectly, other human beings. Production, even in science and art, can never be accomplished by some mythically conceived isolated individual. (5) Finally, this activity is "not a determination with which he [man] is completely identified".[62] Unlike animal, man distinguishes the activity from himself, insofar as he makes it an object of his will and consciousness.[63] It is for this reason that such activity can be free.

Marx called his own position naturalism.[64] And this certainly means that man is considered part of nature to the extent that he is entirely a this-worldly being. There is no metaphysical transcendence about him. However, it does not mean that he is merely one element in nature along with others. Rather than being subject to nature, he controls and dominates it. And it is precisely in his productive activity that this privileged relation to the rest of nature is expressed. Marx's naturalistic anthropology – which is hardly reconcilable with a scientific or cosmological naturalism – is best understood as a view of man's relation to nature, expressed in his characteristic type of activity, which essentially involves an interchange, a *Stoffwechsel* as Marx called it, with the objective world.[65]

2.2. *Alienation as the Loss of Freedom*

In capitalism, man's productive activity is deformed and perverted to such an extent that far from being a fulfillment of human nature, it is its estrangement. Alienation is a radical loss of freedom precisely because it is the negation of genuinely human productivity. This is described by Marx in the *Economic and Philosophical Manuscripts* in four aspects: alienation from the product of work, from the work itself, from one's fellow beings, and from human species-life.[66]

First of all, an obvious fact, which according to Marx can be observed, is the inverse relation obtaining between the growing amount of produced goods and the decreasing amount appropriated by the worker. The world which he has created is becoming less and less accessible to him: "The worker becomes poorer the more wealth he produces".[67] He is alienated from his own *product*, which assumes an independent existence and becomes a power on its own. The more work he puts into his products, the more he suffers a loss of himself, for "The life which he has given to the object sets itself against him as an alien force".[68] This process of objectification is carried so far that the worker himself becomes a commodity, and finally in large-scale capitalism a mere physical entity, whose value does not exceed the bare means of subsistence necessary to keep him alive. He has transformed nature into a world of commodities and has himself fallen into this world, becoming totally an 'object'.[69]

Secondly, Marx points out that the alien relationship of the worker to the product is only an expression of the alienated nature of the productive *activity* itself. Why is this activity alienated? Because it is performed, not as an end in itself or for an end set voluntarily by the worker, but in the imposed service of the system of commodity production. Thus the agent's activity ceases to be his own; it is torn into two parts, its aim and purpose and its physical execution, with only the latter being left to him.[70] The only way in which it is subject to the worker's will is indirectly; it is for him a means of securing his biological subsistence. But it is not the satisfaction of a properly human need, and "we arrive at the result that man (the worker) feels himself to be freely active only in his animal functions".[71] In his properly human functions he is not free at all.

Thirdly, a consequence of alienated activity is that man is alienated from *other men*. The product of labor and the labor activity itself have been dispossessed of the worker. Who could be the dispossessor? Not a god, nor nature, but only another man.[72] The worker himself engenders this "domination of the non-producer over production and its product".[73] He establishes the relation through his alienated labor. The result is that the worker and the capitalist stand to each other as opposed and alien forces. Further, they see each other as mere means to achieving their mutual ends. And this attitude is extended also to fellow members of their respective classes: each person sees his fellow man only as an element in the system of alienated production. There is no positive affirmation of persons as such, for their own value. The basis of genuine social relation is thus totally annihilated.

The situation described by these three aspects of alienation is seen by Marx to represent a loss of human *species-life*. Man is alienated from his own species and thus from himself. As previously mentioned[74], the terms 'species-life' and 'species-being' always carry a twofold meaning: (1) that man is communal being, each individual bearing a relation to a society or to the whole of humanity (to the whole species), and (2) that he has a characteristic activity and characteristic traits which consitute his specific nature (possessed by each member of the species).

Now the alienation from one's fellow man clearly constitutes a loss of species-life in the first sense. Marx believed that truly human 'living-together' was a respectful and unselfish relation; a genuinely human society would be a kingdom of ends, where each person makes the other's welfare his own goal. The paradigm of this condition is marriage, whose very principle is love. But in an alienated society the principle of egoism reigns, so that man's social orientation is perverted into a negative form.

Passing to the second sense of species, we see a similar loss here in two forms: (1) In man's *relation to nature* he is characteristically a universal being.[75] He is the only being who can appropriate either practically or theoretically the whole of nature: "Man reproduces the whole of nature" and thus "nature appears as *his* work and his reality".[76] Now since the product of labor appears as an objectification of this universal species-character, when "alienated labor takes away the object of production from man, it also takes away his species-life... and changes his advantage over animals into a disadvantage insofar as his organic body, nature, is taken away from him".[77] His very transformation of nature has resulted in its disenfranchisement from him in the form of the alienation of the product. (2) But secondly, even a more vital aspect of man's species-being submits to this fate, namely his *relation to his own activity*. The type of life-activity of a being actually constitutes the peculiarity of its species, its 'species character'.[78] And as we indicated above, human life activity is for Marx a conscious and willed operation. For this reason, man is potentially a free being: he can make his own productive activity the object of his consciousness and will. By making the activity itself the end, he excercises his autonomy in a radical way. However, "alienated labor reverses the relationship in that man... makes his life activity, his being, only a means for his existence".[79] In the system of wage labor the properly human life of man loses its free and self-directed character; as it becomes a means, the very species-life of man is transformed into a mere means of physical existence.[80] Man suffers the unfreedom which is a loss of himself.[81]

2.3. *The Overcoming of Alienation Through Communism*

Marx did not restrict himself to description and analysis. He *found* mankind in an alienated condition, which he tried to analyze; but he also *foresaw* the future triumph over alienation through communism. This was to mediate the achievement of genuine human freedom – the free development of each, as he expressed it in the *Communist Manifesto.*

Communism itself is to be conceived as a means. In the *Economic and Philosophical Manuscripts,* Marx notes that "communism as such is not the aim of human development"[82], and later in the *German Ideology* that "Communism is for us not a *state of affairs* which is to be established, an *ideal* to which reality will have to adjust itself. We call communism the *real* movement which abolishes the present state of things"[83]. The goal for which communism is only the mediation is a life for man which corresponds to his dignity and nature.

Now neither Marx nor Engels is overly generous in giving us details on the nature of communism, but their remarks allow us to make at least the following points: (1) Private property will be eliminated. That is, the forces of production will no longer be owned by a particular class but by the whole society.[84] The division between producers and productive forces will be destroyed. (2) All economic production will be organized and controlled according to a rational, all-embracing plan. In this way, economic crises, overproduction, etc., will be eradicated, and production of necessary goods will require the minimum expenditure of human labor.[85] (3) Due to this planned production, which will be both more efficient and more directly oriented towards satisfying the real wants of the people, the distribution of goods can be organized according to need.[86] In this way, no person will be without the basic necessities of life. (4) The division of labor in the new system of production will assume a more flexible character. It will no longer be necessary for a man to devote his total energies to a particular job or profession.

Assuming that such changes could take place in society, it can easily be admitted that they would eliminate most of what Marx thought were the causes of alienation. The basic evil, private property, no longer sets man against man. Economic planning reverses the previous domination of the product over the worker: as a commodity it had assumed a life of its own, oppressing the worker; now it is under his control. Distribution according to need removes the previously overbearing concern for one's purely physical, animal existence; the struggle to survive no longer suffocates all other human functions. And because the division of labor is reduced, the worker is able to engage in several types of productive activity.

The last point, the abolition of the division of labor, already indicates an important element in the final *goal* of communism. Man is set free to develop all of his capacities. In Marx's early writings, as well as in the *German Ideology,* the ideal of the development of the 'whole man' is clearly affirmed.[87] A truly human life is one in which man can exercise the whole range of his capacities. He can "do one thing today and another tomorrow, hunt in the morning, fish in the afternoon, rear cattle in the evening, criticize after dinner", "without ever becoming hunter, fisherman, shepherd or critic".[88] Under the division of labor one particular type of activity is forced upon him; in communism he voluntarily chooses his labor, and since his nature is to be many-sided, chooses *several* types of labor. Further, these activities are performed for their own sake. Creative productive activity – the essential trait of man – becomes the very purpose of life.

Of course, this is not to be an egoistical, selfish activity; in communism the conflict between the interests of the individual and those of the community no longer exists.[89] In the *Exerptheften* Marx depicts a society in which the production of each is not only his own personal expression of life but also the mediation between someone else and the human species[90]; the worker is conscious of the fact that his product will fulfill the needs of another. Thus the worker's essence as a social being is also confirmed in his "immediate, individual activity".[91]

This picture of the final human condition in which man attains full freedom, both in the sense that he voluntarily chooses all of his actions and in the sense that he is fulfilling his own nature, undergoes a certain alteration in Marx's later writings. According to his earlier works, labor is to assume a form very much resembling artistic activity, performed for its own sake and as a free creative expression of the person. However, in the third volume of *Kapital,* Marx admits that man must always, "in all social formations and modes of production", "struggle with nature in order to satisfy his needs, preserve and reproduce his life".[92] Thus material production "always remains a realm of necessity".[93] Does this mean that the older and less optimistic Marx abandoned his ideal of a condition in which man was truly free? No, but yet this realm of freedom is to lie "beyond the sphere of real material production".[94]

Marx clearly distinguishes two spheres of human life: that in which freedom can be achieved in a merely limited sense, and that which allows its achievement in the full and proper sense. The first is the sphere of material production. Man is forced to satisfy his physical needs; thus work is determined by an external finality. And "Freedom in this area can only consist in the fact that socialized man, the associated producers, rationally regulate their interchange [*Stoffwechsel*] with nature, bring it under their common control instead of being dominated by it as a blind power, and carry it out with the least expenditure of energy under conditions the most worthy of and adequate to human nature".[95] Economic planning can gain for man a certain amount of freedom in the sphere of production, i.e., in its form of execution. But this is all. It is only in the second sphere, that of leisure time, that occurs "the development of human capacity which is its own end".[96] This freedom begins only at that point where work ceases. Marx had great faith in man, and expected that he would use his leisure time for artistic and scientific pursuits, thus developing his highest human faculties. This activity fulfills all of the requirements for human species-activity: it is freely chosen, performed for its own sake, a high form of human creativity and a positive contribution to society.

There is no doubt that this represents a real departure from Marx's earlier position. The alienation of the worker in production, according to the later view, is not to be eliminated. And he must therefore seek his fulfillment in another sphere, that of his leisure. However, this division of human life into two segments is not absolute, and a few remarks on the relation between them might serve to correct the impression that we have here 'two Marx's'. First of all, Marx remained convinced that the oppressive character of labor could always be further reduced. While regretting the ineradicable remainder of externality in labor activity, he nevertheless was optimistic that technology would continue to minimize this factor. Secondly, in the *Grundrisse der Kritik der politischen Oekonomie, Rohentwurf,* he remarked that the "increase in leisure time, i.e., time for the full development of the individual itself reacts upon the productive force of work as the greatest productive force".[97] The labor time itself "cannot remain in abstract opposition to leisure time".[98] The personal development which the worker undergoes in his free time results in his greater efficiency in material productive activity. Thus leisure activity indirectly reduces labor time, which permits more leisure activity, and so forth. Thirdly and finally, it must be noticed that Marx did not surrender his ideal of human fulfillment through 'productive activity', if this phrase is taken in the broad sense of 'praxis' rather than in the narrow sense of economic labor. In this connection it is important to recall a point made earlier, namely that it is more correct to state that for Marx man is a 'productive animal' than that he is a 'working animal'. Material labor is characteristic of but not definitive for man. For this reason Marx can still hold onto his basic ideal of free self-development in the future communist society. Man will be able to produce according to his own wishes and ends, during the increasing amount of leisure time afforded him, and thus be able to actualize in a free manner the whole range of potentialities rooted in his nature.

3. HISTORY AS THE LAW-BOUND PROCESS OF MAN'S LIBERATION

The foregoing presentation of Marx's view of freedom as the negation of alienation and the self-realization of man captures only one side of his thought, his *anthropology*. Here Marx expresses his conception of freedom within the framework of his view of human nature. But another equally important dimension of his thought for the purposes of this study is his *theory of history*. This attempts to explain the basic structure and main stages of the historical process through which man will finally attain the goal described above.

Several considerations bound up with Marx's theory of history are relevant and will be treated here: First, his theory of historical development is based on a principle which would seem to weaken seriously the claim that individuals are free in any meaningful sense. This is the principle of the law-bound nature of history: namely, that history proceeds unalterably according to definite laws, independently of the wills of individuals, and that the historical conditions which were formed according to these laws actually exert a determining influence on these individuals. The doctrine known as 'historical determinism' seems to place the freedom of man in jeopardy. Secondly, Marx viewed the course of history as a progressive advance, and – in spite of the previous statement – he considered one of the important criteria of progress to be the degree of freedom attained at any particular stage of this process. And this notion of freedom is notably different from the one outlined above. Finally, practically the entire Marxist tradition has connected up Marx's alleged concept of freedom with that of historical necessity, so that freedom is seen to lie in an attitude towards or a utilization of the laws of historical necessity.

3.1. *The Laws of History*

Marx claimed to have advanced beyond utopian socialism because his vision of the socialist future was based on a scientific understanding of the reasons and conditions for its appearance.[99] This scientific understanding of history was expressed, for example, in the famous *Preface to the Critique of Political Economy* in the shape of general propositions stating the causal relationships both between the various elements in the structure of a socio-economic formation and between one formation and the appearance of its successor.[100] And in *Capital* Marx explicitly characterizes these relations as laws; he speaks of "the natural laws of (a society's) movement" and states as the purpose of this work "to lay bare the economic law of motion of modern society".[101]

Now although Marx compares these laws to those of the sciences of natural history – which are laws in a much weaker sense than, say physical laws – he nevertheless insists that they operate "with iron necessity towards inevitable results".[102] For example, that capitalism grew out of feudalism was a necessity, something which could not have been prevented by any historical accident, human intervention or by anything else. In particular, Marx emphasizes that such a historical development occurs independently of the wills of separate individuals.[103] This obviously does not mean that there can be history without men, but rather that the main course of its development is determined by material factors over which the decisions of men have little control. It is the real economic 'contradiction' in a particular society between its developing productive forces and lagging productive relations which inevitably leads to its collapse and to the establishment of a new social order. Men can do little more than temporarily delay or advance the moment at which this contradiction will burst forth and mediate the appearance of the new society.[104]

In a similar way, the form which the various elements of any one particular social formation will take, and their relation to each other, are just as little dependent on the will of man. In an important letter to P. V. Annenkov, Marx poses the question "Are men free to choose this or that form of society for themselves?" He answers with an emphatic "By no means" and then states his conception of the determined character of an integral social formation: "Assume a particular state of development in the productive forces of man and you will get a particular form of commerce and consumption. Assume particular stages of development in production, commerce and consumption and you will have a corresponding social constitution, a corresponding organization of the family, of orders or of classes, in a word a corresponding civil society. Assume a particular civil society and you will get particular political conditions which are only the official expression of civil society".[105] That the relation between these elements is more than just a functional relation is made clear enough by Marx: "The mode of production of material life determines the general character of the social, political and spiritual life".[106] It is not denied that a certain amount of secondary reverse influence of the latter may exert itself on the primary economic factors[107], but again this may have only accidental significance. In the materialist conception of history the structure of a society and its development are undeviatingly determined in a regular law-bound manner by its economic life.

Nevertheless, while Marx unquestioningly conceived socio-economic formations, economic systems, modes of production, etc., to fall under certain determinate laws, it is not clear whether the same holds for individuals, i.e., whether persons are also, in some sense, instances of universal historical laws.

There is no lack of quotations in Marx's works. The statement that "It is not the consciousness of men that determines their being, but, on the contrary, their social being determines their consciousness"[108] seems to point in that direction, since it is drawn in close analogy to the historical law stating the relation between basis and superstructure. More concretely, Marx seems to establish a determinate relation between the activity of men as economic producers and their activity in general, i.e., as social, political or moral beings. In the *Poverty of Philosophy* Marx notes, "The same men who establish their social relations in conformity with their material productivity, produce also principles, ideas and categories, in conformity with their social relations".[109]

And yet it must be emphasized that when Marx is describing the general relationships between the actions of men and some 'material' factor, he almost always has *groups* of men in mind, not individuals. It is the actions of *classes* which are explained by the laws of historical development: "History... is the history of class struggles".[110] Marx views morality and politics as the expression of a *whole society,* and social relations as typifying an *entire system* of production. It is never stated that the laws which govern these units also apply equally and without exception to each individual member. For example, individual bourgeois ideologists can convert to the cause of the proletariat if they grasp the historical movement as a whole.[111] Individuals can be both behind and ahead of their respective economic classes. Thus it does not seem that historical materialism, as a set of statements governing the structure and development of socio-economic formations, unambiguously entails for Marx a determinism of individuals.

3.2. *The Historical Conditions of Human Existence*

Now Marx often speaks about the relation between men and history in terms of the determining influence on individuals of their concrete economic and social *conditions*. Men make their own history, but only under circumstances for which they themselves are not responsible.[112]

They always inherit a set of productive forces and the corresponding social relations from their predecessors.[113] A set of historical conditions is always given; it cannot be chosen. Further, these conditions can influence an individual to act in a certain manner. Marx gives the example of a producer and a consumer living in a society based on the division of labor. Neither the producer nor the consumer is free with regard to the transactions of buying and selling: "both of these are determined by his social position, which itself depends on the whole social organization".[114] Such statements suggest that Marx held a deterministic conception of individual action which might be formulated in the following manner: every human action can be sufficiently explained by the influences of the social environment on the agent.

And yet if we wish to be totally fair, we cannot attribute this position to Marx. He never expressed his socio-historical determinism in this universal form, nor does a careful examination of the texts allow us to infer it. In particular, the following must be noted. First, the domination of circumstances over individuals is always expressed as the result of a *concrete historical* social order. Even in the *German Ideology*, Marx largely adopts a historical rather than a strictly philosophical point of view. Accordingly, the domination of circumstances was vastly different in different epochs[115]; the primitive man was unfree in a very different sense than the wage laborer. Secondly, there are *degrees* of this domination. It increases, for example, with the progress of a commodity economy into its higher forms. Also, the members of the ruling classes (slaveholders, feudal lords and capitalists), all the while acting under the conditions dictated by the productive forces, are less dominated by these conditions in certain aspects, e.g., their concern for their daily existence.[116] And if we can be allowed to generalize from the tenor of Marx's texts, it would seem that an individual would be more directly and fully determined in his economic relationships than in those remotely connected with his labor activity. This fact alone, that Marx speaks of *degrees* of the domination of the circumstances, indicates that he is not a determinist in the normal sense of the word, for it is part of the meaning of 'determinism' that the subject be fully determined. A 'more or less' determined subject does not have to be unfree. Finally, and this is the most important consideration, Marx thought that this domination by circumstances was a *transitory* historical phenomenon.

In his view, it was not the normal human condition but the characteristic of an epoch through which man had to pass and which will be overthrown by communism. The task of the communist organization of society coincides with "the task of replacing the domination of circumstances and of chance over individuals by the domination of individuals over chance and circumstances".[117] It will bring "the abolition of the state of things in which relationships become independent of individuals, in which... the personal relationships of individuals are subordinated to general class relationships, etc.".[118] With the triumph of communism, individuals will control their conditions, eliminating their character as an alien force and subordinating them to their own ends.

Consequently, Marx cannot be accused of 'historical determinism' insofar as this would indicate that individuals are fully determined in their actions either through the operation of historical laws or by the influence of their historical circumstances. The 'iron necessity' which characterizes the development of history applies only to supra-individual entities in the formation of their general types of economic and social structure.

3.3. *Freedom as a Historical Category*

In Marx's conception of the relation of man to his circumstances are already contained elements of his notion of freedom as a historical category. It is not in the separation or isolation from something, the immunity to external influences, that freedom consists, but rather in power, in "domination over the circumstances and conditions in which an individual lives".[119] That is, the term 'freedom' does not carry a primarily negative connotation, but rather a positive one.[120] Man cannot be free from external circumstances without actually controlling them; there is no neutral state.

This notion is clearly operative in Marx's assessment of the progress in liberation achieved in the various eras. Primitive communism, in spite of its absence of class-exploitation, represented the lowest stage, since man had not yet learned at that time to control his physical environment. He was oppressed by natural forces. With the advent of the division of labor a whole new epoch began. In the slave-holding society, men, being mere chattel, lost their personal freedom totally. However, this permitted a greater development of the productive forces and a consequent increase in man's power over nature. A continuation of this progress followed in feudalism, which also improved the social autonomy of man, since the serf and the free peasant produced their own means of subsistence with land and tools over which they either permanently or conditionally disposed.[121] There is here progress both in the domination of nature and in the control of social relations. But the limited capabilities of private agriculture and especially domestic commodity production forced this era to give way to capitalism.[122] This final stage of the epoch of the division of labor is characterized by two opposing traits: the enormous development of the productive forces and thus the almost unlimited domination of man over nature, and the acute condition of the subjection of man to economic circumstances. Man is lord over nature but not over himself. The resolution of this contradiction, and thus the total domination of man both over nature and over his social existence, can only be achieved through communism.

This last transition deserves to be examined a bit more closely, since it was Marx's main concern. The role of the productive forces is again the key. People previously "won freedom for themselves each time to the extent that was dictated and permitted... by the existing productive forces".[123] The final conquest of freedom will be no exception. However, it will differ from earlier conquests in that it will not be based on *restricted* productive forces. Before, the productive forces were able to supply products sufficient only to fill the needs of a minority of the society – thus the necessary exploitation of one group by another, without which there could have been no development at all.[124] Modern large-scale industry, which concentrates capital and utilizes power-driven machinery, presents a different situation. It has productive forces capable of supplying the needs of all. Thus, the conquest of freedom 'permitted' on the basis of these forces can be of a different kind; it can be universal, in the sense that it frees *all* men from their basic wants and, at the same time, eliminates the need for exploitation.

Why is this final liberation not only permitted but also 'dictated' by the productive forces? From a theoretical point of view, it is seen to lie in the fact that the industrial forces have reached a stage where they are capable of producing the necessities of life for all, but cannot be so employed or even developed further under the capitalist relations of production. This contradiction between the modern forces of production (operated by and sufficient for all of society) and the capitalist relations of production (prejudiced in favor of a few) will have to be resolved, just as all such previous contradictions.[125] This follows from the principles of historical materialism.[126] From a more concrete and historical point of view, Marx sees the inevitability of the communist liberation to lie in two factors: First, capitalism was to be crumbling from within; weakened by unbridled competition, overproduction, periodic economic crises, bankruptcies, etc., it seemed to be hastening its own dissolution. Secondly, the concentration of capital brought with it a concentration of workers. In organizing the great labor force, capitalism produced the class which was to serve as capitalism's own 'grave-digger' – the proletariat. Thrown together in the vast industrial complexes and afflicted by a common state of absolute misery, the workers were to overcome their partisan tendencies and, in view of the manifest mutual advantage to be gained by closing ranks, unite into an organized revolutionary movement. This organized class would represent *all* of humanity[127], since it was a majority class which due to its absolute impoverishment had long lost all claims to special rights, privileges, forms of property, etc., over against any other group; it would be a kind of common denominator for all of humanity. Thus the final liberating act, the seizure of the productive forces by the revolutionary proletariat, would be an act of liberation of all mankind.[128]

By means of the proletarian revolution, the dependence of men on economic factors "will be transformed... into the control and conscious mastery of these powers, which, born of the action of men on one another, have till now overawed and governed men as powers completely alien to them".[129] This revolution will be the first *conscious* act of an entire revolutionary class, since this class will be organized and made aware of its historic role by the world communist movement, and thus mark the beginning of the deliberate rational organization of human conditions. The newly won mastery will be felt in two spheres: in man's relation to *nature* and in his relation to *society*. Regarding the first, the shackles will be removed from the forces of production, permitting them to be developed limitlessly and to be organized to satisfy the needs of all men. Nature will no longer submit men to its violence and fortuity but will itself be turned into a willing servant. Secondly, in man's relation to his *social* structure, the abolition of private property will mark the end of the division of labor and thereby of class relations. These relations had taken on an independent existence, and as such exerted an extrinsic influence on the individuals making up the community.[130] The community was a conditioned one, in which men "participated not as individuals but as members of a class".[131] But "with the community of revolutionary proletarians..., who take their conditions of existence and those of all members of society under their control, it is just the reverse; it is as individuals that the individuals participate in it. It is just this combination of individuals... which puts the conditions of the free development and movement of individuals under their control..."[132] The oppressive class-character of social relations will disappear, and man will be able for the first time to freely construct his own community.

The concept of freedom which Marx employs in his assessment of the progress of history is different from that elaborated in his anthropology. It refers not to individual men but to whole societies. It is based not on a conception of the nature of man but on a historical view of the relation of man to his changing external circumstances. Insofar as these circumstances prevail in giving form to human action, man is unfree; insofar as he learns, not to avoid the influence of these factors, but to control them, to make them work for his own ends, he increases his freedom. However, this *historical* concept of freedom, as power, does not contradict or even replace the *anthropological* concept, freedom as self-realization. The two are complementary to each other. The self-realization of man is impossible so long as he is not able to control his environment. On the other hand, the possession of power itself is not an end but only a means. It can have value only to the extent that it is utilized for the accomplishment of a goal which is good in itself, and this is for Marx the perfection of man.

3.4. *Freedom and Necessity*

Marx's conception of freedom as the historically evolving power over nature and history rules out a formulation of his view as "Freedom is the insight into necessity".[133] This definition, deriving from Hegel, places emphasis on the cognition of and acquiescence to the laws of reality. The free man is here the one who has become reconciled with the forces shaping his fate, by understanding their operation; necessity becomes less 'blind' and foreign only when and to the extent that it is understood. Such a doctrine could not be more radically opposed to the Marxian view. Marx himself rejected such merely 'philosophical liberation' in his early works.[134] And in the preceding section, we saw that his view of the concrete freedom achieved in history centers on the notions of power, control, domination of reality. Marx's view is 'activist' in the most radical sense of the word; the truly liberated man is the one who transforms and refashions reality according to his own ends. The world is not seen as an unalterable order, specified by necessary laws which man can do no more than recognize, but rather as the highly malleable raw material for man's self-oriented activity.

According to one view, Marxian freedom consists in activity 'based on' the knowledge of necessity.[135] However, it is difficult to know what this could mean in the context of Marx's own thought. Marx spoke about two kinds of necessity: external necessity[136] and the necessity of certain laws.[137] The *first* is equivalent to the domination of external circumstances – Marx often called them 'alien forces' – over the individual. Examples of these would be the class-determined social relations, the state of the world market, the working conditions of the laborer, etc. Now assuming that an individual, e.g. a medieval serf, gained insight into the fact that he was the plaything of such forces, it is not clear how he could use this knowledge to free himself from them. If he wished to work at all, he would have to accept the given work-relations, no matter how external, oppressive and forced they happened to be; his insight into the situation would not alleviate and might even increase his misery. The *second* sense of necessity poses similar problems. In this case, necessity is a characteristic of the development of societies, modes of production, classes, etc. This development is supposed to take a determined course, following necessary laws which according to the Marxists are not only knowable but have actually been discovered by Marx himself. Now again, assume that a person has gained insight into these laws; in what sense will this insight change his mode of activity? Marx himself gives us an answer: an enlightened member of society will be able to advance slightly, 'lessen the birth pangs' of the coming social revolution.[138] That is all. The occurrence of the revolution, the emergent economic situation, the form of the new society, etc., are all beyond his reach. But does the essence of freedom for Marx lie in the simple acceleration of social movements? This cannot be taken seriously as a possible interpretation of his view. Further, it is equally questionable that he considered the knowledge of historical laws to be the main contributing factor to the state of freedom which the establishment of communism will initiate. The laws of the capitalist economy will certainly not be valid here. Nor will the general relations between basis and superstructure. And it would be extremely unfair to Marx to burden him with the view that such general laws as 'all history is a history of class-struggle' and 'the conflict between the productive forces and productive relations engenders new social orders' could be used extensively as the basis for the creation of a new social order; in particular, that their being known could be the main reason for the new 'free' and 'human' character of this society. Not only are there no texts to support such a view; it does injustice to Marx's intelligence and keen historical sense.

Therefore, the view that freedom is essentially bound up with 'insight into necessity' cannot be attributed to Marx. As we shall see, it is Engels who introduces this idea into the Marxist tradition. Marx himself considered freedom and necessity to be mutually opposing concepts. The presence of necessity in the world was for him a limitation on freedom and not somehow a constitutive element of it.[139]

4. CONCLUSION: RESULTS AND UNDECIDED ISSUES

Our examination of Marx's views on the nature of freedom has proceeded within the context of diverse aspects of his thought: his breaking-away from Hegel, his social critique and anthropology, and his theory of history. Consequently, it will be useful to pull some of our results together, in order to have a more over-all grasp of his position and its unity. Also, there are two special issues which will have to be examined, not because they are main concerns of Marx, but because they have taken a prominent place in the Western critique of his position: the question of free will and that of the ontological status of the person.

4.1. *The Two Marxian Concepts of Freedom*

As the previous exposition has shown, there are *two* concepts of freedom in Marx: what were designated as the 'anthropological' and the 'histori-cal' concepts.

The *anthropological* concept, as the term indicates, is based upon a certain understanding of man. Marx assumes that man has a nature, that the human species is not merely a group of individuals displaying similar behavior patterns but that each individual is endowed with an essential structure which constitutes him a human being.[140] However, because man is not a monad but a being who must continually interact with nature and society, historical changes in his relation to the latter result in different modes of existence of this essential core. The realization of man's human nature assumes widely differing forms. Now freedom is achieved in a certain type of realization of this essence which is characteristic of man but which can be thwarted by external circum-stances. This is *self-realization,* in the sense that man achieves control both over the exercise and the goal of his properly human activity. Marx felt that in capitalism the species-activity of man was deformed to such an extent that it was no longer really human, or to put it differently, human activity took on a non-human form: instead of being creative, it was mechanical; instead of being socially oriented in a positive sense, it was self-centered, setting men against each other; instead of being the object of conscious deliberation and choice, it was forced upon the agent as a necessary condition of his biological survival. Thus since human activity was perverted, it did not fulfill man's nature, his species-being, but suffocated it. Marx believed at one point that the communist overthrow of capitalist relations of production would lead to the total de-alienation of human activity and thus to the comprehensive freedom of man. However, he later altered this view, noting that produc-tive activity would always fall short of the ideal, and he introduced the thesis that pure or unlimited freedom – activity which is totally devoid of any compulsion coming from outside the individual – could be attained only in the sphere of leisure. Only here can human activity attain that summit of autonomy where its perfection is its own end.

An additional feature of this conception deserves reiterating: man's self-realization is of necessity a process which requires several *diverse* types of activity. Marx fostered the ideal of the all-round development of the person. A human being is by nature many-sided. He has both theoretical and practical abilities. He is capable of engaging in a wide range of pursuits, including scientific, artistic, cultural and social activities. Accordingly, his fulfillment must also involve the exercise of these diverse activities. This is the anthropological basis for Marx's strong rejection of the division of labor: the specialist who can perform well only his trade is not a free man; his life represents a realization of only one side of his nature and is thus a frustration of his humanity. The 'realm of freedom' is the negation of this condition; it is the state of affairs in which man can fully and comprehensively actualize all of the potentialities which lie within him.

The *historical* concept of freedom, which was worked out by Marx in connection with his theory of the development of history, is not a replacement for the anthropological concept but a complement to it. Marx realized that the realm of freedom described above was to be made possible only by the age-long struggle of man to control his environment, to submit the forces of nature and the spontaneous tendencies of social life to his own designs – in short, that the freedom of self-realization could be achieved only by the mediation of freedom *as power*. Marx's own time, the height of the industrial revolution, revealed to him the nearly unlimited potency of man's manipulation of nature, and his own utopian vision completed that with a view of a rationally regulated society.

Freedom in this sense of the term, as power, is understood by Marx as opposed to necessity; it is not, as later Marxists claim, complementary to or 'dialectically related' to necessity. The achievement of mastery is equivalent to the elimination of what Marx called 'external necessity', namely the influence on man of external factors over which he has no control. Freedom does not somehow make room for this necessity – it supersedes it. As for that necessity which designates the law-bound behavior of events, Marx offers no explanation of how this is related to freedom.

It might be further mentioned that while the anthropological concept of freedom applies to individuals, the historical concept does not. It is society, in the collective sense of the whole of mankind, to which the accumulated productive forces and social forms belong. The individual exercises this power over his conditions of life only as a member of this larger group. Without the knowledge and skill passed on to him by past generations, his actions would be primitive and broadly subject to chance; without the co-operation of other men their results would be insubstantial. This also underlines the fact that Marx never conceived freedom as the mere ability to direct one's life without interference from the other members of society. Marx does not deny that a certain measure of this kind of freedom is desirable; indeed, his utopian realm of freedom, with its emphasis on the development of one's personal faculties, would seem to presume it. However, this does not constitute the positive meaning of the historical concept of freedom.

4.2. *The Question of Free Will*

The philosophical discussion of freedom often centers around the question of free will. One form of this question – the answer to which however does not necessarily decide the whole issue – can be put as follows: Is the will of man completely determined by external causal factors or is it at least partially immune to these and somehow able to direct the course of its own operation?

Marx has been accused of supporting the first of these two alternatives and thus of denying free will.[141] He allegedly maintains that since all actions are economically motivated and since the economic factors themselves are independent of the individual, the direction of his will – his choices – are determined by factors beyond his influence. Now is this a correct evaluation of Marx's position?

There are very few texts in Marx's writings which refer to the nature of the will or its relation to causal factors. In an early essay, Marx warns of the tendency to "overlook the objective nature of (political) relationships and to explain everything from the will of the persons acting."[142] A bit later, he rejects Proudhon's thesis that it is man's free will that gives rise to the opposition between use value and exchange value.[143] But in such statements he is not so much concerned with giving an account of the will as he is with emphasizing the 'objective' nature of certain social phenomena, i.e., that these do not depend on individual wills. And this does not imply either an affirmation or denial of freedom of will.

Of a different character are two other statements which do concern the human will. The first does so only indirectly. Marx wishes to show that the consumer is no freer than the producer. Citing the case of "the worker who buys potatoes and the mistress who buys lace", Marx notes that they "both follow their respective opinions. But the difference in their opinions is explained by the difference in the positions which they occupy in the world, and which themselves are the product of social organization".[144] The fact that the consumer is not free to the extent that his opinions are determined by his social position might seem to indicate that his decisions are also not free. A second statement is more explicit. In the *German Ideology,* Marx writes that the co-operation of workers in economic production "is not voluntary but has come about naturally... as an alien force existing outside of them, of the origin and goal of which they are ignorant" and which force not only "passes through a peculiar series of phases and stages independent of human willing and acting", but also in this process "governs this willing and acting".[145] These two statements are, as far as is known to the present author, the strongest expressions of psychological determinism to be found in Marx's works. But do they actually deny the existence of free will?

Consider the first statement. The worker and the mistress decide what to purchase on the basis of their opinions of what would be best for them; and these opinions are determined by their social positions. Now it is difficult to see in what sense this would involve a determinism of the will. If Marx is merely saying that individuals in different situations have different needs and form their practical judgments with a view to satisfying these needs, no deterministic inferences may be drawn. No philosophical weight is carried by the simple admission that individuals are not fully responsible for their particular interests and needs, in function of which they make decisions. On the other hand, if Marx is saying that the concrete situation so completely and forcibly influences the individual that only one decision is possible, then he is in fact rejecting free will. But he does not actually say this, either here or anywhere else. In fact, one passage rather clearly rules out such an interpretation. Emphasizing that the individual does not have the freedom to get rid of the conditions of his life, Marx nevertheless admits that the individual has at least "the choice between definite things which lie within his province", even if it is only the choice of the Irish peasant between eating potatoes or starving.[146]

The second statement, from the *German Ideology,* is equally inconclusive. Marx says that a social force, i.e., the forces and relations of production, passes through a natural development which process 'governs' (*dirigiert*) the volitional activity of man. Now even if we overlook the fact that the word 'govern' could be taken in both a deterministic and a non-deterministic sense, the context of the passage still clearly forbids the inference that Marx is here advocating psychological determinism. In fact, he is discussing the consequences of the division of labor, one of which is that social relations take on an independent existence alien to and often oppressing the individual. And among the human functions affected is volition. However in the very sentence following the one quoted above, he speaks of the abolishment of this 'estrangement'. That is, the will's being governed by alien forces – whatever this might mean – is only a temporary phenomenon. It is not a universal condition of every will but an unfortunate historical situation which humanity passes through on its way to full liberation.

In such passages Marx is obviously speaking as a social historian or sociologist, and not primarily as a philosopher. He is not so much interested in presenting a philosophical psychology as he is in describing and analyzing the historical predicament of groups of men. And only by neglecting this fact and by generally disregarding the context and tenor of his remarks can a Marxian theory of 'free will' or 'determinism' be constructed. In a word, none of Marx's statements concerning the will carry sufficient precision or philosophical import to constitute a properly philosophical position. Marx is not one of the main combatants in the age-old dispute between determinism and free will.

4.3. *The Ontological Status of the Individual*

As was pointed out previously[147], the particular conception of the ontological status of the person can have an important bearing on the notion of freedom. In the case of Marx, if it is correct to ascribe to him a dialectical theory of the individual, whereby the person is just a dialectical constituent of society, then it cannot properly be said that the person is the subject of freedom. The society becomes the subject, and personal freedom disappears.

It was also seen that the young Marx, in his *Critique of the Hegelian Philosophy of State,* turned against the Hegelian dialectical ontology, emphasizing that it is the empirical individual subject which is the ultimate reality.[148] However, later writings have seemed to indicate to many commentators a reversal of this openly Aristotelian position, a return to Hegel, from whose spell Marx was perhaps never fully released. This disparity in the texts poses no small problem of interpretation: are there two totally different Marxian positions (in which case the later position would have to be accepted as Marx's final view) or is there some unity in the Marxian ontology of the person?

The main text indicating a return to Hegel is found in the widely quoted *Theses on Feuerbach,* a series of cryptic statements jotted down by Marx in a notebook in the Spring of 1845. The sixth thesis runs, in part: "the human essence is no abstraction inherent in each single individual. In its reality it is the *ensemble* of the social relations. Feuerbach, who does not enter upon a criticism of this real essence, is consequently compelled: 1. To abstract from the historical process and to fix the religious sentiment as something by itself and to presuppose an abstract – *isolated* – human individual."[149] The difficulty of interpreting such a text is immediately obvious, because of the evident carelessness with which it was composed; for example, the word 'abstract' is used in several different senses. However, an attempt must be made to lift out the main thoughts relevant to our discussion.

The first two sentences, taken together, express a negative judgment: that the human essence is *not* an "abstraction inherent in each single individual". As Marx says, Feuerbach had shown that the religious essence (God) was actually a form of the human essence; this projected and purified transcendental construction turned out to be nothing else than an abstract form of the human essence itself. However, Marx objects that the human essence is not such an abstraction. What does this mean? In the *Holy Family,* written and published immediately before the notebook jottings on Feuerbach, Marx goes to considerable lengths to explain the 'speculative' (and thus false) conception of abstract essences. He writes, with an acid filled pen: "If from real apples, pears, strawberries and almonds I form the general idea of 'Fruit', if I go further and *imagine* that my abstract idea 'Fruit', derived from real fruit, is an entity existing outside me, is indeed the *true* essence of the pear, the apple, etc.; then, in the *language of speculative philosophy* I am declaring that 'Fruit' is the 'substance' of the pear..., that to be a pear is not essential to the pear...; that what is essential to these things is not their real being, perceptible to the senses, but the essence that I have abstracted from them and then foisted upon them, the essence of my idea – 'Fruit'. I therefore declare apples, pears, almonds, etc., to be mere forms of existence, *modi* of 'Fruit'."[150] For Marx an 'abstract essence' is thus an abstract idea which is given independent being both over the thinker and the sensible object, and is in this form conceived as the true reality, of which real concrete things are only modi or incarnations.[151] He categorically rejects this type of thinking, calling it "speculative, Hegelian construction".[152] In his view, the true reality of things does not lie in some imagined construction but in the concrete things themselves. And so also with man: the human essence is not a speculative idea incarnated in the separate individuals; it is the nature of these individuals and nothing else.

Consequently, we must conclude that at the time Marx jotted down his notes on Feuerbach he expressly and consciously rejected the Hegelian conception of essences. His position actually seems to lean toward Aristotelianism, but unfortunately he does not positively develop his own view. He is content with criticizing Hegel.

Now the famous sentence which allegedly announces his *Rückkehr* to Hegel is the following: "In its reality it [the human essence] is the *ensemble* of the social relations."[153] At least two lines of interpretation can be taken in explaining this statement: (1) It can be seen as a formulation of an *ontological program,* rejecting the conception of essence as form or structure in favor of the view that it is only a set of relations, and noting that in the case of man these relations are social. (2) Or it can be understood as an *empiricist counter-charge* to both Feuerbach and Hegel, insisting that the concrete realization of the human essence 'in its reality' is to be found in the totality of the individual's actual social relations. And in fact, the succeeding sentences seem to support this second line of interpretation. Marx chides Feuerbach for neglecting the real essence of man, for abstracting from the historical process, and for being able to grasp the human essence 'only as "genus"'. He feels that Feuerbach's merely contemplative materialism attains only an abstract individual, falsely cut off from its social milieu and conceived after the fashion of an imagined isolation. In these critical remarks on Feuerbach, Marx certainly underlines the social nature of man. But his immediate concern is not to elevate this to an ontological category; it is rather to emphasize the concrete situation in which man really exists, i.e., as a member of a particular historical form of society.[154]

Thus if Marx's statement is understood in its context, it does not seem to provide sufficient evidence of a new espousal of Hegelian metaphysics, in particular of a relationist theory of the person. This conclusion is further strengthened when one considers the consequences such a theory would entail. If men (and their human essences) consisted of no more than sets of concrete historical social relations, human nature would be transformed in each new era. There would then be no subject of human history. Human history, which Marx so fondly speaks of, would not exist; or rather there would be as many as there are different forms of social relations. Secondly, Marx's repeated distinction between the actual condition of man in a certain historical social formation and a condition which would be worthy of his human nature would make no sense. Such a distinction implies an element in man which is not identical with his actual realized state. Without this, for example, his whole discussion of alienation would be meaningless; he would not be permitted to distinguish between an alienated an unalienated state of man. And thirdly, Marx left numerous statements which explicitly depart from the relationist conceptions, both regarding the status of the individual and regarding his human essence. With regard to the first, Marx rejects the idea of a supra-individual being as a subject, i.e., the view that history is "a person apart, a metaphysical subject of which real human individuals are but the bearers".[155] And the frequency with which Marx goes out of his way to emphasize that it is real individuals who make history would be hard to explain if individual being was in fact derived being, and not primary.[156] Regarding the human essence, Marx speaks in the *Holy Family* of *"essential human properties,* however alienated they may seem to be"[157], of the "contradiction between its [the proletariat's] human *nature* and its condition of life which is... the negation of that nature"[158], and in *Capital* of the difference between "human nature in general" and "human nature as modified in each historical epoch".[159]

Consequently, it must be concluded that Marx's ontology of the person did not take a Hegelian turn. It is undeniable that in his later works he put more emphasis on the essential relation of the individual to society and on the variability of human nature's historical modes of existence. But he never deliberately and consequently supports this with

Hegelian ontological underpinnings; and there is some evidence that he was thinking along Aristotelian lines. In short, one cannot accuse Marx of denying the primacy of individual being and the universality of human nature without broadly neglecting both explicit texts and the sense of some of his leading statements.

CHAPTER III

ENGELS

Friedrich Engels and Karl Marx shared an intellectual partnership nearly unequaled in the history of thought.[1] Collaborators from 1844 until Marx's death, they co-authored books, published under each others' names[2] and often manifested complete confidence in the other's ability to speak for them both. After Marx's death, Engels became the editor of his unpublished works and the official interpreter of his thought, and was recognized as such from Bernstein and Kautsky down to Lenin and the Soviets. Indeed, the ideas of Karl Marx took hold among late 19th century social reformers largely due to their clear and straightforward presentation in the writings of his thoroughly devoted partner.[3]

However, their unity of view should not be understood as identity.[4] In areas such as social theory, political economy, contemporary social critique, strategy of the socialist movement, etc., the coincidence of their positions is almost total. But their respective intellectual outputs went beyond this common ground. The young Marx worked out the elements of an anthropology before he began to collaborate with Engels, and in fact never returned to this in a concentrated fashion during their collaboration. And there is not sufficient justification for believing that Engels assimilated these views.[5] On the other hand, the late Engels struck off on his own in fields such as epistemology, natural philosophy and even science. Marx may have given his friend moral support and encouragement to follow such wide-ranging scholarly inclinations; however, there is no indication that Marx actually did any amount of thinking along these lines.[6] Analogies between Marxian social theory and Engelsian philosophy prove only that the two seem to fit well together. They do not prove that Marx either worked out or adopted what was later on called 'dialectical materialism'.[7]

Now these two facts alone – that Engels did not share Marx's early anthropology, and Marx Engels' late philosophy – would justify a separate treatment of Engels. Both of these differences bear relevance to the notion of freedom. But even apart from this, there is a difference between the two thinkers which is not so much one of substantive doctrine but of approach and emphasis. And this must be underlined, especially if one is to understand the Soviet position.

In presenting Engels' views, it will be appropriate to begin with those conceptions which he shared with Marx. This chapter will then turn to examine Engels' characteristic approach to the notion of freedom by analyzing a key text from *Anti-Dühring*. Two following sections will deal with more particular issues: the relation between human actions and historical laws, and the problem of free will. The final section will sum up the results of the chapter.

1. THE CONTINUATION OF MARX'S VIEWS

1.1 *Freedom as Power*

Engels openly shared the Marxian view that freedom consisted not in the absence of restraint but in power, in man's mastery over his surrounding social and physical milieu. This central point is affirmed first in the co-authored *German Ideology*[8] and later in numerous works by Engels alone, including *Anti-Dühring* and the *Dialectics of Nature*. In the former, Engels asserts that freedom does not consist in independence from nature but rather in the "control over ourselves and over external nature".[9] And in the latter, he singles out this mastery as the "final, essential distinction between man and other animals".[10]

In the majority of the texts where Engels speaks of freedom, he means to indicate not a psychological characteristic of the individual but an actual historical accomplishment of mankind. That is, it refers to the real concrete control that man has gained over his environment, achieved through the development of technology and (at least in the coming final stages of history) the application of social engineering. Engels, himself directly involved in an industry (textiles) which many times over was virtually transformed by the development of new techniques, was fascinated by the enormous effect of technical achievements on the life of man. At the beginning of history stands the discovery that "mechanical motion can be transformed into heat",[11] that is, that fire can be produced by friction. This discovery had a great effect on the liberation of mankind, for it "gave man for the first time control over one of the forces of nature" and thus represented "a mighty leap forward in human development".[12] A lesser but still in Engels' view a world-shaking discovery was that of the steam engine. It became in the nineteenth century both the symbolic representation and the real basis of the entire system of productive forces. And it is these forces which will make possible a classless society in which there will no longer be anxiety over the means of one's daily subsistence and "in which for the first time there can be talk of real human freedom".[13]

While Engels sees the technological power of man as growing steadily throughout the course of history, he does not see the same gradual progress in the control man exercises over his own social organization. This control increases dialectically, which means that it must first be negated before it can emerge in a higher positive form. From the first primitive grouping of men up to the last form of monopoly capitalism, the division of labor stamps society with some unavoidable marks: exploitation, class struggle, etc. Men have little control over these.[14] In fact, it decreases until in the last segment of this stage of history, the era of commodity-production, total anarchy reigns and finally leads to the collapse of the entire system.[15] Engels does not say that history is actually proceeding fortuitously, but rather that this development is fortuitous as far as the members of society are concerned; that is, they do not control it. But there comes a moment when this social anarchy is transformed in a dialectical leap into its opposite – total social planning. This sudden about-face is produced by the proletariat's seizure of the means of production: "With the seizing of the means of production by society, production of commodities is done away with, and, simultaneously, the mastery of the product over the producer. Anarchy in social production is replaced by plan-conforming, conscious organization".[16] The organization of production, in turn, makes it possible to place the whole of man's social life under his control. In a statement that closely parallels Marx's description in the *Capital* of the leap into the realm of freedom[17], Engels glowingly paints the state of affairs that will follow the proletarian revolution: "Man's own social organization, hitherto confronting him as a necessity imposed by nature and history, now becomes the result of his own free action. The extraneous objective forces that have hitherto governed history pass under the control of man himself. Only from that time will man himself, with full consciousness, make his own history – only from that time will the social causes set in movement by him have, in the main and in a constantly growing measure, the results intended by him. It is the ascent of man from the kingdom of necessity to the kingdom of freedom."[18] Thus mankind achieves its final freedom when the technological revolution is completed by the social revolution. The latter will even have a beneficial reciprocal effect on technology by releasing its full potentialities which were previously pent up by the limitations imposed by a market economy. In any case, in both Marx's and Engels' view man will emerge as the true master of both nature and society. His whole environment will be subjected to serving his own goals. And this is the meaning of real freedom.[19]

1.2. *Freedom as the Realization of One's Essence*

The majority of Engels' statements on freedom lead one to believe that power over nature and society is for him the final goal and ultimate meaning of freedom. Marx had gone further. He had placed this view within the larger context of a conception of man. Freedom as power is for him only a means for man to achieve something else – the full self-realization of himself as a person. As has previously been noted, the passage in *Capital* describing the leap into the realm of freedom indicates that Marx continued to develop his thought against the background of an anthropology long after the *Frühschriften*.[20]

Now it cannot be denied that Engels did put forward certain theses and descriptions which belong to philosophical anthropology: the doctrine of the origin of consciousness,[21] the characterization of man as a working animal,[22] the description of the nature of human action and volition[23], etc. However, these fragments are more of a consequence of his investigations than a frame of reference. Engels' anthropology does not motivate his thought but incidentally arises out of it, and is partially a result of his inability to abstain from wandering into almost every domain of intellectual endeavor. In any case, there is nothing in Engels' own philosophical writings which compares with the anthropology set down in the *Frühschriften* and which in an analogous manner gives meaning to his total view of history.

This having been said, it must nevertheless be admitted that there is a certain continuity of view also in the conception of freedom as the realization of one's human potentialities, simply because Engels explicitly restates this Marxian conception. In *Anti-Dühring* Engels states that in the new organization of production, "productive labor, instead of being a means of subjugating men, will become a means of their emancipation, by offering each individual the opportunity to develop all of his faculties, physical and mental, in all directions and exercise them to the full – in which therefore, productive labor will become a pleasure instead of being a burden."[24] It is not clear here whether the development of one's faculties occurs inside of or beyond the sphere of productive labor. Marx himself seems to change his position on this point.[25] But what is noteworthy about this statement is that Engels in fact verbally restates here Marx's anthropological notion of freedom. Thus there is a certain literal agreement on this conception also. Only it must not be forgotten that Engels does not reformulate the whole anthropology that lies behind this statement, nor does he offer one of his own. In short, it does not have any deeper roots in Engels' philosophical understanding of man. The statement stands alone, uninterpreted, and, as will be seen, is not repeated in his main statement on the nature of freedom. The emphasis in his writings is placed elsewhere, namely on the notion of freedom of activity.

2. THE FREEDOM OF HUMAN ACTIVITY

If Engels had done no more than reaffirm the 'concrete' conception of freedom as man's mastery over his environment, there would be no justification for speaking of an Engelsian theory of freedom. But he did in fact go further and tried to explain the source of this mastery in terms of the structure of human action. That is, Engels attempted to show that man's power derives from the unique nature of human activity in its relation to the environment.

The reason for which Engels pushed his analysis of freedom in this direction is not difficult to grasp. He and Marx had affirmed, on the one hand, that man becomes free to the extent that he controls and transforms his world; but, on the other hand, they believed that this world was governed by definite laws, independent of and inalterable by human agency. Given these two affirmations, the problem arises: How can man attain mastery over a world which develops according to its own inner necessity? What is it that makes concrete freedom possible in the face of the law-bound necessity of things?

The main text in which Engels gives his answer to this question is found in *Anti-Dühring* under the subtitle 'Freedom and Necessity'.[26] The key paragraphs found here are quoted and re-quoted in virtually every subsequent Marxist–Leninist treatment of freedom. And as we will see later[27], the manner in which Engels approaches the notion of freedom here becomes normative for practically all Soviet philosophers. In short it is *the* fundamental text, not only in Engels but also for most subsequent versions of Marxist conceptions of freedom. For this reason and because the interpretation of this text has often followed errant paths, we will subject it to a rather close analysis.

2.1. *The Insight into Necessity*

After accusing Dühring of presenting a vulgarization of the Hegelian view, Engels briefly states what the genuine Hegelian position is: "Hegel was the first to state correctly the relation between freedom and necessity. To him freedom is insight into necessity." Then he quotes Hegel, "'Necessity is *blind* only *insofar as it is not understood*'".[28] By approvingly citing a central thesis of Hegel,[28a] Engels seems to be asserting that freedom consists primarily in a type of *knowledge,* namely insight *(Einsicht)*. Plekhanov understands it in this way: for him, a cognitive apprehension of necessity removes its character as fate, as a blind force manipulating unsuspecting individuals; necessity loses its alien character through the mediation of knowledge, and this reconciliation is the essence of freedom.[29] As we read in Hegel's *Philosophy of History,* "when the subjective will of man submits to laws, the opposition of freedom and necessity vanishes. The rational, as that which is substantial, is necessary, and we are free insofar as we recognize it as law and follow it as the substance of our own being".[30]

Now in order to judge whether or not Engels actually follows Hegel, it is important to keep in mind that Hegel makes 'thought' not only a precondition of freedom but its very essence. In cognitively apprehending something, the knower assimilates it, makes it his own to a degree which neither will nor action can accomplish. The object loses in a certain way its independence from the knower; instead of the knower being dependent on it, it becomes a mode of and thus dependent on the knowing subject. And this absolute self-sufficiency of the subject achieved in the cognitive order constitutes freedom. Hegel remarks that in logic, "the spirit is fully with itself *(bei sich selbst)* and thereby free, for freedom is just this, to be with oneself in the other". And he adds, "Freedom is only present when there is no other for me which is not myself".[31] Of course, the appropriation of and resultant unity with the other reaches its highest stage only when the absolute spirit achieves full self-consciousness and realizes that its life is, in fact, the reality of everything else.[32] But the point we wish to make clear is only that no matter on what level of development of the Idea, the essence of freedom is seen to lie in some form of thought, whether this be understanding, reason or spirit.

Does Engels actually adopt this Hegelian conception or any variation of it? The fact stands that he explicitly approved Hegel's notion of freedom – although in somewhat cryptic fashion – and he has often been interpreted as following Hegel in this point. Only a close examination of the remainder of the text, in which Engels presents his own position, and a comparison of the results with the Hegelian view outlined here will answer this question.

2.2. *The Structure of the Free Act*

Immediately after the reference to Hegel, Engels writes "Freedom does not consist in the imagined *(geträumten)* independence from the laws of nature, but in the knowledge of these laws and in the possibility this gives of making them work according to a plan *(planmässig)* towards definite ends".[33] Here a pragmatic element is already introduced into the notion of freedom. It is no longer pure insight or knowledge alone which constitutes freedom, but knowledge *and* the capacity it gives for a certain kind of activity. One becomes free through knowledge to the extent that this gives one the possibility for 'making something work'.

Further, Engels has already specified what the nature of this practical activity is: making the laws of nature work for the achievement of definite ends. This very important precision touches the heart of Engels' viewpoint. Recall that we previously pointed out that Engels followed Marx in conceiving freedom as power, as the control man exercises over his environment. Here Engels is explaining how this control is realized. Man is uniquely able to apprehend the laws of nature. Since these laws are objective – they really hold – concrete applications can be deduced, by which nature can be steered in one direction or another. In this way, through the application of science nature is made to serve the definite ends of human beings. Man can never be free from nature, but through the power that knowledge gives him he is free to utilize it for his own well-being.

In the key statement of the passage which we are analyzing, Engels explains more precisely in what type of individual human act this can be accomplished: "Freedom of will therefore means nothing else but the capacity to decide with knowledge of the subject. Thus, the *freer* a man's judgment is in relation to a certain question, the greater is the *necessity* with which the content of this judgment will be determined; while the uncertainty founded on ignorance which chooses in an apparently arbitrary fashion between different and contradictory possibilities of choice shows precisely by this fact that it is not free, that it is dominated by the object which it should itself control."[34] The individual act which can be free is a *judgment of practical reason*. Although Engels begins here by speaking of freedom of will, the full text reveals that it is not primarily in the volitional order that he wishes to locate freedom. As a matter of fact, the greater the role left to mere choice, the lesser is the degree of freedom. Choice is not denied, but it must be fully guided by practical reason. The true locus of individual freedom is a judgment 'in relation to a certain question'. This question is not a theoretical but a practical one: namely, how can one best utilize the environment for one's own ends. It is always a specific case of man's struggle to control nature and society. And accordingly the answer is not to be found in pure insight, that such and such is the state of affairs, but rather in a judgment of the type 'x is the course of action which will best achieve y', where y is some particular human goal. Now Engels is saying that freedom is a quality of this type of judgment, regarding the degree with which its content is determined by knowledge of the subject. Not every practical judgment is free, only those which are well-founded and correct, and thus will achieve results.

In the final sentence of this text Engels rounds out his position, integrating some of what he previously said into a more comprehensive view: "Therefore freedom consists in the control *(Herrschaft)* over ourselves and over external nature which is founded on the knowledge of natural necessity; it is thereby necessarily a product of historical development".[35] If freedom can be said to consist in one sense in knowledge of laws, and in another sense in the correctness and certainty of a practical judgment, it is only because both of these issue in 'the control over ourselves and over external nature'. Without this final stage, the actual transformation of reality, the other two moments would lose their significance. In order to be the *loci* of freedom in any sense, they must have as their result a concrete act which actually exerts power, control, dominance over reality.

By way of summary we might summarize Engels' position as follows: (1) freedom as a historical category means the actual control over nature that man has won; this is accumulated in the form of machines, production methods, technological advances, etc.; (2) freedom as a characteristic of individual human activity describes a chain of action, beginning with (a) the comprehension of the laws of nature, passing to (b) the formation of some practical judgment on the basis of this knowledge, and issuing in (c) an act in which this judgment is realized in the practical order. The results of this act thus become an addition to freedom in the first sense.

The relation of Engels' view to that of Hegel now becomes clear. The knowledge of or 'insight into' necessity is not itself freedom but only the foundation for it. Knowledge is apprized not as spirit, but in the Baconian sense as power, insofar as it supplies the basis for technology and social planning. Quite contrary to Hegel, one does not seek out the laws of necessity 'to follow... as the substance of our own being', but to harness and submit to one's own designs. Ultimately, Engels cannot agree with Hegel's understanding of the relation of knowledge and freedom, because he rejects the identity of subject and object upon which this is based. Thus the Hegelian position, so positively affirmed by Engels himself, turns out to be only a small contributive factor in the formation of Engels' total view, where it is understood in a completely different sense than in the Hegelian philosophy itself.

It must also be noted that Engels' theory of freedom is not merely a re-statement of Marx. It is a development of Marxian ideas along a path which Marx himself would perhaps not have been so anxious to follow. Not resting content with historical analysis, Engels seeks to give a philosophical interpretation of the manner in which freedom is accomplished, with particular reference to the 'laws' of nature and society which so preoccupy him. Now his emphasis on the free employment of the laws of *nature* in technology both renders his theory credible and saves it from comparison with Marx, who said very little about natural science. But as soon as the context is *society*, difficulties arise. We have already discussed some of these in arguing that Marx did not hold the view that social freedom was achieved primarily through the conscious application of the laws of society.[36] This is an Engelsian view.[37] And unfortunately, Engels does not explain in any detail what the mechanism of this process might be.

2.3. *The Determined Character of the Free Act*

A final comment might be made on the relevance of this text to the problem of determinism. On the one hand, it must be admitted that the relation between freedom and necessity described here does not directly imply psychological determinism. Engels says that the degree of freedom is a function of the degree of necessity with which a judgment is determined – a statement which would seem to place him squarely in the determinist camp. But as our remarks already indicated, a more careful look at the passage reveals that Engels here means by 'necessity' something very different than he did earlier when alluding to the Hegelian 'insight into necessity' or when he uses the term in other contexts, as in the phrase 'natural necessity'. In these latter cases 'necessity' is the approximate equivalent of 'necessary laws' or 'occurrence in conformity with law'. That the term is not being used in this sense to characterize judgment becomes evident if one notes what Engels considers to be the opposite of a judgment which is determined by necessity – namely, one founded on ignorance. Engels is not concerned here with the efficient causes of a judgment, whether or not it is fully determined to occur in the way in which it does; in this case, the opposite of 'necessary' would be 'contingent'. He is concerned rather with the *content* of the judgment, its full specification by a correct apprehension of the laws of nature pertinent to the subject. If this distinction is not kept in mind, Engels could be interpreted as representing the absurd position that free judgments are those which occur inevitably while unfree ones are those which are the results of chance.

On the other hand, Engels makes a statement in the context of this passage which is not so innocent of deterministic implications. After stating that freedom consists in the application of laws, he specifies what types of laws he had in mind: "This holds good in relation both to the laws of external nature and to those which govern the bodily and mental existence of men themselves – two classes of laws which we can separate from each other at most only in thought but not in reality".[38] What strikes one here is that Engels affirms the existence of laws governing mental activity and conceives these as being not separated 'in reality', from the laws of nature. Unfortunately, he does not explain how or to what degree these laws govern *(regeln)* mental events. It could mean that every mental event is thoroughly and exhaustively determined by a set of operative laws; or it could mean only that there are certain laws according to which mental activity proceeds, e.g., that perception always precedes desire, that intellectual knowledge is based on sense knowledge, etc. If only the latter is meant, no psychological determinism is implied. This question will be discussed more extensively later on. But here it can at least be conjectured that the weaker sense of law is intended. Engels says that by apprehending these laws we have the power to gain 'control over ourselves', that is, we should be able even to alter our mental activity according to our goals. If strict determinism were meant, it would be difficult to conceive in what real sense this control could be exercised.

3. Human action and historical law

Just as Engels went beyond Marx in elaborating a theoretical conception of the nature of free activity, so also did he try to explain in a more general fashion the relation between individual human actions and historical laws. Marx was content with describing the influence of certain historical conditions on human behavior. Engels assaults the much more difficult task of explaining how individual actions fit into a historical process which is determined by necessary laws.

There is a significant difference between natural and historical process: "In nature... there are only blind, unconscious agencies acting upon one another, out of whose interplay the general law comes into operation. Nothing of all that happens... happens as a consciously desired aim. In the history of society, on the contrary, the actors are all endowed with consciousness, are men acting with deliberation or passion, working towards definite goals; nothing happens without a conscious purpose, without an intended aim".[39] This is a straightforward observation: in history, unlike in nature, events occur as the result of conscious, goal-directed activity; results are intended and executed through conscious action. However, although Engels admits that history is a unique process, different from nature, this does not exempt it from being "governed by general laws".[40] This characteristic it does share with nature. Now the question arises: does not the statement that history is in some form governed by laws seriously weaken the claim that it is a product of conscious human activity? Although men consciously sketch and execute plans and thus naturally consider themselves to be the authors of historical events, the fact of the matter, according to Engels, is that these events are determined by general laws. How does Engels explain this apparent contradiction?

He appeals to two distinctions, both of which tend to resolve the problem by reducing the importance of human acts without at the same time openly denying their reality. First of all, he distinguishes between that which is consciously intended by the agent and that which actually happens: "That which is willed happens but rarely; in the majority of instances the numerous desired ends cross and conflict with one another, or these ends themselves are from the outset incapable of realization or the means of attaining them are insufficient."[41] Although the ends of human actions are intended, as a matter of fact the results and consequences are not.[42] It is the normal human condition to be incapable of realizing one's goals and projects; it is only rarely that the chain of human activity proceeds successfully from initial conception to actual realization. Of course, Engels does not trouble to substantiate or illustrate this point, nor does he offer any empirical evidence that this is in fact the situation in the majority of instances. What is more evident than the truth of the observation itself is the function it serves in his argument: since the planned actions of individuals do not normally accomplish what they set out to do, they do not provide the ultimate explanation for historical events. And the ground is cleared for explaining the rational development of history in another fashion, namely by the appeal to laws. Secondly, in order to relate these human acts to the laws of history, Engels appeals to the distinction between appearance and underlying reality. Although "historical events... appear on the whole to be... governed by chance", because all we allegedly see is a mass of floundering, ineffectual and conflicting human agents, the fact of the matter is that "where on the surface accident holds sway, there actually it is always governed by inner, hidden laws".[43] There are two different levels: the level of observable phenomena and that of concealed underlying factors. It is of course the latter which in the last analysis really count, and these are the reputed laws of history.

Thus we have the following situation in history. An event is the resultant of "many wills operating in different directions".[44] Many lines of purposeful action come together unintentionally and produce a result which would normally be labelled a chance event. However, it is not a chance event but the result of the operation of definite laws, which one only needs to uncover. Now Engels makes it clear enough that these laws do not directly govern the historical events, bypassing the human actions. They in some way operate *through* human actions. How is this to be explained?

Behind human actions lie definite motives of various kinds. But these motives themselves are not ultimate factors: there are driving forces which "stand behind these motives", "historical causes which transform themselves into these motives in the brains of the actors".[45] It is these driving forces which are the ultimate causes of historical events. Only by investigating these forces can we be put "on the track of the laws holding sway both in history as a whole and at particular periods and in particular lands".[46] Fortunately, Engels himself knows what these forces are: class struggles, brought about ultimately by the "development of the forces of production and relations of exchange".[47]

Thus the total scheme in Engels' analysis of history would include four elements: (a) the driving forces, (b) the motives of human actions conditioned by these forces, (c) the actions themselves, and (d) the resultant historical event. The statement that history is governed by laws can be taken to mean that there is a regular co-ordination between *a* and *d,* and that *a* is somehow the ultimate cause of *d.*

Now it is difficult to assess whether or not this position involves 'historical determinism'. First of all, if by this phrase is meant the view that the leading historical events (which set the general trend of the development of society) are brought about by factors uncontrollable by subjective decisions, then Engels *is* a historical determinist. If it is meant that *all* events occur in this way, he is not. Engels never expressed his conception of the determined nature of the course of history in such a universal formula. Secondly, if 'historical determinism' is taken to designate a conception not of the determinateness of events but of the fact that human actions are nothing but mere moments in the historical process and as such have no independence, then it is very difficult to decide whether or not this term is applicable to Engels. The relation of *a* to *b* is certainly a necessary one, in the sense that men cannot escape the influence of economic factors on their motivation. But it is important to keep in mind that just as when Engels speaks of history he normally means a broad process of the development of economic, social and political movements, and not momentary occurrences, so also when he affirms that there are driving forces which determine human motivation, he means not so much "the motives of single individuals" as "those motives which set in motion great masses, whole peoples, and again whole classes of the people in each people".[48] For example, the political struggle in early 19th century England is to be explained as a struggle of three conflicting classes whose origin is seen to lie in economic differences.[49] Here to be 'historically determined' would mean to act as a member of a group which is motivated in its political action by its own economic interests. More than that does not seem to be implied.

Thus it does not seem that Engels presents a deterministic interpretation of human actions in their relation to the laws of history alone. Men are motivated by the driving forces of history, but this does not preclude the influence of other motivating forces. In fact, Engels, in his later years, himself took pains to refute the conception of Marxism as an economic reductionism: political, legal, philosphical, and religious views in the minds of the participants in history "also exercise their influence upon the course of the historical struggles and in many cases preponderate in determining their *form*".[50] Consequently, the (economic) 'driving forces' determine human action as limiting conditions only; they do not in a necessary and sufficient manner univocally specify the form that action will assume.

4. FREEDOM OF WILL

The general theory of historical determinism, including the thesis that human actions are motivated by economic factors, does not rule out a certain freedom of choice. However, Engels was not always content to remain within the bounds of social theory, but occasionally ventured remarks which present at least the fragments of a psychology of human decision. And this *does* appear to be deterministic.

A distinction which sets off Engels' fragmentary psychology from his other remarks on human will and decision was provided by himself. In explaining the nature of the will of the state by comparing it to individual will, Engels writes: "As all the driving forces of the actions of any individual person must pass through his brain, and transform themselves into motives of his will in order to set him into action, so also all the needs of civil society... must pass through the will of the state... That is the formal aspect of the matter – the one which is self-evident. The question arises, however, what is the content of this merely formal will... and whence is this content derived?"[51] Two aspects of the will are here distinguished, the formal aspect and its content. The latter designates the actual, concrete specifications of the will, the types of decisions, the actual directions which the will gives to the subject, etc. One might dispute, for example, whether decisions are motivated chiefly by economic or by moral factors, or whether they are wise or unwise. But the settling of such issues would say little or nothing about the structure of human decision, about the formal aspect the will considered not for its content but for its structure and mode of operation. The formal characteristics of the will would be those that apply to all and not to just a few wills, that abstract from individual differences among particular wills and describe human will in general. Now it is true that Engels disapproved of the formal approach; he speaks perjoratively of the 'merely formal will'. This is consistent with his (and Marx's) strongly empiricist inclination to examine everything within its concrete material (especially social) context. Nevertheless, he does make remarks about the formal nature of the will, and these are relevant to the question of whether or not the will is free.

Engels sketches the functioning of the will in the following way: "The will is determined by passion or deliberation. But the levers which immediately determine passion or deliberation are of very different kinds. Partly they may be external objects, partly ideal motives, ambition, 'enthusiasm for truth and justice', personal hatred or even purely individual whims of all kinds".[52] The direct movers of the will are passion and deliberation. Apparently Engels does not differentiate the way in which each of these affects the will. They are not set off as separate faculties. And thus their peculiarity must be interpreted at face value: individuals sometimes make decisions which are unpremeditated and are a more or less spontaneous outcome of their emotional state, while at other times their decisions are preceded by long consideration and a measured judgment of the alternatives. But both processes (or some combination of the two) determine the will; there is no provision made for an intermediate factor. In their turn, passion and deliberation are determined by a multitude of 'levers'. These are the components of the psyche, in particular those which function as motives: ideals, desires, prejudices, etc. Again, Engels nowhere explains precisely how these factors determine passion or deliberation: whether they all contributively constitute a passion, whether it is merely the strongest motive which prevails over all the rest, etc. But however they work their influence is decisive. On the other hand, they are not the primordial determinants. The chain of causality stretches back even further: "we simply cannot get away from the fact that everything which sets men acting must find its way through their brains... The influences of the external world upon man express themselves in his brain, are reflected therein as feelings, thoughts, impulses, volitions – in short, as 'ideal tendencies' and in this form become 'ideal powers'".[53] All of the factors which contribute to the determination of the will are products of the influence of the external world. More precisely, they are reflections of this influence. Consequently, the final explanation for any act of the will is not to be sought in the human psyche itself, but outside of it, in that particular segment of the external world which forms its milieu.

There is no doubt that such an analysis of the functioning of the will leaves little room for freedom. Not only is no provision made in the inner functioning of volition for either an indeterminate or superdeterminate element, but the course of this process is subordinated, in the last analysis, to factors lying outside of its sphere. The will thereby also loses its autonomy.

The vagueness of Engels' analysis may lead one to speculate that perhaps Engels did not intend his remarks to be taken so literally, as the formulation of a deterministic view. However, other occasional statements leave no room for doubt. In a letter to Bloch, Engels talks about "individual wills, of which each in turn has been made what it is by a host of particular conditions of life"; and further on he described "individual wills" as those "each of which wishes what it is impelled to by its physical constitution and external, in the last resort economic circumstances (either its own personal circumstances or those of society in general)".[54] The latter statement is particularly important because it directly relates the act of will to the circumstances of life. It interprets the whole chain of action – which Engels analyzes into act of will, passion or deliberation, motivating elements, and reflection of the external world – as a single process in which the will is impelled to act in the way it does. If any of the intermediate stages would allow the intrusion of a 'free' influence, this direct coordination between the first stage, the act of the will, and the last, the conditions of life, would not obtain.

As a final remark, it might be noted that Engels rejected the attribution of any proper meaning to the concept itself of free will. At the beginning of the classic text on freedom in *Anti-Dühring* he speaks condescendingly of "so-called free will".[55] And then in his actual presentation of the theory of freedom, he reduces free will to something else: "Freedom of will means the capacity to decide with knowledge of the subject".[56] He thereby deprives the first of its status as a separate and legitimate philosophical concept. What is implied by this is that free will as it has been traditionally understood is a fiction; the individual has no spiritual autonomy vis-a-vis the totality of his determining factors. This is, to use Engels' own word, merely a dream.

5. SUMMARY

The examination of Engels' remarks concerning freedom shows not so much that he departed from Marx, but that he turned his attention to different aspects of the notion and thereby expanded the Marxist tradition which Soviet philosophers would later have to interpret. Whether Engels' additions are compatible with Marx's basic principles has been questioned.[57] And one ought to examine the problem of the internal consistency of the Engelsian view as a whole. But since the problems inherent in Engels' view also reappear openly in the Soviet discussions, their treatment will be deferred to later sections of this work. For the present, it will be useful to summarize the results of our analysis of Engels' position.

(1) Following Marx, Engels interprets freedom not as a negative category indicating some absence of determination, but as an expression of man's positive, active relation to nature and society. This is clearly in evidence in Engels' re-affirmation of Marx's *historical concept* of freedom, which characterizes the growing control, the mastery of the human environment – in Marx's early language, the humanization of nature – made possible by the increasing transformative capabilities of the productive apparatus. This process is to culminate in a dialectical leap into the realm of freedom, where not only natural forces but also social forces will be subject to man's conscious control.

(2) Although Engels does not take over the early Marxian anthropology or orient his thought within the context of a conception of man – his thought is more cosmocentric than anthropocentric – nevertheless he also repeats literally Marx's anthropological concept of freedom: i.e., that human freedom consists in the realization of all the human potentialities, in the all-round fulfillment of man. But again this does not seem to be an organic element of his thought.

(3) In spite of Engels' positive evaluation of the Hegelian position, the thesis that freedom is 'insight into necessity' does not express his own view either (a) in the sense that freedom consists in cognition, or (b) in the related meaning that it lies in the cognition of and acquiescence to necessity.

(4) Freedom is predicated of individual human *activity* by analogy to the historical sense of freedom as power; the former is seen as free insofar as it is the cause of the latter. Expressed in different terms, Engels' account of free activity is one attempt to explain how the control which man exercises over his environment can be traced to his categoreally unique form of activity.

(5) Free activity comprises several different stages: (a) the entertainment of a definite goal to be accomplished; (b) the cognition of the laws of nature or society which govern the relevant sphere of reality;

(c) the formulation of a practical judgment based on the knowledge of these laws and suited to the achievement of the goal, and (d), the issue of this process in actual practical action.

(6) The *judgment* alone is designated 'free' in still a third sense, insofar as it is seen as the pivotal stage in the whole process. Its degree of freedom is specified by the extent to which it is informed by the knowledge of the necessary laws covering the situation. It is thereby opposed to 'free choice', i.e., a decision made arbitrarily due to the indifference of ignorance concerning the relative merits of the various alternatives.

(7) The thesis that a judgment is free to the extent that it is determined by necessity concerns not the causal conditionedness of the act but the degree to which it is based on true knowledge.

(8) Engels' conception of the relation of human acts to objective *historical* factors is certainly deterministic in spirit, but it does not necessarily imply the universal and univocal determination of these acts. For various reasons, it is only rarely that an individual agent is able to achieve the very same goal which he has posited. However, this does not mean that these acts have no efficacy; they are contributive factors which together constitute the resulting concrete historical situation. Further, while it is true that the laws of history lie beneath and give form to the conglomeration of individual acts, thus imposing a unity of development on history, they determine these acts only in a general, average sense. That is, they are necessary but not sufficient conditions for the precise form any individual act will take.

(9) On the other hand, Engels' psychology of volition does appear to be deterministic. Acts of will are determined through a chain of causality in which the primary factors are the physical constitution and external milieu of the individual. The 'ideal' components of the mind, such as ideals, desires, thoughts, etc., and the immediate levers of volition – passion and deliberation – are mere intermediate links in the total process. There are no indeterminate relations permitting the subject to exercise any autonomy over against this causal mechanism.

CHAPTER IV

LENIN

Of the three classic authors, Lenin contributed the least in the way of a philosophical development of the notion of freedom. His works are full of scathing remarks on the so-called democratic freedoms – freedom of trade, of the press, of assembly, of voting, etc. – repeating Marx's critique that these are freedoms enjoyed only by a certain class.[1] And of course he is no less voluble in insisting that the goal of the proletarian revolution is to free working mankind from exploitation.[2] But aside from these remarks, which are mainly sociological and political in character, there is very little serious discussion of the notion of freedom from a philosophical point of view. Furthermore, the few passages which are relevant do not manifest any radically new thinking on Lenin's part. This was evidently the effect of his conviction that the problem of freedom had already been fully solved by Marx and Engels. In particular, he held *Anti-Dühring* in great esteem, expressing full agreement with the passage in this work where Engels described the relation between freedom and necessity.

Nevertheless, Lenin's remarks concerning freedom, however few and uninspired they might be, carry extraordinary weight among Soviet philosophers, simply because it was Lenin who made them. Especially since the death of Stalin, Lenin's authority in theoretical matters has been enormous. Just as Engels' interpretation of Marx was considered as normative by Lenin, so also is Lenin's view of the entire Marxist tradition considered by contemporary Soviet philosophers. Thus even if Lenin did not essentially revise the Marxian-Engelsian heritage, the very fact that he repeated some points and omitted others bears some importance for the understanding of the Soviet position. Moreover, as will be seen, the confusion which plagues his interpretation of Engels was thereby passed on to his unfortunate philosophical heirs. And finally, it must be admitted that Lenin's political activity and the revisions of historical materialism which this required have indirectly but nonetheless decidedly influenced the general frame of mind within which the problem of freedom is considered.

In the present chapter we will first examine Lenin's early defence of Marxism against the charge of fatalism. It is here that he makes his most substantive statement on free will. Secondly, we will discuss his adoption and interpretation of the Engelsian view on freedom and necessity. Thirdly, we will present his conception of the relation between objective laws and human activity as found in the *Philosophical Notebooks*. And finally, we will assess the importance of his alleged voluntarism.

1. DETERMINISM, FATALISM AND FREE WILL

One of the first problems with which Lenin had to grapple in his defense of Marxism was the apparent incompatibility of determinism with an activist view of the role of individuals in history. Some of the Russian populists had claimed that Marxism was a fatalistic theory.[3] They objected that men became little more than puppets in the pre-determined drama of history, and that determinism robbed them of the possibility of moral responsibility; in short, that Marxism was a fatalism and thus implied quietism and indifferentism. Lenin denied this vociferously: "Determinism not only does not pre-suppose fatalism, but, on the contrary, it supplies a basis for intelligent activity."[4]

What is interesting about Lenin's defense of Marx against alleged deterministic excesses is that in the course of that defense he puts forward a more comprehensive and tight determinism than Marx himself proposed. It is certainly not a voluntaristic revision of Marxian determinism, as has been suggested,[5] for if Lenin's text is closely examined, it becomes clear that his arguments do not actually serve his intentions.

In seeking to counter the charge that (Marxist) determinism and morality conflict with each other, Lenin writes: "The idea of determinism, which establishes the necessity of human actions and rejects the absurd tale of free will, does not in the least do away with either the intelligence or conscience of man, or the appraisal of his actions. Quite the contrary, only on the basis of a determinist view is it possible to make a strict and correct appraisal, instead of attributing everything you want to free will."[6] There are two facets of Lenin's conception of determinism which deserve to be underlined here. First, he extends the principle of determinism fully to individual actions. Marx never said that all human actions were necessary, nor does this seem to be assumed by his theory of historical materialism. But Lenin, perhaps under the influence of Plekhanov, states it categorically. His determinism here seems to reach much further than Marx's; it is a universal explanation of reality rather than a limited thesis applied to a particular type of phenomena. Human actions, like everything else, are determined by their conditions and causes. Secondly, this determinism entails a rejection of free will. We might surmise that Lenin rejected free will because he understood this to mean nothing more than 'indeterminism'. But elsewhere he manifests his opposition to any notion of free will. He denies that free will is a fact of experience.[7] And he places the notion in the same category as that of God and immortality (the three Kantian ideas) as products of idealism and as inimical to a "philosophy of materialism".[8]

It is obvious that in this text Lenin does not explain how moral appraisal is *justified* from a determinist point of view; he only states that determinism makes a 'strict and correct appraisal' *possible*. The same weakness plagues his attempt to show that historical necessity does not nullify the significance of human actions. After insisting that "all history is made up precisely of the actions of persons, who are undoubtedly active", he explains how these actions can be appraised, namely in relation to their circumstances: "The real question that arises in appraising the social activity of a person is: in the presence of what conditions is this activity ensured of success? what guarantee is there that this activity will not remain an isolated act, drowning in a sea of contradictory acts??".[9] It is not difficult to see that such a type of appraisal, which evaluates the worth of actions solely in relation to the favorable or unfavorable conditions for success, actually depreciates the act itself. Historical conditions become everything: they are not only the cause but also the criterion of judgment of actions.

Thus, Lenin's earliest substantive statement concerning freedom does not move away from determinism: human actions are necessarily determined, free will is a fiction, and consequently the moral quality and social significance of human activity is to be assessed only on the basis of its conditions and consequences.

2. FREEDOM AND NECESSITY

In spite of Lenin's rejection of free will and affirmation of the necessity of human actions, he did not refrain from speaking positively of *any* notion of freedom. He explicitly stated his acceptance of the Engelsian view of the relation between freedom and necessity and often quoted with approval the central text from *Anti-Dühring* which we analyzed above.[9a] In *Materialism and Empirio-criticism,* he devotes a whole section to 'Freedom and Necessity'.[10] His immediate purpose is not to explain what freedom is but to refute the Russian Machists, who, all the while accepting the Engelsian conception of freedom, do not see that it is based on 'materialist' (i.e., realist) epistemological premises.[11] In order to make his point Lenin quotes nearly the entire passage from *Anti-Dühring*. This is accepted as true, to serve as the basis for his argument against the Machists. Lenin could not have paid a higher compliment to a doctrine than to judge it a proof for materialism. In another place, a short essay on Marx written for *Granat's Encyclopedia,* Lenin also makes use of Engels' famous text. It is interesting that he quotes it as a statement of *Marx's* position: "It is especially important to note Marx's view on the relation between freedom and necessity: 'Freedom is the consciousness of necessity. "Necessity is blind only insofar as it is not understood"' (Engels, *Anti-Dühring*)".[12] This second text shows that Lenin regarded Engels' conception of freedom and necessity as definitive for the entire Marx-Engels tradition, as *the* Marxist position.[13] Consequently, it is a position with which Lenin himself can be identified.

However, it was noted above that Engels' text is open to various interpretations: the emphasis can be laid either on the conscious acquiescence to or the activist utilization of necessity.[14] Lenin, unfortunately, gave support to *both* lines of interpretation. The chief comment on Engels' text which Lenin puts forward in *Materialism and Empirio-criticism* is by itself non-committal. After praising Engels for not contriving any 'scholastic definitions' of freedom and necessity, Lenin describes Engels' procedure: "Engels takes the knowledge and will of man, on the one hand, and the necessity of nature, on the other, and instead of giving any definitions, simply says that the necessity of nature is primary, and human will and mind secondary. The latter must necessarily and inevitably adapt themselves to the former."[15] Lenin here equates the solution of the problem of freedom and necessity with that of the relation between mind and nature. Just as the knowing mind must reflect nature, so also must the will conform to its necessary laws.

How is this relation between will and the laws of nature to be understood? If it is at all similar to copying, reflecting, etc. (i.e., the epistemological relation), then it would seem that Lenin understands freedom in a passivist sense. Such a view is indicated by his remarks in the *Karl Marx* article: "This", i.e. Engels' statement on freedom and necessity, "means the recognition *(priznanie)* of objective law in nature and of the dialectical transformation of necessity into freedom (in the same manner as the transformation of the unknown, but knowable 'thing-in-itself' into the 'thing-for-us', of the 'essence of things' into 'phenomena')".[16] What is important to note here is that the transformation of necessity into freedom is understood as similar to and very closely connected with a cognitive process, if not a cognitive process itself. It happens in the same manner as the process by which the thing-in-itself is transformed into a thing-for-us. This is also indicated in the earlier work: "The development of consciousness... presents us at every step with examples of... the transformation of blind, unknown necessity, 'necessity-in-itself', into the known 'necessity-for-us'".[17] The transformation of blind necessity, i.e., the achievement of freedom, is the same as or at least is directly correlative to and thoroughly dependent upon the attainment of knowledge by which man correctly reflects nature. Thus, Lenin in these texts seems to be much closer than Engels to understanding the Hegelian formula, 'Freedom is the insight into necessity', in a Hegelian manner.

On the other hand, Lenin also makes statements that support the activist conception of the relation between freedom and necessity – which is Engels' actual view. According to this interpretation, the insight into necessity is merely a means, a first step towards achieving freedom. In *Materialism and Empirio-criticism,* Lenin writes, "... until we know a law of nature, it, existing and acting independently of and outside our mind, makes us slaves of 'blind necessity'. But once we come to know this law, which acts (as Marx repeated a thousand times) *independently* of our will and our mind, we become the masters of nature. The mastery of nature manifested in human practice is a result of an objectively correct reflection within the human head of the phenomena and processes of nature…"[18] There is quite a difference between saying that freedom consists in the knowledge of necessity, and saying that it is a *result* of such knowledge and actually consists in the control, the mastery over nature. In the latter view, freedom is achieved not in the realm of spirit but that of practice. And Lenin emphasizes that "Practice is higher than (theoretical) knowledge".[19]

Thus there is a certain ambiguity in Lenin's statements on freedom and necessity. He wishes to interpret Engels in a manner in which the reference to Hegel makes sense. But he also approves Engels' anti-Hegelian view that freedom lies in the realm of practice. This ambiguity, unfortunately, continues to this day to becloud the discussion of freedom by Soviet philosophers.

3. PURPOSEFUL ACTIVITY AND NATURAL PROCESS

Lenin's early rejection of free will and his stumbling interpretation of the relation between freedom and necessity did not enrich the Marxist tradition in any significant way. They were variations on themes by Engels. And yet it cannot be said that Lenin added nothing. In the *Philosophical Notebooks* he makes a number of cryptic remarks relevant to the notion of freedom, which, although lacking in explication, are important in their suggestive power.

While commenting on the transition in Hegel's *Logic* from the doctrine of 'essence' to that of 'concept', Lenin writes, "NB Freedom = subjectivity ('or') goal, consciousness, endeavor".[20] He is thereby calling attention to the fact that in Hegel freedom is connected with a special mode of being, namely subjectivity. Further, he is emphasizing the teleological nature of subjective activity: to operate as a subject means to have conscious goals and to strive to realize them. This can be taken as defining a type of activity which is proper to man only and in which his freedom can be seen to consist.[20a] It is important to note that the emphasis here falls on the 'inner subject' as the locus of freedom, and not on the external world of practical activity. Thus, this fragment may have served to suggest to Lenin's followers that freedom might be sought in the person himself, that there can be such a thing as a theory of personal freedom as well as a social and technological conception.

Also suggesting the view that human activity has a unique structure of its own is a discussion by Lenin of the different forms of 'objective process'. In a passage entitled 'Materialist Dialectics' where Lenin is unquestionably stating his own position, he distinguishes "two forms of objective process: nature... and the purposive *(celepolagajuščaja)* activity of man".[21] What is intimated here is that human activity constitutes a level of reality categoreally different from nature, and that consequently the way in which it is caused or acts as a cause must not be understood after the fashion of natural causal explanation. Lenin indicates this in a reverse manner by emphasizing that the specific character of natural processes which enables them to serve human activity lies in the fact that they are "determined by external conditions (the laws of nature)".[22] The obvious inference to be drawn from this statement is that human activity is determined by internal conditions, and that the leading internal condition is the consciously entertained goal, the purpose of an action.

However, although Lenin is willing to set off human activity from natural process as qualitatively different, he takes pains to insist that it is not independent of nature. The goal which functions in purposive activity is not a pure creation of the human spirit. At first glance it "*seems* to man as if his goals are taken from outside the world, and are independent of the world ('freedom')".[23] This arises from the fact that while consciousness reflects nature, nonetheless there is no simple coincidence with it; thus man's conscious goals appear foreign to nature. But "in actual fact, men's ends are engendered *(poroždeny)* by the objective world and pre-suppose it".[24] Lenin wishes to stress that goals are derived from the external world. Although he does not say that the goals of individual actions are *no more* than a consequence of the natural conditions of the agent (goals might be only *partially* caused by nature), his intention is to devalue their spontaneity and autonomy in consciousness and to emphasize the fact that they are determined from without. It is relevant in this connection that he underlines, with the marginal note 'Hegel and historical materialism', the following passage from Hegel's *Logic*: "In his tools man possesses power over external nature, although as regards his ends, he frequently is subjected to it".[25]

4. VOLUNTARISM AND DETERMINISM IN HISTORY

Lenin is nearly always classified as a voluntarist[26], since he is supposed to have given greater importance to will than did Marx. But one must be careful in attaching this label to Lenin, for he is not a voluntarist in every sense of the term. He is certainly not an ontological voluntarist: will is not for him constitutive of reality. Nor is he a voluntarist in the psychological or moral senses: will does not take precedence over intellect, nor is it the main factor which determines the moral goodness of an act.

It is normally specified that Lenin's voluntarism is a *historical* conception, to the extent that it revises Marx's determinist explanation of history.[27] According to the Marxist view, history proceeds in accordance with necessary laws which are independent of the will of man. The main motive factors are not social contracts, reform movements, etc. – conscious schemes of great men – but material forces, namely the forces and relations of production. Lenin is seen to have violated this view to the extent that he sought to substitute, for the law-bound socio-economic evolution, his own personal agency and thus to force history along an arbitrary path. In particular, he is famous for two specific revisions of historical materialism: (1) He advocated and successfully led a socialist revolution in an unindustrialized country, in which the working class still constituted a minority; in the Marxist view it should have been necessary first to pass through the stage of full industrial capitalism. (2) His doctrine of the party as a small band of professional revolutionaries trained to carry out the revolution replaced the Marxist view that the revolution would be carried out by the mass army of impoverished workers. In these two points, Lenin went much further than was justified by Marx's concession that the actions of individuals might speed up (lessen the birth pangs of) the course of history. His revolutionary impatience led him to alter the very *form* of historical development, by substituting political action for the natural occurrence of certain intermediate stages of history.

Now Lenin's historical voluntarism has one important implication for the conception of human freedom: the actions of individuals are not fully determined by historical laws. If history is considered to be subject to the transforming influence of men, then the latter cannot be fully subject to history's own natural rhythm. Their actions may be subject to other laws, but they retain a certain autonomy vis-à-vis history. However, bearing this point fully in mind, one must not over-evaluate Lenin's 'voluntarist' revisions as an entirely new juncture in the development of the Marxist view of the freedom of the individual. And this for three reasons: (1) As we saw earlier[27a], Marx and Engels themselves did not understand historical laws as totally regulating the behavior of men. These are 'iron' laws only with regard to the development of socio-economic formations. Thus the implication of Lenin's voluntarism that human actions are not fully determined by historical laws has some precedent in the Marxist tradition. (2) Further, Lenin's voluntarism was in a certain sense more practical than theoretical. He repeatedly affirmed Marx's theory of history in quite orthodox fashion,[28] but was forced to make some *ad hoc* revisions to justify his own revolutionary activity. And it goes without saying that he always considered his views to be absolutely faithful to the principles laid down by Marx.[29] (3) Finally, Lenin's historical voluntarism is certainly not backed up by an anthropological voluntarism. His conception of man and man's relation to the environment does not include any significant role for the human will. What little Lenin says which might be construed as an anthropology seems rather to emphasize the inconsequence of volitional functions.

5. SUMMARY

In general, Lenin's scattered remarks on freedom do not amount to much more than an affirmation of the views of Engels. He does not actually clarify these views; in fact he seems rather to add some confusion. As was seen, his comments on Engels' text in *Anti-Dühring* vacillate between an activist and a passivist interpretation of the relation of freedom to necessity. Insofar as the purely psychological problem is concerned, he follows Engels' determinist tendencies, at least in an early work; and he does not think much at all of the notion of free will. However, some cryptic jottings in the *Philosophical Notebooks* on freedom and subjectivity are important, because they underline the teleological structure of human activity as a unique form of determination and as the proper locus of freedom. Soviet philosophers later place great emphasis on this, just as they accept his canonization of the *Anti-Dühring* text. Perhaps Lenin's most significant legacy to the Soviet view of freedom was his own revolutionary action which demonstrated quite clearly that a single individual can, through his plans, ideals, decisions, etc., exert a quite extraordinary influence on that social reality of which he is alleged to be the product; in other words, that he is no mere product of society but very significantly its architect.

PART II

SOVIET PHILOSOPHY

CHAPTER V

GENERAL CONCEPTIONS CONCERNING THE PERSON

The general philosophical understanding of man elaborated by Soviet philosophy is relevant to its more specific conceptions of personal freedom for two reasons. First of all, *any* theory of freedom which interprets freedom as a quality of human activity must situate it within the total context of what man is and how he is related to his environment. Inasmuch as freedom is not a thing, a self-contained entity, but an aspect of a very unique type of being, the categoreal structure of this being largely determines the form which this aspect will assume. Further, free acts are not isolated from every context, but are integrated within the ensemble of man's other acts and are conditioned by the physical and social factors which constitute his situation in the world. Consequently, the precise explanations of how man is free will depend to a large extent upon some more general conceptions of the nature of the human condition. Secondly, as was already noted in the introduction and in the chapter on Marx, certain characteristic theses of Marxian and Soviet philosophical anthropology seem to rule out the affirmation of personal freedom. The strong emphasis on the social nature of man and on the fact of his essential integration in a concrete society is seen as endangering freedom, by totally socializing man. The following assertions are characteristic of this view: man is the ensemble of the social relations, the individual is subordinate to the society, there is no inherent human nature remaining untouched by social change, the person is nothing but the conglomeration of his social qualities, the individual has no intrinsic value apart from the value of society, etc. The consequence of a view containing such assertions would be the negation of the autonomy of the person. The person becomes so totally integrated into society that, in this conception, he loses his status as an independent agent, as a genuine subject of action. He is not a whole, but just a part of a larger entity. And whatever activity can be attributed to him, in the reduced sense of being a subject, is nevertheless in the last analysis determined by his social connections. Such a conception of man evidently imposes severe restrictions on one's understanding of the freedom of the person.

Now Soviet authors themselves insist upon the necessity of correctly understanding the relation between the person and society as a precondition for grasping the Marxist conception of freedom. But they vigorously deny that they totally socialize man and thus endanger the reality of the subject. T. I. Ojzerman rejects the Western criticism that Marxism reduces the individual to his relations to society, thus denying personal freedom.[1] This is a mere 'caricature'; "Marxism does not reduce the social person to human individuality any more than it reduces the individuality of man to his social position."[2] A correct understanding of the relation between person and society requires, G. Glezerman underlines, the avoidance of both extremes: the individualist conception, according to which the individual is an isolated monad, self-sufficient even apart from society, as well as the organic or universalist view, which sees society as a higher unity in which individuals are integrated as are parts of an organism[3]. Both the individualist *and* the organic conceptions are seen as opposed to Marxism–Leninism. Nevertheless, Soviet authors do sometimes admit that there was at one time a tendency to over-emphasize society and the social nature of man, thereby neglecting the individual.[4] M. I. Petrosjan attributes this to two factors: First, during the period of the socialist revolution and the construction of socialism in the USSR, Marxist–Leninist theory had to lay the main weight on the dictatorship of the proletariat, the socialist state, the role of the masses, etc.[5] Secondly, the peculiar situation prevailing during the Stalinist period retarded the theoretical elaboration of the problems concerning the person, and those of socialist humanism in general.[6] However, it is claimed that this state of affairs has been corrected, beginning with the works of V. P. Volgin, P. N. Fedoseev, A. F. Šiškin, V. P. Tugarinov, and L. M. Arxangelskij, to which in recent years numerous studies concerning diverse aspects of the person have been added.[7]

Thus, the difference between the Western interpretation of the Soviet concept of man and its own self-appraisal poses a question: does Soviet philosophical anthropology lay so much weight on the social context of the individual that his personal autonomy is endangered, or does it preserve a balance, at least in the post-Stalinist period, between person and society? In order to clarify this situation the present chapter will present some of the recent Soviet discussions which concern several notions basic to a categoreal understanding of the person.

1. THE ONTOLOGICAL STATUS OF INDIVIDUAL BEING

Soviet anthropology is in its main lines cosmocentric. Unlike existentialism, which radically divorces human existence *(Existenz)* from natural being, underlining the fact that man is an exception to the laws of nature, Marxism–Leninism considers man as only one type of being among others and one which conforms to the structure and laws of all of reality.[8] Consequently all the propositions of general ontology, elaborated in the branch of philosophy called dialectical materialism, also hold as principles in philosophical anthropology.

Now this ontology has often been characterized as collectivist.[9] This means that, following Hegel, it allegedly does not recognize the ontological autonomy of individual beings. According to this position – which is alleged to be the Soviet view – only the collective, the whole, is genuinely real, and individuals have reality only to the extent that they are moments of the whole. Further, in such an ontology the ultimate structure of any secondary reality is relational. The individual is in the last analysis a kind of nexus of relations. And these relations are both internal – they constitute the very being of the individual, and universal – they connect the individual to and make him ontologically dependent on the whole unitary universe. Such a conception is diametrically opposed to the Aristotelian view, which admits a plurality of independent beings and places their ground for existence not in their relation to something else but in themselves, designating them as substances. Further, the collectivist ontology has been regarded as the basis for the Soviet concept of man. Just as all things are ultimately complexes of relations, so is the human individual, to use Marx's phrase, the ensemble of social relations. Only the social collective really exists; the human individual is real merely as a moment of this social whole. In short, the ontological principles of dialectical materialism seem to entail necessarily an explanation of the person as a non-substantial entity, one whose ground of being does not lie in himself.

It is not easy to judge whether or not Soviet ontology actually is collectivist, both because this involves indirectly the whole question of the adaptation of the Hegelian dialectic to a materialist view and because there are few explicit discussions in Soviet writings which directly pose this question. However, one may approach the matter from a slightly different point of view by inquiring as to the status given by Soviet philosopers to the notion of substance, and thereby test the radicality with which this collectivism is (or is not) carried through.

1.1. *The Substantialist View*

V. P. Tugarinov, who is both an ontologist and a leading proponent of philosophical anthropology, explicitly *defends* the substantialist view. The basis of his position is a classification of all existing reality into three categories: things *(predmety)*, properties *(svojstva)* and relations *(otnošenija)*.[10] Of these three categories, he argues, Marxist philosophy, taking the materialist position, underlines the "primacy of things, of substrata in relation to properties and relations," because it is only to things that the notion of materiality directly applies.[11] Further, there is a natural relation of dependency among things, properties and relations. Things are the support *(nositel')* for properties and relations, and to that extent are the basis of the latter.[12] Properties are never found separately, all by themselves, but always as belonging to a thing, and relations pre-suppose the existence of at least two things.[13] Thus, things are ontologically prior to properties and relations, a status which they owe to the fact that only they possess separate "individual existence".[14] Tugarinov expressly uses the word 'substance' *(substancija)* when he refers to things as the basis of all phenomena and processes in the world.

This special structural inter-connection between things, properties and relations rules out for Tugarinov the reduction of the first to either the second or the third. A thing is not just an aggregate *(sovokupnost')* of properties, for it remains constant through their many changes; it is in a real sense their support.[15] And, above all a thing (or its properties) cannot be reduced to a *set of relations*. Tugarinov vehemently attacks relationism as a form of metaphysical idealism. It actually explains away the real existence of things of our experience and naturally leads to the conceptions that this reality is subjective.[16] But this contradicts the substantiality and objective reality of matter. As a matter of fact, relations are far from having primacy in being. They are weaker than *both* things and properties: "A property is always the property of a certain thing. But a relation is, so to speak, without individuality *(bez-lično)*. It is only possible between different objects which it connects or separates."[17]

It is clear that this ontological position is anti-collectivist and does not endanger the ontological autonomy of the person. This becomes even more explicit where Tugarinov applies his ontological principles to the notion of society. He points out that the Marxist conception of society as a system of relations does not involve the assumption of pure relationism. On the contrary, the foundation of all social relations, in his view, is the connection between "living individuals, i.e., substantial *(predmetnye)*, material beings".[18] In other words, the human individual is the ontological basis of society rather than one of its dialectical moments.

1.2. *Individuals as Systems of Qualities*

Clearly, Tugarinov's openly Aristotelian position is neither representative for the whole of Soviet philosophy nor is it even widespread. Closer to what might be considered the generally accepted explanation of individual being is the position of A. I. Uemov. This philosopher has produced the most extensive discussion of the categories 'thing', 'property' and 'relation'[19] and has written some of the pertinent articles for the *Filosofskaja enciklopedija*.[20] While Tugarinov presents a substantialist view of discrete individual beings, Uemov explains them as systems of qualities. He sets out from a criticism of the 'traditional' conception of the thing as a body whose individuality is defined by its spatial boundaries.[21] Since modern physics has shown that several different things can occupy the same spatial boundaries, this conception must be rejected.[22] In fact, as dialectical materialism maintains, matter contains an innumerably variety of qualities of which spatiality is only one, and not even the most important.[23] An individual thing must be set off, as a discrete entity, from all other things by the *totality* of its qualities. It is all of these together which constitute its individuality and separateness. Thus, Uemov arrives at his qualitative conception of things: "A thing is a system of qualities."[24]

Now it is not easy to judge exactly what status the category 'thing' has in such a conception. On the one side, Uemov can reduce both qualities and things to relations. He quotes Hegel with approbation, "the quality is the interconnection itself and the thing is nothing outside of this."[25] Things differ from 'other relations' only in that they are not simply relations in general but relations to 'definite objects'.[26] And when the relations change, so does the thing itself: this is a consequence of the fact that things are made up of properties, and properties are just a special case of relations.[27] But although Uemov here explains things as complexes of qualities and relations, he elsewhere states that the latter are in fact different from and dependent on things. He underlines Engels' statement that qualities alone do not exist, only things with qualities.[28] And since qualities characterize a thing, are immanent in it, they must be different from that which they characterize.[29] Just as in the definition of these three categories one is defined by the other, but the "central, basic category is the category 'thing'",[30] so also in reality while things, qualities and relation exist in mutual interconnection, "a thing possesses a greater autonomy *(samostojatel'nost'ju)* than a quality or relation. One can speak simply about a thing, but a quality is always a quality of something and a relation always a relation between something."[31]

As a matter of fact, Uemov refuses to grant ontological primacy to *any* one category: all three represent for him 'necessary elements of reality'.[32] In spite of the fact that he shows how one category can be subsumed under another (e.g. things as sub-species of qualities) this is only a relative subsumption (qualities are not primary in relation to things[33]). The result of reducing all three categories to any one primary category is one of three *false* positions: reism, attributivism or relationism.[34] Only the triadic model of reality which recognizes the irreducible reality of all three aspects is valid.[35]

This anti-reductionist conception, which explains individual discrete beings as relatively autonomous systems of qualities *in* relation to other beings, is supported by much of the official literature on the theme. In the *Filosofskij slovar'*, a 'thing' is defined as "any part of the material world which has a relatively autonomous and stable existence".[36] It is characterized by the totality of its properties and depends upon the totality of its relations[36a]; but neither properties nor relations exist independently – they inhere in and hold between things.[37] A similar view is assumed in the discussion of qualities in the *Osnovy marksistskoj filosofii.*[38] And besides Uemov's articles on thing and property in the *Filosofskaja encikopedija,* one finds an article on relation, by M. Novoselov, which is interesting in that it seeks to defend the reality of relations. Although the author denies that a thing is more real than a relation, he must admit that the latter's "ontological status in a given case is expressed in the existence of the basis," i.e., it is rooted in the subjects which are standing in relation and has no reality outside of them.[39]

1.3. *The Relationist View*

Besides Tugarinov's view, which affirms the primacy of substance, and the view which attributes more or less equal status to all three categories, one also finds in Soviet philosophy the defence of relationism. I. B. Novik criticizes the conception that the world is an aggregate of things as the antiquated position of 18th century materialism.[40] In his opinion, behind things and their qualities lie hidden their internal relations; behind these lie even more profound internal relations, and so forth.[41] Thus what is phenomenally a thing is in reality a complex of relations. Other philosophers emphasize that all phenomena are universally connected with all *others,* insofar as they are all parts of the unified material world.[42] According to V. S. Bibler, an object is characterized not by its general properties but by an intertwined system of relations[43]; and in the end it is only a moment of the universal process of development.[44]

However, the reduction of all discrete, individual being to ensembles of relations is hardly widespread in Soviet philosophy. There is first of all the built-in restriction on any relationist theory (and in a reduced manner on any attributivist theory), that it must not explain away the *material* character of the world. It is a fundamental thesis of dialectical materialism that there is nothing in the world which is not either matter, a property of matter or a product of the development of matter.[45] And although there is not much agreement as to precisely what the word 'matter' means, there is no question but that one of its basic characteristics is its substantiality. It is the "substratum of all of the various properties, relations and inter-acting forms of movement."[46] A relationist ontological conception which would draw the full consequences of its position would be hard-pressed to preserve this basic principle of dialectical materialism. Secondly, it is in fact more common

– as well as more compatible with the materialist principles of diamat – to try to respect both the relative substantiality and autonomy of individual being and its inter-connections with the rest of reality. A new development in this direction is the increasing use of the category 'dynamic material system' to describe the complex structure and relations of material objects.[47] By distinguishing the different degrees of unity and stability which systems possess, Soviet philosophers seek to account for both the relativity of physical phenomena and the much greater individual autonomy of higher organisms. In any case, Soviet ontology as a whole cannot be simply described as 'collectivist', at least if that word is taken in its most radical sense. There is a significant attempt to account for the autonomy of discrete individual being.

2. MAN AS THE ENSEMBLE OF SOCIAL RELATIONS

Now although all Soviet *ontological* positions do not imply a collectivist conception of individual being, there seems to be nothing more evident than that Soviet anthropology, following Marx, characterizes man as a product of the *social collective*. Man is a social being. But this is meant in a much stronger sense than in the Aristotelian conception. Man not only lives *in* society, but he is formed *by* it, determined by it in all aspects of his properly human activity to such an extent that he can be described as society's 'product'. The famous formula which Marx used to describe the nature of man is quoted in literally every Soviet work concerning philosophical anthropology: man is the 'ensemble of social relations'. Can this be taken as an affirmation of the total integration of the person into society?[48]

Both before the recent upsurge in publications on the problems of man, and even today, certain texts justify such a judgment. Marx's formula is taken quite literally in a recent philosophical dictionary: the totality of man's social relations "is not something external in relation to man but constitutes his essence."[49] This conception also provides an appropriate philosophical basis for the goal of the formation of the new man in communism. Because man is the product of his society, time and social position, and his essence is the totality of definite concrete-historical social relations, "it is possible to change man's essence" by a "radical transformation of the existing system of relations".[50] Here man in his very nature becomes a function of the social whole.

Such conceptions are not rare, but they are almost always stated cryptically, programmatically, without much argument or explanation. In fact, it would not be an exaggeration to say that Marx's famous phrase is, in the vast majority of cases, simply cited as proof of the fact that man is a social being rather than being interpreted and analyzed for its full ontological meaning, And when it *is* interpreted, by those Soviet philosophers directly interested in philosophical anthropology, the emphasis on collectivism is very moderate.

2.1. *The Bio-Social Nature of Man*

Both N. M. Brežnoj and I. S. Narskij warn against a one-sided understanding of Marx's statement as a totally social characterization of man.[51] They interpret it in its historical context as a correction to Feuerbach's one-sided psycho-biological treatment of human nature. Marx had to correct Feuerbach's narrow, abstract understanding of corporeal man, in which all attributes and specifications of human life and history are deduced from the 'natural man'.[52] But this did not mean that Marx intended to cast aside the "anthropological foundation of the human essence".[53] Marx always considered man a natural being, but one in which his "natural functions are covered up, pushed into the background, socialized".[54] Thus man is more correctly described as a 'biosocial' being, as a unity of the biological and social.[55] In this view the ontological basis for social relations is not the society as some supra-individual being, but individuals as *natural beings*. Society is seen as a high stage in the development of living beings, where man (the human animal) distinguishes himself from other animals by the fact that he not only adapts himself to his milieu but appropriates and changes it.[56] A qualitatively new stage is reached in the development of nature: Narskij interprets the meaning of Marx's definition of man as "the indication that man is a product of his own activity in its necessary interaction with the activity of other people".[57] A. V. Drozdov also cautions against the exclusive emphasis of either the biological or the social side of man.[58] Even though the appearance of man and society marked a qualitatively new stage in the development of nature, and thereby man was distinguished from nature, yet he remains a part of nature.[59] He possesses all the characteristics of a material body and in particular of a higher living organism. His social life surpasses this, but only at the same time building *upon* it. If sociology does not recognize this, man is transformed into "a dead social schema".[60] Not only is the biological organization of man "the substantial, material basis, the substratum of his social properties", but it "also plays a role in his social life".[61] A consideration of these facts, in Drozdov's opinion, reveals that the description of man as an ensemble of social relations "is, strictly speaking, not completely exact", for while this expresses man's social essence it does not account for the whole man.[62] Consequently, these authors modify the literal interpretation of Marx's phrase in two ways: (1) they point out that man is not only a social being, but a bio-social being, and that his social nature rests upon the biological basis; and (2) they emphasize that society and social relations do not so much produce man as they are produced by him in the process of his natural development.

2.2. *Human Nature and Human Individuality*

T. I. Ojzerman, V. P. Tugarinov and others see in Marx's statement a description of man's *essential* nature, to be distinguished from those other non-essential factors which make up his *individuality*.

Ojzerman argues against the bourgeois critique which sees in Marx's definition of man the absolute reduction of the individual to society, thus implying the negation of freedom.[63] One cannot draw this conclusion, he maintains, because the essence of man which Marx is talking about does not include the whole of his individual being. The essence of several things belonging to the same class indicates their commonness: two things in the same class have the same essence even though they are distinguished by their individual properties. The same applies to man: he "possesses a certain (historically changing) essence, but his immediate existence is a *phenomenon* which is richer than the essence, and is characterized by definite qualities the most important of which is his individuality."[64] Ojzerman is here utilizing the principle of diamat that the phenomenal reality of a thing exceeds the essence lying behind it: the fact of man's being an ensemble of social relations would thus be only a partial determination of a concrete person. In other words, a person is a man because of certain social relations which connect him with other people, but his individuality lies outside of this. When

Marx formulated his famous definition, I. S. Kon explains, he did not have in mind the individual person, but man as a *generic concept*. Thus the definition does not apply to the "separate, empirical individual"; the essence of man and the concrete person are not one and the same thing.[65] These authors do not go so far as to say that man's individuality is a-social – it is an "expression of the general human essence".[66] But the limitation of the notion 'ensemble of social relation' to the essential core of man is very significant. What is implied is that although the nature of the individual's being is determined by the general social relationships prevalent in a society, his accidents, including his individual actions, lie outside of this influence.

Tugarinov states that Marx's phrase "means that the essence of man lies in the fact that in him are reflected and concentrated qualities, features of that society in which he lives. Every man is a child of his times."[67] But this characterization must be interpreted in terms of the relation between the universal and the particular: the particular is only partially taken up in the universal.[68] There is a dialectical relation between the universal (here the social essence of man) and the particular, i.e. the individual. In support of this explanation, Tugarinov quotes Lenin: "the individual exists only in the connection that leads to the universal. The universal exists *only in the individual* and through the individual... Every universal only approximately embraces all the individual objects. Every individual enters incompletely into the universal, etc., etc.,"[69] If this is the type of relation which exists between the society and the human individual, then one can hardly speak of the total socialization of the person. In fact, Tugarinov distinguishes *three* levels of the individual's determinations. The individual is a unity of the universal, the particular and the singular: (1) the universal in him is his human nature, all of the human traits which are proper to him as man, and distinguish him from animals; (2) the particular is the sum of the characteristics which he shares with some, but not all other people, such as race, sex and nationality; (3) finally he possesses his own proper individual qualities, which belong only to him.[70] Now only the first is meant when he says that man is a concentration of the features of his society, that he is an ensemble of his society's relations. This is what is general to all men, but what *really* exists is "only concrete individuals, which also have, besides the general human features... particular and individual traits".[71]

Now these interpretations of Marx's definition of the nature of man do not so much directly concern the categoreal structure of the person in relation to society (i.e., either as the substantial support of society or one of its relational moments) as they explain the content of what it means to be a human individual – some emphasizing that man is both a natural and a social being, others distinguishing his general social nature and his individual characteristics. But both intend to limit in some manner the extent of the social dimension of man, and they clearly pose obstacles in the way of any conception which would, in fact, seek to explain man as totally sub-ordinate to society.

2.3. *The Individual Subject and His Social Relations*

In order to understand the definition of human nature as the ensemble of social relations, one must clarify the meaning of the term 'social relation', for it is not immediately clear in this context just what a social relation is. One could ask: is it any connection between men; is it a connection between institutions and social formations; is it an internal or external relation, functional or causal, conscious or unconscious, primary or derivative? Soviet philosophers devote considerable attention to distinguishing the different *kinds* of social relations (material and ideological, antagonistic and non-antagonistic, etc.), but make little effort to explain the meaning of 'social relation' in the generic sense. Nor do they specify what meaning the term has in Marx's definition of man. A. V. Drozdov, who accounts for the regrettable situation partially by the influence of Stalinism[72], presents what is perhaps the most extensive attempt to characterize the generic nature of social relations. And his work is not without interest.

A social relation is conceived by Drozdov as a particular kind of connection *(svjaz')*. Not all connections are relations, but only those which are proper to the life of man.[73] Strictly speaking, the word 'relation' should not be applied to inorganic or even to living nature; for in these realms there are connections and interactions, but things do not "relate to each other" *(otnosjatsja)*.[74] What is characteristic of a social relation is that it is a connection between a subject and an object. Thus the first condition of a social relation is the setting apart *(vydelenie)* of the self from the surrounding world, a conscious realization of one's separateness – the appearance of the *subject*.[75] Further, when the subject establishes a relation with something, he is *conscious* of his own activity.[76] Drozdov underlines the fact that men, unlike animals, who act instinctively, are not simply related but are always conscious of the relation. The same point is contained in the definition of social relations given by G. L. Smirnov: social relations are "relations between people, realized with the participation of consciousness when man relates a part of his self *(ja)* to another man or to other people in general."[77] Drozdov's description goes a bit further in specifying that the act in which man relates himself to an object (another person) is a "process of the accomplishment of a pre-determined goal".[78] Social relations are, in short, the conscious activities of men by which they are related to each other.

It is interesting that Drozdov attributes to social relations a normative character.[79] This arises from the fact that social relations are, in general, mediated relations. Only a few personal relations can be considered immediate, and even this immediacy is highly conditional.[80] Now among the mediating factors is a system of norms of social behavior present in the society. And it is with the system of norms that the individual co-ordinates each one of his actions.[81] Drozdov points out that not only the higher and more complex social relations display a normative aspect so also do some natural relations which have taken on a social character, such as the relations between the sexes.

The most striking feature of this characterization of social relations is the fact that the leading role is given to the *subject* of the relation, the individual person. Social relations are viewed not as objective impersonal factors but as the result of the activity of human agents: "man is not simply a side of the relation but its subject".[82] When Drozdov states, as all Marxists do, that man can exist only within the system of social relations, he does not imply that man is a pure moment or product of society. He means that if the person would not be actually entering into any social relations, he would not be functioning as a human being, since his social functions are his properly human activities. The individual carries, over and above his biological functions, an additional 'pay load' *(nagruzku)*, insofar as he is "the bearer, the substance of social functions, properties and connections".[83] And if he would cease to carry this pay-load, i.e. cease to enter into relations with other people, he would in fact be living only a biological existence.

Such an explanation of the relation between the human individual and his social relations is neither exceptional nor does it lack support in the classics. Tugarinov states that human subjects are the "real bearers *(nositeli)* of social relations"[84], and with full justification he refers to Marx, who often repeated that it is the real concrete individuals who make history. Textual support for this position is also found in Lenin, who states: "The materialist sociologist who studies definite social relations thereby also studies real persons out of whose activities these relations are formed."[85] There is no doubt that there is a significant collectivist strain running through the whole tradition which begins with Marx. But an examination of both Marxian and Soviet texts reveals that this is far from a pure strain, and that in recent years a concerted attempt has been made to balance the former collectivist emphasis with a recognition of the real autonomy and basic role of the individual subject. I. S. Kon reflects that more balanced point of view in his refusal to consider society either as an aggregate of individuals or as the sum total of social relations: the starting point of the materialist conception of history "is not separate individuals (they do not exist outside of society), nor is it impersonal social relations (they are relations between individuals), but practice as the combined activity of the people."[86]

3. THE PROBLEM OF A GENERIC HUMAN NATURE

A consequence of the conception of man as a mere product of society is the *historical mutability* of the human essence, for as society develops historically into different forms so also must its elements and products. We have seen that Soviet authors have begun to moderate their emphasis on man as a purely social product. It may now be asked: has this resulted in a different approach to the concept of human nature? In the opinion of certain Western and Soviet philosophers, Marx's sixth thesis on Feuerbach implies a denial of the universality of human nature. The argument runs as follows: Since human nature is for Marx a historically changing phenomenon, there is no common human essence which each individual in history shares. The unity of humanity consists only in the fact that all individuals participate in the same common *history,* and not in their possession of a common essential structure.

The implications of such a conception for the explanation of human freedom are obvious. Any statements about the nature of human activity, about the relationships between the agent and his determining factors, the character of his intelligence, will, moral judgment, etc., would describe only man in a particular historical era. Insofar as there is no generic concept of human nature, there can be no generic concept of human freedom. But such is exactly what the philosopher is seeking to explain. Even the Marxist–Leninist who accounts for freedom as a result of social development distinguishes between what social freedom is, and what degree of social freedom is attained in any particular society. He is in fact employing a generic concept of freedom to distinguish and compare its different embodiments. But how is this justified in the absence of a generic concept of human nature?

We have already argued that Marx himself both widely assumed and explicitly affirmed the existence of a common human nature.[87] Does Soviet philosophy take a similar position, or does it defend a radically historical interpretation of man?

3.1. *The Interpretation of Marx*

S. Rodriges, writing in the *Vestnik movskovskogo universiteta,* claims that Marx, in his later works, rejected the notion of the generic essence of man.[88] This allegedly appears as a part of the break in Marx's thought between the *Manuscripts* and the *German Ideology* with regard to the notion of alienation. While in the former alienation is conceived as the effect on the generic essence of man of a certain kind of work, in the latter it is merely a product of the appearance of a commodity economy, surplus products, exchange, etc.[89] Rodriges claims that Marx ceases to conceive alienation in relation to human nature.

Now it can be stated without qualification that the leading Soviet Marxologists, e.g., T. I. Ojzerman, E. V. Il'enkov, and I. S. Narskij[90], openly disapprove of any such dualist interpretation of Marx's historical development. In their view the mature Marx did not abandon the notion of essential alienation; he merely turned to its more concrete manifestations, hoping that this empirical analysis would in fact serve as a tool to achieve the concrete social order which would free man from this alienation. Even M. B. Mitin, whose orthodoxy in the Soviet philosophical community is beyond question, argues that one cannot draw a sharp line between the early and the mature writings of Marx with regard to alienation, and speaks approvingly of the notion of the human essence.[91] Marx continued to see the abolition of alienation as "the appropriation of the human essence for man", which is a "basic idea" of Marxist humanism.[92] In fact, Mitin seems to go a bit far in his praise of the unity of the Marxist tradition by claiming that in the resolution of the problem of the humanization of man, of the 'embodiment *(vosploščenii)* in life of the real essence of man", one can clearly see "a single theoretical line from Marx's *Economic and Philosophical Manuscripts* through *Capital* to the works of Lenin, in which a *concrete* program is given for the liberation of man from all forms of alienation."[93]

The notion of a general supra-historical human essence is approved not only by implication but also in categorical affirmations by several important Soviet philosophers.

I. S. Narskij criticizes the widespread assumption that Marx and Engels rejected the concept of human nature as unscientific.[94] What was rejected in their critique of Feuerbach's anthropology was only the purely natural, biological interpretation of human nature, which was blind to the social dimension of man.[95] In fact, historical materialism "simply cannot do without the concept of the essence of the human species, since it singles out general features proper to all human societies", which distinguish them from other (non-human) societies.[96] Narskij admits that Marx concentrated his efforts on the specific differences (as opposed to the generic essence) of the various historical forms of human nature. But this emphasis did not entail the denial of a human species which possesses general properties, even though these properties might be diversified in different ages, sexes, generations, nations, etc.[97] In Narskij's opinion, Marx employed a special methodology for studying human nature; this consisted in considering the generic properties of man *in* their movement and development, *in* the changes of their specific differences.[98] Consequently, both extremes must be rejected: the absolutist view, which conceives man as immune to any alterations whatsoever; and the purely relativist view, which refuses to see any general properties among the people of different classes and socio-economic formations. In order to strengthen the point that Marx did not discard the notion of a generic human essence in his later works, Narskij quotes Marx's comment on

Bentham's utilitarianism in *Capital,* that in order to know what is useful for man one must first know what human nature is in general, and then how it is modified in each historical epoch.[99]

3.2. *The Distinction Between Class-Conditioned and Universal Human Factors*

One of the most interesting developments in recent Soviet philosophy – which actually concerns issues extending far beyond philosophical anthropology – also presents positive support for the notion of a generic human essence. It is the distinction between the eternal and the concrete-historical, or the universally-human and the class-conditioned, applied to all social phenomena in general. For example, the class-conditioned content of social consciousness is distinguished from its supra-class content[100]; some basic moral norms, as well as the 'logical structure of moral consciousness', are designated as universally-human[101]; and values are classified as either unconditioned, universally-human or class-bound[102]. This development is indeed a long-needed counterbalance to Marxist historicism. But what interests us here is the more precise point that it affirms the existence of a univeral human nature. The universally human in man lies in his possession of "properties which belong to all people in distinction from animals and even more so from inanimate things."[103] What is designated by the term 'human individual', i.e. a being which possesses certain properties characteristic only of man, is, within the limits of human history, an 'eternal phenomenon'.[104] This does not mean that man undergoes no historical changes. One must distinguish, according to Tugarinov and others, between the notions of the human individual and the person. The first applies to human beings insofar as they possess general human traits found in individuals of *every* society.[105] The notion of the person, however, includes the historically developing features of the individual conditioned by the society and class within which he lives. Thus man evolves with society as a *person* but holds constant throughout the historical process in his status as a *human* individual.

3.3. *The Critique of Anthropologism*

Although this partial exemption of man from the historical dimension of the social process is a clearly visible trend in recent Soviet philosophy, there are those who remain adamantly opposed to what is called 'anthropologism', i.e., a non-historical approach to human phenomena. They are normally those authors who specialize in criticizing 'bourgeois' philosophy rather than those who develop their own views systematically, and it is well-known that the basic weapon of this group is deliberate hyperbole. K. N. Ljubutin, in an article on West German philosophical anthropology, interprets Marx's definition of man in so literal a fashion that he finds it impossible to give a definition of the human individual which would be applicable to more than one class.[106] To this, O. I. Džioev counters: "But is not the definition of man as the ensemble of social relation applicable to representatives of both opposing classes?"[107] In a similar fashion, Z. M. Orudžev attacks the notion of the human essence which T. V. Samsonova, presents in her article on Marx's theory of the person in *Capital*.[108] He was annoyed by Samsonova's explanation of the all-round development of the person as a realization of the human essence, and warns that this could lead to an understanding of this development as a mere "restoration of the true, generic essence".[109] But none of the Soviet anthropologists have ignored the importance of historical development in the realization of the person, nor does their position imply that personal fulfillment is simply a return to some prior condition.

Thus one can hardly say that Soviet philosophy as a whole rejects the notion of a generic human essence. What it does reject is on the one hand, the conception in which the essence is separate from the individual (either as a self-sufficient kind of being or as an element of the supra-empirical development of an Absolute), and, on the other hand, what might be called the 'immutabilist' view, according to which types of being are completely untouched by their historical development. Individual Soviet philosophers have argued that other alternatives remain open to them. And there is no reason why more of their colleagues could not take the same direction. In fact, the recent tendency to analyze the philosophical problems of man from a genuinely descriptive point of view, rather than by reducing all solutions to the final resolution of everything in communism, would seem to support such a development. Soviet philosophers have come a long way from their clinical diagnosis of philosophical anthropology as a symptom (and product) of the crisis of bourgeois society. One can hardly disagree with the recent assessment by T. I. Ojzerman of the philosophical approach to the problems of man: "As long as humanity exists, the problem of man will retain its actuality, and any solution will remain just as incomplete as the history of humanity. Even the definition of man as a being different from all other beings will always remain a problem, since it is precisely man who is giving this definition to himself, and he apparently will always do likewise."[110]

4. THE NATURE OF THE PERSON

The description of man as a member of the human species, as an element in a class of things which are distinguished by their possession of certain common properties or functions, refers exclusively to the formal generic aspect of man. As such it is an insufficient ontological account of the subject of freedom. Both tradional philosophers and Soviet Marxist–Leninists emphasize that the subject of free acts is not man insofar as he is a member of the human species, i.e., seen from the aspect of his common nature, but man as a *person*. One traditional conception explains that it is not natures which exercise actions, but supposits; and a human supposit, i.e., one possessing a rational nature, is what is designated by the term 'person'. The Soviets however do not analyze this concept in such explicitly ontological categories, but rather in terms of man's psychological and social constitution. In general, they point out that while the concepts of man and the human individual are abstract (in the sense of being very general), the concept of the person refers to the concrete existence of the human individual with the inclusion of his specific (and especially social) characterstics. In the *Filosofskaja enciklopedija* the distinction is made in the following manner: "The concept 'human individual' means only membership in the human species and does not include the concrete social or psychological characteristics"; "the concept of the person denotes the integral man in the unity of his individual features and the social functions (roles) carried out by him."[111] Such a concrete notion of the person serves to indicate for Soviet authors that there are no agents in general that perform actions, but only concrete agents endowed with a specific set of qualities and subject to the specific conditions of some particular social order.

4.1. *The Normative and Descriptive Notions of the Person*

One of the most important early attempts by a Soviet philosopher to clarify the notion of the person – and one to which other Soviet philosophers often refer – is that presented by Tugarinov in an article entitled 'Communism and the Person'.[112] First of all, taking advantage of the dual meaning in Russian of the term 'person' *(ličnost')* either as a person or as personality (in the sense of the quality of being a person[113]), Tugarinov defines *ličnost'* as a 'property' of man. That is, he speaks of *ličnost'* not as something which the individual man *is,* but something that he *has.* It is a characteristic possessed by the individual, and not the individual itself.[114] In Tugarinov's own division of the categories, the category of personality would not fall into the group of substantial categories but would be classified as an attributive category. Secondly, Tugarinov presents a description of what is contained in this property of being a person. It is constituted by the following basic characteristics: rationality, certain rights and obligations, specifically personal behavior and activity, freedom, individuality, and personal worth.[115]

Now Soviet critics were quick to point out that many of the characteristics this description of the person refer exclusively to positive values.[116] Freedom and responsibility are positive traits of the person. And, Tugarinov's critics object, if only that activity which springs from one's sense of responsibility to society can be called the activity of a person, then how can one call a reactionary a person? His activity certainly does not spring from his social responsibility; but to deny him the appellation 'person' would be an abuse of language.[117] In fact, the possession or lack of such positive qualities does not determine whether or not one is a person. Tugarinov's view is similarly criticized by a Western author as an 'honorific' concept of the person, because it sees personality as something morally good to be achieved,[118] which is not a necessary, intrinsic part of every individual man. Because this concept is a normative one, i.e. carries a value-content, "not every man is necessarily a person", but only those who possess a certain value, derived ultimately from the society in which they live.[119] Thus it is judged as entailing the anti-humanistic thesis that not every individual possesses the intrinsic worth of personhood.

As a matter of fact, Tugarinov's position, as it is clarified in a later work, is more differentiated than this critique assumes, although it still continues to suffer from considerable confusion. He also distinguishes between the normative and formal concepts of the person, the latter (which he considers too general) being identical with the concept of the individual man; the former including also in its content an *ideal*.[120] According to the normative concept, not every man can be considered a person: "A person must possess such characteristics which are proper only to a mature and mentally normal man."[121] Thereby excluded are young children, lunatics, and anyone who is not able to answer for his actions because of some special reason.[122] Now, this is actually not as broad a restriction as his critics assume, for it is obvious that Tugarinov excludes here, not those men who do not in fact achieve a certain ideal, but only those who are not even *capable* of achieving it, due to some inherent deficiency.[123] He clarifies this point by distinguishing between the extension and the content (intension) of the concepts person and man: "In their extension, the concepts *man* and *person* are actually identical; the three billion people in the world are three billion persons (minus the above-noted exceptions). But these two concepts are far from identical in their content. The concept *person* refers to a *property*, [i.e., the sum total of the above-noted characteristics of the person] while man is the *bearer* of this property."[124]

Now there are several parts of this theory of the person which can be distinguished and compared to other Soviet positions, especially those which are explicitly critical of Tugarinov:

First of all, there is the categoreal problem of whether the term 'person' refers to an individual thing or to a property. Here Tugarinov definitely stands outside of the mainstream of Soviet philosophy, where the term is used predominantly in the substantive sense. In both official, collective works[125] and in individual treatises and articles[126] the term 'person' is taken as denoting the individual man. One author even claims that the conception of the person "as the living individual, the bearer *(nositel')* of social and biological properties", is the one to which the Party Program corresponds.[127] Further, Tugarinov himself extensively *uses* the term *'ličnost'* to designate the individual person as the substantial support of qualities and the subject of action. This indeed can hardly be avoided. For example, when Tugarinov is speaking of the 'duties of the person to society'[128], he is obviously not thinking of the person as a property; properties simply do not have duties to fulfill.

Secondly, there is a question as to the *extension* of the term 'person'. As G. M. Gak points out, there are Soviet authors who, in distinguishing the person from the individual, consider the person as a late product of history.[129] Some consider the break-up of primitive society, others the rise of capitalism as the moment in which individuals became persons.[130] This kind of a historical limitation is seen by Gak as contradicting statements by Engels with regard to persons in primitive societies and by Marx and Lenin in reference to capitalism.[131] For example, Marx and Engels explicitly state in the *German Ideology* that landlords and capitalists do not cease to be persons because of their particular class status.[132] Other Soviet authors have pointed to the fact that a social or ethnic limitation on the extension of the term 'person' would open the door for a philosophical justification of nationalism or racism. Thus the term must be taken as universally applicable to all human individuals.[133] Tugarinov's understanding of the concept of the person as normative, i.e., as an ideal, would seem to rule this out; an ideal is something *to be* achieved, and not already achieved by all those who are able to do so. How then can he consider all sane, adult men to be persons? In answering his critics he states: "Not only does the young child only gradually become a person, to the degree to which the characteristics of personality... are developed in him, but also the adult man is formed into a person in the process of development of these traits. Every man in every social formation is a person in the sense that *he possesses the characteristics (traits) of personality, even though to a minimal degree*. But these characteristics are able to be developed, and it is in this process that the person of full value *(polnocennaja licnost')* is developed."[134] It is obvious that Tugarinov uses the term 'person' here in two senses[135]: (1) as denoting any individual who possesses certain characteristics, irrespective of the degree to which they are developed; (2) as denoting an ideal, a level of perfection of these characteristics relative to and higher than some previous state. In Tugarinov's own writings, and those of practically all other Soviet writers considering the development of the person, this second sense is usually specified as the 'full' person, the 'all-round' person, the 'fully developed' person. It is in this sense also that one speaks of the 'communist person'. Unfortunately the distinction is not always obvious, and one has the impression that the term 'person' is being restricted to some special historical type (i.e., the socialist type of person). But Tugarinov's work, and the strong reaction to it insisting on the universal extension of the notion of the person to all human beings, has somewhat clarified this ambiguity.

4.2. *The Specification of the Nature of the Person*

There is a third aspect of the theory of the person put forward by Tugarinov and other Soviet philosophers which because of its importance requires more extensive consideration. This is the matter of the content or *intension* of the term. The question is: what is added in the Soviet's notion of the person which is not already contained in their notion of the individual man? Several Soviet authors object to a purely formal concept of the person, but then fail to describe what its material content is. For example: "one should understand by person not man in general, but the concrete given man in the unity of his typical and individual traits. Of course, such a concept of the person is a formal concept; content is given to it by the study of the concrete historical epoch, the social formation which gives rise to definite social types embodied in concrete person, and of those characteristics of the individual which are connected with the specific character of his own fate."[136] What this statement amounts to is an admission that philosophy can only point out that the concept of the person refers to the individual in the totality of his concrete traits, and that one must look to sociology to fill in the content. Another author defines the person as a unity of the universal and the particular: "The universal is that which connects the individual with a historically given totality of social relations, a class and a social group; it is also that which is proper to all vital activity, to every human organism (its anatomy and physiology and its psychic properties) Particularity is that which is unique and unrepeatable in the appearance of the universal; it is that which distinguishes one individual from another."[137] Again, to point out that the person is a concrete unity of social, biological and psychological traits (those which are common to all as well as those unique to one person) is not to advance very far towards a material concept of the person. The further specification of the nature of the person is left to the other sciences (sociology, biology and psychology).

One group of Soviet philosophers specify the concept of the person more fully by excluding from it all non-social qualities of the individual man. While 'man' designates a bio-social entity, 'person' is applied to an individual only insofar as he is a social being.[138] Tugarinov defines the person as "man, taken in the totality of those properties (qualities), which are realized in him in the process of his inter-relation with society".[139] However, with the exception of Tugarinov, these authors fail to describe or list these social qualities except in the most vague terms. I.S. Kon, for example, explains the person in terms of the various 'roles' he must fill.[140] Because of the plurality of the social groups to which he belongs (family, factory, etc.), he fulfulls qualitatively different roles, each one of which is relatively independent of the other. And the sum of these, taken in their unity in the particular person, "form the structure of the person".[141] But to point out that a person is a father, a laborer and a citizen does not indicate the person's characteristic qualities; it simply describes his behavior. Such an explanation may be sufficient for a sociologist (which Kon is) but it does not satisfy the philosopher.

Before looking at Tugarinov's description of the nature of the person, it should be mentioned that several Soviet psychologists are not in full agreement with the exclusively social concept of the person. B.D. Parygin objects that the neglect of the psychic content of the person turns him into a mere personified socal function, a cog in the impersonal social mechanism.[142] The error of the socialization of the person is that it overlooks the relative independence of the individual's psychic world, his self-consciousness and unique psychic processes.[143] In his opinion, a more balanced account of the person would include both his psychic properties and functions, and his properly social aspects. K.K.Platonov goes further in explicitly defining the person in terms of his highest psychic functions: "A man is a person insofar as he possesses consciousness *(soznanie)*. The highest form of consciousness is self-consciousness, that is, man's realization of himself as a person. Thus the basic property of the person is his conscious activity *(soznatel 'nost')*."[44] S. L. Rubinštejn places an equally strong emphasis on consciousness as the basic characteristic of the person: "Man is a person by virtue of the fact that he consciously determines his relation to the environment... Consciousness has fundamental significance for man as a *person,* not only as knowledge but also as a relation."[145] However, this consciousness is for Rubinštejn in no way isolated from the natural and social milieu of the person. Psychic functions are a result of the causal convergence of external influences and the internal factors through which the former are 'refracted'.[146] Thus what is characteristic of the person is the conscious manner in which he reacts to his environment. And this principle allows Rubinštejn to say, all the while emphasizing the capital importance of consciousness, that 'person' is a *social* category; for man's most essential activities are those in which he interacts with his social environment.[147]

Now as far as the present author knows, the only Soviet philosopher who has presented a generic material concept of the person, which goes beyond a merely formal description (in terms of the relative importance of social and psychological factors) is Tugarinov. As was mentioned above, Tugarinov explains the property of being a person by listing several characteristics. Five of these are singled out as basic: rationality, responsibility, freedom, individuality and personal worth. The first, *rationality*, characterizes the person as a being who has attained a highly developed level of intelligence; it does not refer to a faculty but to an achieved capability. It is, further, the basis of all other personal characteristics.[148] For example, responsibility and freedom depend upon rationality insofar as rationality gives man the possibility of changing the nature of his reaction to the influence of the external world. The importance of rationality is obvious in Tugarinov's definition of the second trait – *responsibility* – as the ability of man to predict the results of his activity and to determine this activity according to the principle of the harm or good it will bring to society.[149] The third trait, *freedom*, is characterized by Tugarinov in quite traditional terms as the "possibility for man to think or act not from external compulsion, but according to his will".[150] More will be said about this characteristic in the following chapter. In naming *individuality* as the fourth trait of the person, Tugarinov provoked some criticism from Soviet commentators. G. Gak has argued that the note of individuality, taken generically, actually applies to all material beings and thus is not an exclusive property of persons.[151] However, Tugarinov's discussion makes it obvious that he merely chose an unhappy term. What he means by individuality is something like creativity, personal initiative or even originality; and these are certainly applicable only to persons.[152] Finally, *personal worth* is a trait of the person which stands out from all the others. It not only describes the person but expressly attributes to him a value. And the fact that Tugarinov attributes to all persons a certain value *as persons* places him in opposition to the former nearly universal Soviet view that the worth of the person is dependent upon and derivative of society, a mere function of his social usefulness.[153] Tugarinov does not categorically condemn this social instrumentalism, but rather reduces its total character by distinguishing two senses of personal worth – relative and absolute. He admits that one can talk about a person's *relative* value, i.e., to the extent that the person serves the good of society. But what is more basic is the *absolute* value of the person, insofar as the person is not a social means but the end of society: "The absolute value of the person means that the society recognizes the value of the person *as such*."[154] And in this connection Tugarinov refers to the Kantian principle that the person ought to be regarded not as a means, but as an end-in-himself. He points out that the concrete realization of this imperative is the goal of communism (capitalism, in totally exploiting the lives of men, turns them into mere means). Without going into an extensive examination of the various Soviet views on this point, let us only remark that Tugarinov's stand is not unique. A. F. Šiškin, the dean of Soviet ethics, expressed a similar viewpoint in an article entitled, 'Man as the Supreme Value'.[155] He also referred positively to Kant's categorical imperative, defending the view that the person ought to be regarded as an end and claiming that this formal demand is concretely embodied in socialism and communism.[156] Such factual claims are not directly relevant to the philosophical problematic, but it is significant that several Soviet philosophers have found it possible to adopt the Kantian principle of the absolute value of the person and to fit it into their general social theory. This opens the way for a further conceptual clarification of the value of the person and his relation to society.

4.3. *The Emphasis on the Social Determination of the Person*

The discussions concerning the nature of man and the person which we have thus far examined have been those which sought primarily to explain the characteristics of the person from a structural point of view. That is, the human individual was regarded as a particular type of being, as a man and as a person. But this is only one aspect of the matter. To point out that the individual possesses certain characteristics does not explain how these characteristics arose in him, under what influences they were formed, or to what extent their specific character derives from internal or external, psychic or material, biological or social causal factors. What remains to be explained is the nature of the causality through which the concrete aspects of the person are formed.

Now it is typical of Soviet anthropology to stress the causal influence on the person which comes from his *social* environment. Not only is the person always a being living *within* society, but he is also formed *by* it. And the use of the current phrase 'product of society' to describe the origin of the person seems to indicate that the social causation of the person is, in the Soviet view, both comprehensive and decisive. In other words, the strong emphasis on the role played by objective social factors seems to warrant the judgment that Soviet Marxism presents a version of social determinism. As the previous section has shown, Soviet philosophers understand the person as the individual insofar as he is a unity of concrete characterstics, of which the social characteristics are the most essential. Here the question must be posed: are these concrete characteristics causally derivative of the person's social position – in which case the person could literally be called a 'product of society' – or are they somehow independent of objective social factors?

The standard explanation of the formation of the person invariably underlines the dominant influence of the social milieu. Soviet authors refer abundantly to those passages in the *German Ideology* where Marx and Engels state that the development of individuals is determined by their productive relations, the form of society in which they live, the technical and cultural tradition into which they are born, etc.[157] The totality of the social relations is conceived as the determining factors in the formation of the person.[158]

It is difficult to find out, however, exactly what this thesis entails, for the Soviet philosophy of society has not yet developed a sufficiently technical conceptual framework to handle such questions in a satisfactory manner. More often than not, the Marxist–Leninist position is described by contrasting it to 'erroneous' views, which are presented in extreme, one-sided formulations and then refuted very cheaply with references to common, every-day knowledge. Individualism and spiritualism are frequently cited – especially with explicit reference to existentialism and Thomism[159] – as counter-points to the Marxist view. In opposition to individualism, which allegedly sees the person as completely free of any social determination, Marxism–Leninism affirms the social conditionedness of every human phenomenon. In opposition to spiritualism, which assigns the leading role to spiritual functions or even to a transcendent spirit, Marxism–Leninism has repeatedly demonstrated the prevailing importance of the person's material situation, i.e., his work relations, every-day needs, membership in various social units, etc. Such general statements hardly serve to clarify the nature of the social determination and what degree of influence it exerts on the formation of the person.

What one Soviet philosopher termed the 'law of the formation of the person' was formulated by him in the following manner: "as the society is, so also is the person."[160] This general correlation is understood by many as indicating that the social relations of historical socio-economic formations gave birth to many historical *types* of persons, such as slaves and slaveholders, serfs and feudal lords, workers and capitalists.[161] Within the social structure, the economic patterns forced every man to assume one of these characteristic roles, and thus to develop the personal traits arising from this activity. Further, since definite political and spiritual forms also appeared in each society, its members acquired from it definite spiritual qualities.[162] In this way, Soviet Marxists use their structural division of the elements of society to indicate the different ways in which society produces the person. The various concrete characteristics whose totality constitutes the nature of the person are regarded as "nothing else but the specific concrete expression" of the different types of social relations.[163]

On the other hand, no Soviet philosophers go so far as to maintain that this influence *sufficiently* explains the social traits of the person. That is, although the broad structural elements of a society determine the traits of the person in a general way, they do not set the individual form the latter will assume. There is the obvious fact to be accounted for that in one and the same society there is a vast variety of individual differences: not all persons in one society have the same needs, interests, temperament, social ideas, etc. A standard explanation of these differences points out that no social milieu is a pure type. There are always in each society traces of the past and germs of the future, which also exert their influence on the development of the person.[164] However, although this might serve to explain the individual differences in the capitalist or socialist societies, it will not do for communism, since this is to be a society purified of the influences of the past and final in the sense that it will have no successor. But it is openly admitted that individual differences in the traits of personality will continue to exist. How then is the formation of these specific, individualized traits to be explained?

There are two ways to account for this individual formation of the person which are represented in Soviet philosophy. One explains it as the influence of the person's milieu, the other as deriving from the person himself.

The first view is a consequent application of the principle of social determinism. It points out that just as the person lives and develops in the conditions of his society at large, i.e., those which characterize the society as a whole, so also he is subject to the influence of his own 'micro-milieu' *(microsreda)*, his immediate surroundings.[165] Among these are to be counted his family, school, particular work-collective, neighborhood, etc. Taken together, these form the prism through which the influence of his general social milieu (the relations of production, legal relations, ideological forms) are refracted.[166] And this is what constitutes his individuality. Because there is an innumerable variety of empirical conditions, so also is there an innumerable variety of individually different persons. Thus the concrete traits of any person, which taken together make up his individuality, are seen as the product of the inter-action of two sets of social factors in which the final determining influence is exercised by the immediate environment. In short, the peculiar make-up of the person is determined in the end by his micro-milieu.

Now it is often asserted that this does not imply a rejection of the person's autonomy. Quoting Marx, Soviet authors emphasize that not only are men products of circumstances, but they also themselves change the circumstances.[167] However, this general statement must first be interpreted before it can take on an anti-determinist meaning. It could mean simply that although men are the products of the circumstances into which they are born, their activity changes these circumstances for the formation of future generations. And this point is in no way incompatible with social determinism.

The second explanation of personal individuality considers the social factors (both the macro- and micro-milieu) to be only partial causes, and explains that their causality is mediated by the inner world of the person.[168] That is, it is the person himself, considered as a micro-system of psychic qualities, which is the prism through which the influences of the social milieu are refracted.[169] The person is not formed exclusively by the particular social causality but is himself an element in the formation of its own character. In this way, the social causality is reduced to the status of a partial cause. It is not man's micro-milieu but the person as a unique prism which explains "the individual differences in the reaction of the person to social influences", and it is this also which accounts for "the autonomy of the person in relation to the immediate conditions of his being".[170]

This conception, however, itself requires further precision. If the determination of the new qualities of the person is considered to be mediated by this unique prism only in virtue of its already-formed characteristics, and if these in turn were previously products of other social factors, then the autonomy of the person in this regard is only relative, and is real only within a temporally restricted framework. If on the other hand there is a factor which belongs to the nature of the person as such and which always serves as the prism through which the external influences are refracted, then the absolute character of social determination is genuinely broken. Unfortunately, Soviet philosophers have not formulated in a rigorous manner the various forms and alternatives which social determinism might assume, and consequently it is difficult to pinpoint their position regarding these alternatives. Yet there is a fairly consistent practice of pointing to one factor in the human make-up which reduces the comprehensive character of social determinism. This factor is human *consciousness*. Although it is always stated that individual consciousness is derivative, both because it is a reflection of being and because it is a product of social conditions (including the supra-individual social consciousness), nevertheless it also "lives its own life".[171] It has not only a passive side but also an active function; it not only mirrors, reflects reality but also 'creates' it.[172] The external social factors which exert their influence upon the person are 'worked over' by consciousness according to its own laws.[173] Thereby, insofar as consciousness mediates the influence of the social factors, these lose their character as immediate causes.

The interpretation of consciousness as an active, creative function may seem to contradict the classical Marxist-Leninist understanding of it as reflection. There is nothing creative indicated by the usual terms such as 'copying', 'reflecting', 'mirroring', etc., which are used to describe the relationship of consciousness to reality. How then can it be termed active? An examination of the texts reveals that the word 'consciousness' and its derivative 'conscious activity' are used in two different senses. In one sense, 'consciousness' means approximately the equivalent of perception or apprehension. That is, it indicates the simple sensible and intellectual grasp of the objects which stand before it. And in this sense it is certainly passive, to the extent that the formal determination in such an act comes from without. But in a second sense, 'consciousness' is used much more broadly to include all conscious intellectual functions of the person. For example, one speaks about the ability of consciousness to 'predict' the results of activities, to 'regulate' the inter-action of man with society, to 'evaluate', to 'choose', etc.[174] Here consciousness is conceived as the totality of the spiritual life of the person. And in this sense, it is undoubtedly active and plays an important role in the development of the person.

The explanation of the person's individuality and autonomy in this manner however amounts to an essential difference in approach. It goes beyond the conception of the person as a totality of qualities, a micro-system of elements. Instead, it lays emphasis on the person's characteristic *activity*. L. V. Bueva agrees with Adam Schaff's statement that "man is the process of his activity".[175] Applying this to the discussion of the person, she writes, "Man in the totality of his social qualities (i.e. the person) is not something static; it is precisely in his activity that he appears as the creator of his own life and fate."[176] Man's characteristic activity, conceived as the exercise of certain conscious functions and issuing in a form of practical influence upon the environment, is itself one of the factors which contributes to the development of the person. It is only in and through his activity that his concrete qualities are formed.

By placing the accent on the role of the person's activity in his formation, Soviet philosophers do not, of course, solve the problem of social determination. The direction and precise character of this activity could itself be the mere product of the confluence of social influences. To put the problem more generally, the autonomy of the person's development depends directly upon his freedom of activity. If the person's individual activities are not free, then neither is the formation of his character, his individuality.

5. CONCLUDING REMARKS

In the foregoing discussion it has become clear that Soviet philosophical anthropology, as it has developed in the last decade, does not present a conception of man as a being totally integrated into society. It does place major emphasis on the social nature and relations of the individual, but it falls very short of social monism, in which the person is a mere element in the social whole; it defends only a modified type of socio-historical relativism (which, in the pure form, asserts the relativity of even the nature of the person); and it is struggling to re-interpret the thesis of social determinism in a way in which the behavior of the person retains a certain autonomy over against the social factors which exert their influence upon him.

This is not to say that it has solved any of the philosophical problems which arise from a reflexion on the relation between man and society. As a matter of fact, it does not even appear to be very well equipped to handle these problems. The ambiguity in the Soviet ontological position already militates against it. The ontological explanations of individual being which have achieved any degree of clarity and coherence are the extreme positions (substantialism and relationism) embraced by only a minority. The more widespread compromise view – according to which an individual being is some sort of system of properties, with a substantial material basis and standing in necessary relations to other things, but with none of these elements having ontological priority – must still be given philosophical clarification (if its syncretism will even allow this) before it can be usefully employed in philosophical anthropology. Another serious difficulty is presented by Marx's unfortunate formula that man is the ensemble of his social relations. Although it is always cited, Soviet philosophers do not take it at face value, i.e., as a formulation of social reductionism. There is visible a certain tendency to interpret this phrase historically, as a reaction to Feuerbach's naturalism, instead of giving it dogmatic truth value. But it will continue to pose a serious exegetical problem until the Soviet philosophical community follows one author's admission that Marx's phrase is 'not completely exact'. There does not seem to be any comparable difficulty in reconciling the idea of a generic human nature with Soviet historicism, given the current limitation on the historicist principle in general. Marx himself had distinguished between a historical and a non-historical sense of human nature. But no serious attempt has yet been made to clarify or give technical terms to these different senses, much less to consider their ontological presuppositions or their application in social theory. Where Soviet anthropologists are most active, in the consideration of the nature of the person and his relation to social determinants, perhaps the greatest number of problems have arisen. There is no agreement as to whether the notion of the person is social, social and psychological, or social, psychological and biological. There is still considerale confusion in the usage of 'person' in the descriptive sense (as a universal, anthropological category) and the normative sense (indicating a particular state of perfection of personality). And there is yet a thoroughgoing lack of precision and consequent analysis in the Soviet discussion of the typology of social determinants, and the manner and degree in which they exert an influence upon the development of the person. On the whole, Soviet philosophical anthropology is beset with numerous difficulties and ambiguities. This is partially accounted for by the fact that, although now a flourishing discipline, it has been developing for less than a decade, and there has not yet been time for systematization and consolidation of its principles.

It is significant, however, that although the Soviet discussions are deficient in themselves, the position defended therein cannot be rejected on the basis of its alleged collectivism, historicism, relativism and social reductionism, as is typical of the approach of most Western critiques. This critical approach, whose main lines of attack were presented in the introduction, is simply no longer warranted by the Soviet texts. The preceding presentation has, it is hoped, shown this in its description of the individual discussions. This is not to say that the negative critique has served no purpose. Many Soviet authors presented their more moderate view of social determinism precisely as a response to the 'bourgeois' critique; they have been very conscious of the charge of anti-humanism leveled against them from many quarters. And although this response cannot be considered to constitute a viable philosophy of man, much less a humanist philosophy, it has corrected many of the previous one-sided formulations of those characteristic principles which Marxism–Leninism claims to have contributed to a correct understanding of man.

CHAPTER VI

GENERAL PRINCIPLES OF A THEORY OF FREEDOM

The previous chapter indicated that the Soviet discussion of man is beginning to work its way out of the general categories and forms of thought proper only to historical materialism, and is emerging as a genuinely philosophical anthropology, as in its philosophical explanation of the person. Previously, whatever reflexions were made on the nature of man tended to be mere consequences of the theory of society. Man was discussed only from the point of view of general social theory. And even the present discussions are incomparably more oriented toward sociology than, say, other philosophies of man developed in the West. Now the situation is quite similar in the Soviet discussion of freedom, only perhaps still more unsatisfactory. There is here the added difficulty that the word 'freedom' is used in several different senses, and that among these not the least important are the economic, social and political senses. It is quite understandable that Soviet philosophers place much of their emphasis here, for Marxism–Leninism publicly proclaims itself to be the ideology of the liberation of man from economic, social and political oppression. But this preoccupation with social freedom, legitimate in itself, all too often beclouds the properly philosophical issues, since the two are practically always treated together. To put the matter more directly, the freedom of the person is often taken as an instance of the freedom of the society as a whole, and this tends to bypass the properly psychological problem of the freedom of individual acts.

As we have already seen, the tradition which Soviet philosophers inherited from the classics contains several notions of freedom. First of all, there is Marx's *anthropological* notion of freedom – opposed in the strict sense to alienation – as the full self-realization of the person, the development of the whole range of the person's creative functions as an end in itself. Secondly, the largely predominating notion, that which is mentioned and developed most extensively by Marx and Engels, is the *historico-social* understanding of freedom as the historical conquest of mankind over the forces of nature and its own social organization.

Thirdly, Engels' explanation of the structure of *free activity* in relation to necessity shows how this freedom of control, exercised by the society at large, is accomplished in individual human acts. And finally, there is, if not a proper conception of *free will,* at least a series of remarks, mostly negative, in the writings of all three of the classics, pertaining to this more specific notion. Now the Soviet discussions retain *all four* of these notions, and their approach is not significantly different than that of the classics. That is, they remain preoccupied with essentially the same problems, and they deal with these problems in the same categories and general contexts. This does not mean that the Soviet position is identical to that of the classics or that there is no development, but rather that it is worked out strictly within the conceptual framework provided by the tradition. Even the emphasis of the various aspects is similar. The main emphasis falls on the historico-social sense, unfortunately the least interesting from a philosophical point of view. For example, among the several book-length studies on freedom, all but two are devoted chiefly to freedom as 'the product of historical development'[1]; and three-quarters of the *Filosofskaja encyclopedija* entry 'freedom' is devoted to social freedom.[2] The least amount of attention is devoted to the notion of free will – which Lenin had previously dismissed with contempt. Since free will is considered by many to be an idealist notion, the discussions are mostly historical rather than systematic.[3] What we have termed the anthropological notion of freedom has been treated in recent years with growing frequency and enthusiasm, due both to the renewed interest in the writings of the young Marx and to the need for Soviet ideology to consider, in view of the 'imminent' approach of full communism, those problems concerned with the destiny of man.[4] But it is the notion of free activity, often treated under the rubric 'freedom and necessity', which has received the most substantial discussion that can be considered genuinely philosophical. Soviet philosophers seek in this conception the solution to the age-long dispute between freedom and determinism, and they group around it their discussions of the various aspects of the problem, such as the extent of universal determinism, the social conditionedness of the agent, the role of knowledge in freedom, the autonomy of human goals, the character of the causal nexus of free acts, etc. It is in these discussions that one can find a Soviet conception which is developed on a sufficiently elevated philosophical niveau to be placed within the long philosophical tradition of attempts to explain the nature of human freedom.

It must be noted at the very beginning, however, that the Soviet discussion of freedom suffers from several general deficiencies.

First of all, it lacks conceptual differentiation. There is very little attempt to distinguish one sense of freedom from another, to distinguish and consider separately the various aspects of one type of freedom, or to assign technical terms to these. The only oft-mentioned division is that of Engels, the threefold division of freedom – over nature, over society and over ourselves.[5] But this is of little value philosophically, since it distinguishes different kinds of freedom according to their objects and not according to their structural types. It appears as if this is a division of freedom into the socio-historical (over nature and society) and the individual (over ourselves), but, individual activity actually cuts across all three domains; it is not always self-directed. Nor is this division the guide for the ordering of the exposition, either in books or articles. The standard development rather begins with a presentation of erroneous non-Marxist views, moves on to the Engelsian 'solution' of the problem of freedom and necessity (treating together, without any explicit distinction, freedom of will, freedom of activity, and the freedom of self-development), and leads into, for the sake of both confirmation and completion, a final discussion of social liberation, especially as it is realized in socialism.[6] There is no further standard articulation of the various aspects of the problem of freedom and necessity. In this respect the discussion of freedom lags considerably behind other parts of Soviet philosophy, such as ontology and epistemology. An exception in this regard is D.T. Axmedli, who carefully distinguishes between freedom of action, freedom of choice and freedom of desire. However, he employs this distinction only for his analysis of pre-Marxist views, and abandons it in his systematic presentation of the Marxist–Leninist position.[7]

Secondly, there have been no discussions of freedom in Soviet journals where various authors confront each other with opposing interpretations. With few exceptions, the differences in the presentations of freedom can be reduced to differences of emphasis. This lack of confrontation and polarization of philosophical positions can be partially explained by the fact that any view which would develop in a consequent manner either a predominantly determinist or a predominantly libertarian explanation would be immediately subjected to ideological censure, since these extremes are considered to imply quietism or, respectively, adventurism – which are both capital sins. In any case, this tacit unanimity deprives Soviet philosophy of the opportunity for clarifying and developing its conception of freedom through mutual criticism. In this regard it differs in extreme from the discussions of freedom in Western publications.

Thirdly, there is a serious ambiguity in the formulation of the 'basic problem'. This is presented as the problem of the relation between freedom and necessity, or more concretely "between the activity of people and the objective laws of nature and society."[8] But what this problem is about depends directly on the understanding of the reference of 'necessity': this can refer either to the natural and social laws which govern the nature of the individual acts whose freedom is in question, or to (the laws of) those domains of reality which form the object, the terminal field of influence of free human acts. If 'necessity' is taken in the *first* sense, the problem is that of freedom and causal determinism. What is considered here is the relation between the person's acts and their efficient causes, and the degree to which the former might be independent of the latter. Freedom in relation to this 'necessity' is the ability of the person to act (or choose) without being univocally determined by a set of necessary and sufficient causes external to the act itself. In the philosophical tradition this has taken the form of the problem of 'free will and determinism.' On the other hand, if 'necessity' is taken in the *second* sense, as indicating the law-bound nature not of the causal nexus but of the objects of human activity, the problem is quite different. It concerns the relation of human activity to an environment which might or might not submit itself to this activity's finality. This second problem arises in Soviet thought because of two lines of thought native to Marxism–Leninism: there is first the affirmation of 'praxis', which is the active, transforming power of man in relation to his natural and social milieu; but also, this same nature and society is considered to be governed by universal and unchangeable causal laws operating independently of human will or action. The second problem, then, is: how can man, in his activity, submit to his own finality a world which develops according to its own inner necessity?

Now it is obvious that an answer to one of these problems does not necessarily entail a similar answer to the other. To affirm the freedom of choice does not entail the affirmation of the freedom over one's environment; if, for example, free choice is explained as the pure indifference of the will in the presence of its motives, it would even seem difficult to explain the effectiveness of human action as a whole. On the other side, the freedom of man to submit nature to his ends does not imply whether these ends themselves were freely chosen or were the products of preceding or external causal factors. Thus there are two different problems, or rather sets of problems, one of which (the psychological) is both more limited in scope and more demanding of precise metaphysical analysis. However, in most Soviet treatments both fall under the rubric of 'freedom and necessity' and are treated as parts of a single philosophical problem. Or to put it more precisely, the psychological problem of freedom of will (or of choice) is treated as part and parcel of the general conception of free activity. There are exceptions to this. One occasionally finds separate treatments of 'the problem of free will'[9], also designated as the 'inner freedom' of man[10], and a few pertinent discussions by psychologists treating the nature of volitional activity.[11] But in general the two problems are taken up together, and often confused.

It would not be entirely fair, however, only to underline that it is unsatisfactory from a *methodological* point of view not to treat these different problems separately. As a matter of fact, it must be mentioned here that it is also part of the Soviet *teaching,* that freedom is not a quality of the will alone but of the whole person, and that the person's free choices cannot be considered in abstraction from either his cognition or his practical activity.[12] In this regard it simply follows Engels, who in *Anti-Dühring* presented the freedom of will as a mere element of practical action: it follows the knowledge of necessity and leads into the attainment of control over the environment.[13] The close inter-relation of willing and acting is affirmed even by those authors whose main attention is directed to man's inner psychic life. S. L. Rubinštejn, for example, maintains that since volitional processes are more closely connected with action than, say, emotional processes, the study of them "immediately leads into the study of action, or more correctly, the study of the act of the will is at the same time the study of action, as the way in which the latter is regulated."[14] Thus the methodological difficulties entailed by the wholist approach to the various types of human freedom does not stem only from a lack of technical philosophical development, but also springs from the content of the theory itself.

Fourthly and finally, the discussion of free activity (including free choice as an element) does not distinguish carefully enough between the *structure* of a free act and its *content*. This is particularly evident where one finds a discussion of the general structure of free activity followed by statements that, in fact, it is only in socialism that man is really free; or where moral acts are designated unfree because they do not conform to socialist moral precepts. On the one hand, freedom is taken as a descriptive characteristic of a certain type of human activity, irrespective of its content or value; on the other hand, and more frequently, it specifies these acts as correct, successful, well-informed, moral, etc. – as measured by some particular norm.[15] Only by unconsciously exploiting this ambiguity can Marxist–Leninists simultaneously assert that freedom (in the material, normative sense) is a product of social development, presupposes a high degree of knowledge of objective laws, etc., and also that it (in the descriptive sense) is a generic feature of human activity. Such an ambiguity creates a problem for the student of the Soviet notion of freedom, for it is not always clear whether in considering a text he is in the presence of a discussion pertaining to philosophical anthropology or one belonging more properly to the social sciences.

Now in view of these methodological deficiencies, our presentation of the Soviet view of freedom will not be able to follow, except in a very general way, what might be called the standard Soviet development of the material. Most of the purely social and political considerations, which actually outweigh the properly philosophical analyses, will be left out. And since there is, strictly speaking, no systematic order, all that one can do is to put the discussions on the various philosophical aspects of freedom in the order that seems to be dictated by the general conception of the freedom of human activity. The difficulty presented by the confusion of the senses of freedom and necessity will be solved by considering the freedom of the will in relation to causal determinism as a special problem, but within the context of the more comprehensive total structure of human activity.

The purpose of the present chapter is to present and analyze the

Soviet discussion of the general principles of a theory of freedom, including the epistemological and ontological principles which they bring to bear on the problems involved. These considerations are relevant to all four types of freedom distinguished – freedom of activity, freedom of will, freedom of self-fulfillment and historico-social freedom – but in this chapter are brought to bear primarily on the freedom of activity. In the following chapter will be presented some Soviet attempts to clarify certain special aspects of the structure of free acts. Explicit reference will be made to the Soviet explanation of the three other types of freedom, in order to reach a comprehensive view of their diverse conceptions.

1. THE CRITIQUE OF VOLUNTARIST AND DETERMINIST EXTREMES

Since Soviet philosophers devote considerable effort to the critique of other conceptions of freedom, it will be helpful to look at this critique, to see how they orient themselves within the traditional alternative positions. This will indicate at least in general their philosophical stance.

Ignoring for a moment the Soviet context, one can reduce, in a broad sense, the various philosophical explanations of the relation between freedom and determinism to three types: voluntarism (or libertarianism), determinism and reconciliationism.[15a] *Voluntarism* is the view that human actions are free because the activity of the will (or some kind of volitional function) is not subject to any causal law. In presuming the general thesis that freedom is incompatible with the principle of the causal determinateness of events, it affirms freedom by rejecting the universal scope of this principle. *Determinism,* in the strict sense, also accepts the general thesis of the incompatibility of freedom and the determinist principle, but instead of adjusting the determinist principle to make room for freedom, it draws its full consequences and denies that freedom is real. This view normally explains freedom as an illusion which springs from man's imperfect knowledge of the causes of his own acts. Finally, *reconciliationism* maintains, against the first two views, that freedom is not incompatible with the causal principle. It affirms determinism and at the same time finds a way to account for the reality of freedom. Let it be noted that this is not simply a compromise or a comfortable eclecticism, for many of the reconciliationist authors assert that the free act itself makes sense only on the assumption of the determinist principle.

1.1. *The Critique of Voluntarism*

Now Soviet philosophers are extremely critical of the first view. Voluntarism is defined as the "idealistic trend in philosophy and psychology, which declares the will to be a supreme principle of being, which opposes the principle of will to the objective laws of nature and society and which affirms the independence of the human will from its surrounding reality."[16] This trend is traced back to Duns Scotus, and in modern times to Kant, and is considered to include Schopenhauer, Nietzsche, Wundt, James, Dewey, Bergson, and the existentialists.[17] In general, it is criticized by Soviet authors for three of its traits: its idealism, its indeterminism and its irrationalism. *First* of all, it is rejected on account of its *idealism:* it violates the materialist solution to the 'basic question' of philosophy, according to which mind is secondary to matter, is matter's product and must conform to all of the general laws which govern matter. Freedom cannot be explained as an exception to the laws which apply to all of reality, as a characteristic of some separate, unique, non-objective being; this sharp division between will and objective reality amounts to a dualism of mind and being which is unacceptable in view of the material unity of the world.[18] *Secondly,* voluntarism is criticized in numerous ways because of its *indeterminism*. It is incompatible with the general principle of diamat that every event has a cause. But it is also rejected in view of the Soviet understanding of free activity. When voluntarists assert that freedom is the "subjective possibility of arbitrary choice determined by nothing,"[19] they are, in the Soviet view, ignoring the obvious fact of experience that human activity is severely limited by its external circumstances. Since free activity is considered to include the accomplishment of a goal, the external circumstances become capital. An example often quoted is the case of the man who decides to fly, and jumps off a building to accomplish his deed.[20] His free choice here is illusory, since his action is in fact enslaved by the law of gravity which brings him to his destruction. If attention is turned from the accomplishment of free activity to its inner psychic structure, indeterminism is also considered untenable. The act of the will, the choice itself, cannot be fully undetermined. If the will is considered as having the ability to turn away from, to reject certain motives acting upon it, then it can do this only because it is influenced by other motives.[21] And the relation between the act of will and the carrying out of the intention also depends upon the principle of determinism. Unless any act whatsoever is going to follow purely spontaneously and arbitrarily upon a decision, there must be a determinate causality within the structure itself of free activity.[22] *Thirdly,* voluntarism is considered false on account of its *irrationalism.* Soviet authors criticize strongly the justification of free choice on the basis of the arbitrariness of the will. The will is not free to the extent that it chooses independently of any reason. Quite the contrary, "a choice must be intelligent, or, in other words, *justified."*[23] Again, given the fact that free activity is finalistic, an arbitrary choice of a goal or means would only frustrate the activity as a whole. This is the reason for the continual insistence that freedom must be founded on the knowledge of necessity.

It is interesting to note that among the voluntarists coming under criticism, by far the most frequently and categorically attacked are the existentialists, especially Sartre.[24] Against the Sartrian thesis that man is absolutely free, based on the view that man is bare of any essential qualities and thus is free to choose even his own essence, the formal objection is made: "if the existentialists deny that man is endowed with any original properties, with what right do they ascribe to him the property of 'freely' thinking and acting?"[25] In the Soviet view, freedom is a property of man, but far less than being the source of the human essence, it is consequent upon other more basic structural characteristics, e.g., consciousness, reasoning, motivation, etc. Against the Sartrian thesis that human choices are absurd and without any reasoned basis, it is objected: "does this not mean that there is no freedom, that man acts under the influence of blind passion, undermined by any motives and unrestrained by the voice of reason?"[26] The Soviet 'scientific' understanding of free choice always affirms the rational character of this act. Against the existentialist thesis that "man is free insofar as his acts are isolated",[27] it is pointed out that the isolation of an act from other acts or from the acts of other persons does not insure that these acts will be free. An isolated act can be as unfree as a totally integrated act, depending on its specific character. Of course, it is the Soviet contention that no properly human acts are isolated; they always take place within a natural and social context. Not only is the existentialist doctrine of freedom itself erroneous but it is seen as entailing disastrous consequences, such as the justification of any human action (even when it contradicts moral principles), the impossibility of any socially unified action where individuals must submit their activity to common goals, and the deprivation of human life of any positive meaning.[28] In sum, the existentialist view is attacked from every possible angle as the antipode of the Marxist–Leninist conception of freedom; it is not considered to have any positive qualities, with the possible exception that it served to call attention to the problem.[29] This exclusively negative critique of existentialism, however, stems only partially from a philosophical motivation; it must also be kept in mind that Soviet ideology considers existentialism to be the product of the contemporary 'crisis' of bourgeois capitalist society.

1.2. *The Critique of Rigid Determinism*

The Soviet attitude towards the strict determinist view, called 'fatalism', is considerably more positive. While voluntarism contains an implicit rejection of materialism, many versions of strict determinism are based upon materialist principles. This places it on the correct side of the option posed by the 'basic question' of philosophy. Further, almost all forms of strict determinism are rationalistic in the broad sense of the term, the most important (for the Soviets) taking science as their model of explanation. This accords well with the rationalistic and scientific tendencies of dialectical materialism. However, certainly the most important factor influencing the judgment of strict determinist trends is the fact that Soviet philosophy itself affirms the universality of the principle of determinism; it is consciously a determinist view. Thus the following definitions are meant to apply to dialectical materialism as well as to the aberrant, fatalistic forms of determinism: "determinism recognizes the universal law-bound connection between phenomena, i.e., it considers every phenomenon to be connected with other past phenomena which condition it";[30] determinism is the doctrine of the "universal causal conditionedness of all phenomena."[31] The critique of the fatalistic versions of determinism concerns the manner in which this principle is applied or integrated in a broader philosophical view-point, and, unlike the critique of voluntarism, does not involve a rejection of the principle itself.

There are three forms of fatalist determinism which are rejected on the basis that they are incompatible with human freedom: supernaturalist determinism, mechanical materialism and idealist monism.

The first type is certainly the most virulently attacked, as are all doctrines which have a religious basis. The Moslem and Calvinist theologies are considered to be the most patently fatalistic, but Orthodox, Catholic and other Protestant theologies are also judged fatalistic on the basis that any doctrine of divine providence is incompatible with free will.[32] The Soviet critique, unfortunately, often consists in simply pointing to those difficulties of which theologians themselves are fully aware. One author indicates two 'insoluble' problems: how can the creature possess free will without weakening the omnipotence and omniscience of God; and how is God's good will compatible with the existence of evil?[33] A more philosophically argued critique, and one which is rooted in the principles of dialectical materialism, refers to theology's *teleological* conception of the universe. In the Soviet view, theology states that all phenomena of nature and society, including man, "develop according to an order previously established by God."[34] The finality attributed to the universe means that nothing contradicts the determinations of God's will; the development of the world is nothing but the "realization of the fore-ordained purpose of the Supreme Being".[35] The result of this conception is that contingency no longer possesses any objective reality. Dialectical materialism usually explains contingency as the quality of an event which arises not from the inner direction of some phenomenon but from the chance intersection of several phenomena. But if these events are themselves determined from without by a fore-ordained purpose, they are just as necessary as those events which do not appear to have a chance character. And what is called contingency becomes nothing more than our "ignorance of the ways of divine providence."[36] This fatalistic teleological view is considered to have been refuted by numerous philosophers, including Spinoza and Holbach, by Darwin, and by science in general. The basic error was allegedly revealed by Spinoza, who showed that teleology arises out of the assumption that events in nature realize goals in the same way as human actions, and thus that it is an anthropomorphic conception.[37] As such, all non-human teleology, including that of Providence, is false.

The second set of views which the Soviet reject as overly deterministic are the 'non-dialectical' or, in a narrower sense, the 'mechanistic' versions of materialism. These views are judged false, generally on the grounds that they offend against the principle of categoreal pluralism. Following Engels and Lenin, dialectical materialists generally affirm the partial irreducibility of essentially different types of phenomena to one another, and in particular the irreducibility of higher order phenomena to lower order phenomena. In view of this principle, mechanistic determinism is false, since it seeks to "reduce the whole diversity of cause to outward, mechanical influences."[38]

It is explicitly recognized that mechanism entails a denial of any real freedom. R. Gal'ceva points out that man's psychic life is in this view a mere derivative of the movement of material particles; the mental process is thereby considered as a product of the displacement of material bodies.[39] Hobbes' account of the origin of human action as lying in an external impulse rules out the possibility of freedom: "since the primary cause of the action is found outside man, then the very action itself is beyond his control."[40] The French materialists of the 18th century openly denied that man possessed any real freedom – Holbach is quoted as saying that "man in each moment of his life is a passive tool in the hands of necessity"[41] – and for this view they are soundly denounced as fatalists. The determinist who is most often mentioned, described and criticized is P. S. LaPlace, the classical representative of mechanical materialism. LaPlace had maintained that given the co-ordinates and impulses, at a given moment, of all the particles in the universe, its states could be determined for any past or future moment. And this allegedly applied not only to physical states but to all others as well, including the psychic states of individuals. The Soviets consider this position to be just as fatalistic as the doctrine of religious predestination.[42] For freedom to be possible, future states of the individual and of the environment which he may alter have to be open to previously undetermined alternatives[43] – a condition which could not exist in the LaPlacian world. One Soviet author, though rather sympathetic toward LaPlace, points out that the position rests upon the assumption that there are absolutely isolated systems which are not subject to any chance influences from without. Since in his opinion such systems do not exist in nature, and in any case one cannot have exhaustive knowledge of the state of a system, its future behavior cannot be predicted.[44] However, the Soviets most often repudiate the LaPlacian threat to the reality of human freedom by recalling not merely that this mechanistic conception is inapplicable to organic and social life, but that it fails even in the physical world; consequently it is hardly acceptable elsewhere. Quantum mechanics is praised for discrediting LaPlace by having shown that in the micro-world only probably relations are determinable.[45] Besides LaPlace, other mechanists such as J. Priestley and in the 19th century E. Büchner and J. Moleschott are found equally unacceptable.

It might be remarked here that in most Soviet discussions of freedom there is a total absence of any consideration of the physical and physiological factors which may influence the individual in his decision making. The context is almost always society, and only rarely nature. Consequently, those philosophies which tend to trace back human acts to man's physical nature (as those just considered) are not taken seriously on their own grounds. This is rather surprising in view of the fact that Soviet philosophy claims to be a materialist, naturalist world-view. In fact, it seems to underline the dichotomy between nature and society more sharply than its ontology should allow. A case in point is V. E. Davidovič's critique of mechanistic determinism. He claims that this type of fatalism arises from a 'naturalistic interpretation of history', one in which natural necessity is carried over to society without taking into consideration the specific nature of social process bound up with the conscious activity of men.[46] The determinism which exists in nature, he says, cannot be carried over into the realm of society and still leave a place for human freedom.[47]

Among the materialists whose views are rejected as overly deterministic a special place is reserved for Spinoza. First of all, this great rationalist is seen to have forerun the development of dialectical materialism in some of its main theses: that the world is a material unity, that its laws are totally immanent, that there is no extrinsic divine cause, and that everything is determined by certain causes.[48] But also, beyond praising his general philosophical position, the Soviets consider him to be "the first to formulate more or less clearly the problem of freedom and necessity."[49] Unlike previous philosophers, who considered freedom and determinism to be mutually exclusive, Spinoza saw that there was a relation between freedom and necessity; that far from being mutually exclusive, one actually presupposed the other.[50] The real antagonism is not between freedom and necessity but between freedom and compulsion.[51] A free being for Spinoza is precisely one who exists and acts out of the necessity of its own nature. Unfortunately Spinoza's ontological principles allow only one being – substance – to be free in the strict sense; man, as a mere mode, is as predetermined in his behavior as the rest of nature.[52] However, Spinoza introduced another important idea which saved his postion from explicit fatalism and later formed yet another integral part of the Marxist–Leninist conception: a human act is free to the extent that it is based upon knowledge, the knowledge of necessity.[53] Knowledge in some way mediates between the individual and the necessity reigning in the universe. For Spinoza, of course, this meant something different and more precise than it means for the Soviets; the latter, as will be shown, understand the role of knowledge in a more instrumentalist and activist fashion. And more importantly, this idea did not come into Marxism–Leninism directly from Spinoza; it had to pass first through Hegel.

Thus both the voluntarist and the rigid determinist positions are rejected by Soviet philosophers. They are both branded 'metaphysical', which means, more simply, one-sided. But besides the fact that each errs by excess in its own direction, there is an aspect of these positions which is very nearly identical (in the Soviet judgment) and which leads to their failure. Both understand freedom in an absolute sense as the complete independence of acts of will from causality: as if our will were entirely its own cause and were independent of all external causal factors. If such a conception of freedom is accepted, one Soviet author writes, "the affirmation of free will unavoidably excludes necessity, causality; and, on the other hand, the affirmation of the latter excludes free will."[54]

2. THE APPRAISAL OF HEGEL

The general importance of the Hegelian philosophy for dialectical materialism is a well-known fact. The dialectic, the basic notions of man, history and knowledge are all strongly influenced by Hegel. There is no doubt that the same holds for the Soviets' concept of freedom. Both by their own admission and as is evident in their discussions, numerous

leading ideas are taken over from Hegel. On the other hand, there
is no truth in the claim that the two views are essentially the same.
The Hegelian heritage undergoes a rather thorough transformation, and
what emerges from the seminal Hegelian ideas as the 'Marxist–Leninist
solution' is something with a considerably different character. However,
a final judgment on this matter will have to await further development
of the Soviet view. For the present, it will be enough to recount the
Soviets' own appraisal of Hegel.

2.1. *Hegel's Contributions*

First of all, Hegel is credited with the 'unquestioned historical contribution' of having shown, for the first time, that there is a 'dialectical
relation' between freedom and necessity[55] (Spinoza had shown that
the two were related, but he explained this relation in a 'metaphysical'
way). Freedom and necessity had been radically divorced by Kant, who
assigned them to the separate realms of noumena and phenomena;[56]
nature was determined, necessary, and spirit was free. In destroying
the noumenon-phenomenon dichotomy Hegel undercut this – as he called
it – 'abstract' understanding of freedom. He is quoted with approval
as saying, "Freedom which would not have within it any necessity,
and necessity alone, without freedom, are abstract and consequently
untrue determinations."[57] Thus, Hegel provides the basic premise of
the Marxist–Leninist treatment of freedom: both freedom and necessity
must be accepted as real, and understood in their relation to each other.

Secondly, Hegel showed that this relation consists, at least in part,
in the appropriation of necessity by man through knowledge. Engels'
statement in which he quotes Hegel as saying that freedom is the knowledge of necessity is referred to in practically every Soviet work on
freedom.

Thirdly, it is taken as established by Hegel that *liberum arbitrium*
is not genuine freedom, at least insofar as it is considered by itself.[58]
Some sort of choice is certainly a component part of a free act, but
this is not freedom itself; it is only the formal aspect. One cannot separate
the act of choice from its content, as if the two were independent.
The content of an act of choice, Hegel showed, is given; its ground
is "not to be found in the will itself, but in the external circumstances."[59]
And the content is extremely important; where it is not well determined,

the freedom of the act is abstract and minimal. Thus Hegel rightly stated that a man who decides only on the basis of his own wishes and caprices will find that his actions will often turn out completely different than he intends.[60]

Fourthly, Hegel is praised for having made the first historical approach to the solution of the problem of freedom and necessity.[61] For him freedom is not something given once and for all, but is the product of historical development. In what sense? Hegel realized that the knowledge of necessity is not basically an individual process; rather it is a social, objectively conditioned historical process.[62] Therefore, say the Soviets, it is clear that freedom is by no means merely a natural property of the will, independent of historical conditions. It is, as Hegel says, a historical product, and its full realization is possible only at a definite stage of social development.

Because of these four 'insights', and several other minor points, Hegel is credited with having contributed more to the solution of the problem of freedom and necessity than any other non-Marxist thinker. On the other hand, there is no question of accepting Hegel's position en bloc; the Marxist–Leninist position is far from identical with the Hegelian. And the Soviets, in their criticisms of Hegel, show that they are well aware of this.

2.2. Hegel's Alleged Shortcomings

The first objection to Hegel's view concerns his monistic conception of the subject of freedom. According to Hegel, full and genuine freedom belongs only to the absolute idea.[63] Man is free only to the extent that he submits his wishes to the march toward self-consciousness of the absolute. In this conception, according to Ojzerman, freedom is equivalent to fate, and the freedom of man is reduced to a single self-consciousness.[64] The Soviets' opposition to Hegel's monism is primarily concerned with its theistic character; man is thereby deprived of his role as the maker of history, But they also oppose the monism as such and clearly endorse the thesis that there is a plurality of subjects of freedom – namely, individual men, who (although they may not be able to accomplish their freedom separately) possess freedom in a primary, and not just a derivative sense.[65]

Secondly, Hegel is criticized for placing the relation of freedom and necessity on its head, so that freedom turns out to be primary and necessity secondary. What does this mean? For Hegel, the essence of reality is ultimately spirit; the empirical world is nothing more than the product of spirit at one of its stages of development. Now what is the essence of spirit? Freedom. Hegel is quoted as saying that just as weight is the substance of matter, so freedom is the substance, the essence of spirit.[66] Thus freedom becomes, in a sense, the essence of reality, and matter merely its by-product. And the Soviets conclude from this that Hegel reduces necessity to a derivative status. This critique is obviously based on a misunderstanding of Hegel's position – he certainly distinguished clearly enough between the external necessity of matter, which was secondary, and the internal necessity of spirit, which was not – but it exemplifies a basic Marxist–Leninist principle: necessity is primary, and freedom secondary. In what sense 'primary' is meant, however, is never clear. If one takes its minimal meaning, it indicates that the 'necessary' laws of reality set the boundaries for the possible acts of freedom, i.e., the limits beyond which human acts, individually or collectively, cannot pass. Most Soviet authors speak of the primacy in this way. Fewer use it in a stronger sense. But a full discussion of this will come later.

A third ciriticism of Hegel is of greater consequence for the Marxist–Leninist explanation of freedom. It is that Hegel reduces freedom to the knowledge of necessity.[67] In Hegel's system, the entire history of humanity is in the end the history of knowledge, of the self-knowledge of the Absolute. But, the Soviets complain, this leaves out practical activity.[68] In their view, the knowledge of necessity is one of the conditions for freedom, but it is not freedom itself. As Lenin pointed out – following Engels – *practice* must be included in the definition of freedom: "freedom is the *practical mastery of necessity*, the conscious and purposeful realization of necessity."[69] It is admitted that the degree of knowledge one possesses is a kind of indicator of the successfulness of an action. But it is not true that all knowledge leads to freedom, either in the sense of the practical mastery of nature or as the autonomy of the decision of the subject.[70] The over-emphasis on knowledge is a one-sided, 'contemplative' and 'fatalistic' view, and therefore must be clearly rejected. It is often stated by Western writers on Marxism–Leninism that the Soviet position on freedom is equivalent to that of Plekhanov.[71] That this is not the case is evident from the Soviet critique of Hegel. Plekhanov was very close to Hegel in his understanding of freedom; he stated explicitly that "freedom *means* being conscious of necessity".[72] Freedom is for him the subject's consciousness of the objective impossibility of acting any differently than he does: the realization of his lack of free will, and, at the same time, of the desirability of the inevitable course of acts that he must accomplish.[73] It is only by identifying one's intentions, *in the mind*, with necessity, that the subject ceases to feel its restraint and becomes free.[74] Soviet authors not only do not support this view (or even refer to Plekhanov much at all); they explicitly reject such a view as fatalistic.[75] Knowledge does not in their opinion serve the function of reconciling oneself to necessity; it is only a means to utilize and control necessity in accordance with one's needs and interests. In short, knowledge is a component of freedom as practical knowledge and not as contemplative knowledge.

3. THE ROLE OF KNOWLEDGE IN FREEDOM

The Soviet critique of Hegel's 'contemplative' view of the role of knowledge in freedom does not carry with it, however, a general de-emphasis of the importance of knowledge in freedom. Quite the contrary. Most of the Marxist–Leninist 'solutions' of the problem of freedom and necessity seek to demonstrate, with long references to the progress of science and technology, that the growth of knowledge is precisely the means by which man liberates himself from necessity. And as has already been mentioned, the main text from Lenin concerning freedom is actually a discussion of the epistemological presuppositions of Engels' view. Few Soviet works on freedom omit a treatment of these epistemological presuppositions. Consequently, a brief look at this is necessary to have a full picture of the Soviet view. Also, there are several Soviet philosophers who go somewhat beyond the Leninist line and seek to locate freedom in the creative function of the cognitive act itself.

3.1. *The Epistemological Presuppositions of Freedom*

Following the order and the spirit of Lenin's text, Soviet philosophers list four epistemological presuppositions of freedom. The first is the recognition of the existence of the objective world independent of human consciousness.[76] This is meant to exclude all idealist epistemologies; only in a realist philosophy can freedom be correctly explained.[77] In particular, it implies that nature and history develop according to objective laws which, far from being products of thought, really hold in external reality. As one Soviet philosopher puts it, "in this presupposition the principle is asserted, that nature develops according to laws which are not dependent on the consciousness of man, and through the action of which necessity realizes and manifests itself in nature and society."[78] The need for this presupposition lies in the fact that if man is to achieve mastery of his environment by learning its laws, then these laws must actually hold sway in reality; otherwise any action based upon them would be ineffective.

The second so-called presupposition is that "the necessity of nature is primary, and the will and consciousness of man secondary."[79] This is not much more than an elaboration of the first principle: given that the laws of nature hold objectively, the mind must adapt itself to them, and not vice versa. It might be noted here that only rarely is this statement taken to mean that necessity 'rules' the consciousness and will of man; that is, that the inner life of man is characterized by necessary relations or events.[80] This would be, in any case, a psychological view and not an epistemological principle.

The third presupposition is that man is capable of knowing objective reality in its very essence.[81] Lenin had said, against Kant, that there is no basic difference between the thing-in-itself and the thing-for-us. The former is just reality insofar as it has not yet been discovered. The mind continually reaches a deeper understanding of reality. Consequently, Engels makes sense when he speaks about a blind necessity, which the mind does not yet know but can at some time discover and put to his own use.[82]

Reference is made to the 'dialectical character' of our knowledge.[83] This means that we can acquire true knowledge of the world, but that this knowledge always remains relative. It remains relative for two reasons: the world is infinite in space, time and depth (not only can we not know the whole perfectly, but we cannot even exhaust one aspect of it); and further, the world is constantly changing, engendering new phenomena and new laws.[84] Special emphasis is laid by one author on the point that necessity (the necessity of laws) not only appears in different forms but itself changes, thus requiring that a new effort be made to cognize the new reality. The inference is explicitly drawn from this observation about knowledge that human freedom always remains *relative*. If, as one author reasons, freedom is realized as a result of the knowledge of objective reality, and this knowledge always remains relative, then "one can never speak of the absolute freedom of men, of their absolute mastery of natural and social necessity."[85]

The fourth epistemological presupposition is that practice and theory are inseparable. [86] Lenin praises Engels, against the Machists, for his *salto vitale,* his leap from theory into practice. In fact, as all Soviet philosophers point out, theories must pass over into practice to be substantiated, for practice is the criterion of truth.

What is the understanding of freedom for which the unity of theory and practice is a presupposition? Clearly, freedom not as pure cognition but as the practical mastery of nature and society made possible by knowledge. Almost all of Lenin's recent interpreters understand the text in this way, as expressing an activist view of freedom, contrary to Hegel and Plekhanov. N. N. Pospelov remarks, in this context, that the genuine freedom from blind necessity can only be achieved through a socialist revolution, consciously and systematically mastering the forces of nature.[87] And I. V. Byčko, one of the more recent thinkers, laments the fact that Marxists have not always been precise in their formulation of the relation between knowledge and freedom and thus gave rise to the 'completely unjustified' attribution to Engels of the formula, 'freedom is the knowledge of necessity'.[88] He states that Engels in no sense identified freedom with the knowledge of objective necessity; Engels, and Lenin after him, "only pointed out that such knowledge is an indispensable *condition* of freedom",[89] which must issue in practice. What is the precise meaning of this epistemological condition? In Byčko's view, this could hardly be the knowledge of "the reigning necessity, tying man down to the given situation"; this kind of knowledge of necessity, such as that of the law of gravity, only furthers man's adaptation to necessity, not his liberation from it.[90] The knowledge of necessity, as a condition for freedom, must be understood as the "objective possibility for surmounting the current, given necessity."[91]

3.2. *The Liberating Function of the Creative Cognitive Act*

It has been shown that the standard Soviet view of the role of knowledge in freedom is that it is not freedom's *essence* but only one of its *conditions,* namely a condition for freedom as practice. Now there are a few Soviet philosophers, especially those who have published very recently, who have rejected in a more radical way the idea that man is a passive spectator of the march of history. V. P. Tugarinov, G. S. Batiščev and I. V. Byčko are three such philosophers. The latter, in a book entitled *Knowledge and Freedom,* not only rejects the view that freedom is just a sub-species of knowledge; he makes knowledge itself subordinate to freedom. He tries to mediate the somewhat abstract and mechanical scheme of 'objective knowledge plus practice equals freedom' by situating an element of freedom, or as he often says, 'creativity', in the cognitive act itself. It will be worthwhile to take a closer look at this somewhat unorthodox position.

Byčko places his whole discussion of freedom in the context of an understanding of human nature. Since the problem of freedom is concerned with the human possibilities and capabilities of exerting an influence on the surrounding world, "it is closely connected with the solution of the problem of man, of his essence."[92] For this anthropological basis, the author turns directly to the early writing of Marx, especially the *Manuscripts.* Man is a universal being in the sense that he can transform the whole of nature into his inorganic body. In virtue of what human activity can he do this? Practice. Consequently, practice is the "essential manifestation of man's specific nature", it is "*the mode of being (sposob bytija) of man in the world.*"[93] Now if man and only man is free, and the reason for this freedom must lie in his specific mode of being, then any inquiry into the nature of freedom must base itself upon an analysis of the structure of practice.[94] Or in other words, the question is to be asked: what is there about the structure of this characteristic of man – practice – which makes him a free being?

Practice, which has as its goal the transformation of the present state of reality, always points to the future. This implies, according to Byčko, that one of its necessary conditions is an anticipation of the future.[95] What is this anticipation of the future? It is not simply the knowledge of the complex of possibilities which might be realized, because not only do many possible courses of action exclude one another, but also man is really interested only in those which correspond to his needs. The anticipation of the future, which is part of practice, is a kind of selection of the future.[96] Consequently, the second essential element of practice, i.e., besides the requisite knowledge of objective laws, is freedom, the freedom to choose. Byčko may seem to be arguing in a circle here – man is free because of his practice, and his practice can occur because he can choose freely. Actually the point he wants to make is that free *activity,* which is practice, is only possible because the very cognitive act by which future courses of action are conceived *includes* a component of free *choice*.

The foundation of this view is an understanding of knowledge at variance with any simplistic copy-theory. The results of man's knowing activity, referred to as 'cognitive forms of reality', are according to Byčko nothing like substantial copies. Although knowledge always includes reflection, all cognitive forms, from the most concrete to the most abstract, are actually 'schemes of activity' (*sxemy dejstvija,* perhaps better translated more freely as 'operational rules').[97] Cognitive forms, the content of knowledge, are not formed in a vacuum but in accordance with man's needs and interests. Rather than simply mirror reality, knowledge, as an 'ideal transformation of reality', endows it with a specific meaning which then serves as a basis for practice.[98] In a somewhat different expression of the same point, Byčko emphasizes that knowledge is a 'creatively active' reflection of things – not a substantial copy of them but a reflection of their 'constructive principle' (*konstruktivnogo principa*), in accordance with which practical activity can create new, previously non-existent things.[99]

Finally, it is important to note *how* the knower arrives at these schemes of activity, these constructive principles. The answer is indicated by the title of part two of Byčko's work: 'Freedom as Gnoseological Choice'. Any significant advance in knowledge must overcome, even sometimes contradict the prevailing conceptions. How does it do this? There must be a free choice of a new direction of investigation, irreducible to elements of the present body of knowledge.[100] It is clear that by 'free choice' here is meant an act which is not purely volitional, but one with cognitive and volitional elements closely intertwined. The cognitive side is specified as intuition: intuition is "the core of all genuinely creative thinking,"[101] enabling it to go beyond the merely logical extrapolation of present knowledge. However, this particular intuition is more than just an act of intellectual vision. It includes choice: "intuition appears as a free choice of fundamental principles of a new system of knowledge."[102] The author is careful to point out, on the other hand, that the free choice which is an element of creative thinking is not arbitrary choice. But his explanation of this is very curious. It states that the choice must be determined by some objective criteria, but that these are not founded on the existing state of affairs but on some future state: "they possess a type of being which is future being, i.e., possibility."[103] In another formulation: free gnoseological choice is valid only if it in some way apprehends a form of determination which derives not from the present or the past, but from the future.[104] It is surprising that such a position can find any room in an epistemology based on the notion of reflection, but the author apparently sees no incompatibility between this traditional Leninist notion and his own 'free cognitive choice of future being': "One can speak of the freedom of man in the genuine sense of the word only when man is a being capable of reflecting not only that which is, but also that which is *not yet, but will be* (or can be)."[105]

4. THE ONTOLOGICAL DIMENSION: DETERMINISM AND THE POSSIBILITY OF FREEDOM

As was mentioned before, Marxism–Leninism is a cosmological philosophy. It asserts that the world is a unity and that there are universal laws governing the whole. As such Marxism–Leninism could not possibly account for human freedom by assigning it a type of reality radically different from that of the rest of the world, as is done by Kant. This entails, however, a serious problem. The principle of determinism applies to the whole of reality, *including* human activity. How can freedom find room in a philosophy which asserts the universality of the principle of determinism? This problem has already been touched upon briefly in the above discussion of the Soviet critique of other, 'fatalistic' types of determinism. Soviet philosophy sees its own position, in contrast to the others, as a moderate rather than a hard determinism. To recapitulate, two specifications of its view are brought forth to explain that difference: (1) it rejects reductionism and affirms that on each level of reality there is a categoreally unique form of determination irreducible to any other; (2) it rejects the notion of pre-determination, according to which events are univocally determined by some previous state of the universe. However, these two negative specifications, although they fence off the dialectical materialist position from other unacceptable views, do not sufficiently explain how *its* understanding of determinism is acceptable, i.e., reconcilable with the reality of freedom.

Soviet philosophy tries to meet this problem mainly by analyzing the categories of necessity and contingency. This is not unexpected, because the notion of freedom is always paired, in the Marxist tradition, with that of necessity: one always speaks of 'the problem of freedom and necessity'. The category of necessity, in turn, is usually contrasted with that of contingency in most ontological discussions. And while there is never an attempt to equate contingency and freedom, the chief means by which the Soviets seek to show that their determinism is not so rigid as to disallow freedom, is precisely to affirm that there is real contingency, that events can take place which are not causally determined in a necessary fashion.[106] By this they seek to make room, in some vague way, for freedom. A second set of ontological categories which is brought to bear on the discussion of freedom is that of possibility and actuality. In this case the orientation is somewhat more positive. The intention is to show how the world is structured in such a way that it is open to the influence of human efficacy. Thirdly, the whole question of how the agent himself can *be* a kind of first cause, i.e., choose with some degree of freedom vis-à-vis all of the external causes which force themselves upon him, is illuminated by recent Soviet philosophy of cybernetics in its discussion of 'self-regulating systems'.

4.1. *Necessity and Contingency*

Although there are significant differences in the understanding of these categories by Soviet ontologists, the standard presentation in the *Osnovy marksistskoj filosofii* and other such works is the basis for their considerations pertaining to the explanation of freedom.

Dialectical materialism asserts that all phenomena are connected according to laws; they are all law-bound (*zakonomernye*) in some respect.[107] Further, although causal connection is just one type of law-bound connection, all phenomena also have their causes; nothing happens which is uncaused.[108] This is the basic assertion of determinism. Now does this entail that everything which happens in the universe could only have happened in the way in which it did? No, it is answered, because this would mean that, for example, a particular dog's tail had to be just five inches long and no longer, or, taking another example from Engels, that a person had to be bitten by a flea at exactly four in the morning and not at three or five, and just in this place, etc. These examples are cited to show that absolute causal determinism is ridiculous. All events are caused, but not all events are necessary. There are some that happen by chance, that is, are contingent *(slučanjnye)*. By asserting the reality of chance, as one Western author puts it, dialectical materialism hopes to "set limits to the absolute reign of necessity."[109]

Necessity and chance are defined in the following way: "The *necessary* is that which proceeds from the essence, from the inner connection of things, and must inevitably occur." "Contingency is changeable; it is not internally or necessarily connected with the essence of a process. A contingent phenomenon can occur but also can not occur, can happen in one way or in another. Necessity has its cause in itself, contingency in another."[110] Two characteristics here distinguish the two kinds of phenomena: while one arises *internally,* the other arises *from without;* while one springs from the *essence* of a thing, the other is an *inessential* happening. The classic example illustrating the difference is that of the life of a tree, whose growth process is called a necessary phenomenon, while its having rooted in a particular spot or its being struck down by lightning is a chance occurrence. Its life did not 'have' to come to an end in that particular way. The Soviets distinguish between the two types of phenomena but do not in fact separate them. Just as the universal always appears in the particular, and vice versa, so also necessity always manifests itself in chance, and chance always appears as a form of necessity.[111] Consequently, it is not just some events that can be singled out as chance occurrences. All events have a contingent dimension.[112] Now what does this mean – that events, or certain aspects of them, although they are caused, could have occurred differently than they did? Where precisely does the contingency come in?

In a very curious shift of position, the *Osnovy marksistskoj filosofii,* after previously having defined causality as "necessary connection between phenomena where whenever one is present the other inevitably follows", then distinguishes between necessary causes, arising from the inner logic of a process, and "causes of a contingent character".[113] What seems to be meant here is that some causes produce effects which would not necessarily have occurred merely because of the inner nature of the particular process, as the lightning brings the life of the tree to an end. These are called contingent phenomena. Structurally they are seen as the result of the crossing of several lines of causality which have essentially no natural connection with each other but for some reason come together: "Contingency occurs at the point of intersection of different causally conditioned phenomena. The intersection of these phenomena precisely at that point is not required; it is the result of the confluence of many circumstances. The absence of one of them would prevent it from happening."[114] Thus the Soviets do not understand contingency as 'pure chance'; it is the form of an event which is the product of interlacing and 'essentially' unrelated chains of causality. It is in this sense that a contingent event is causally conditioned but not necessary.

Now it must be asked: does the assertion of this kind of contingency really qualify the thoroughness of the determinist principle and make it any easier to explain the existence of free acts in the world? On this point, the criticism of a previous Western treatment of Soviet ontology seems conclusive.[115] Although the Soviets wish to deny by the doctrine of contingency the mechanistic position that everything in the world is necessarily determined down to the last detail, their assertion that the contingent is still causally determined actually entails the same thing. Taking the previous example: the fall of the tree is not necessary if one looks at it from the standpoint of the tree's pattern of growth, or just from the standpoint of the lightning's attraction for a ground. But if one does not artificially separate the sides of the situation and considers all of the factors together, it certainly is necessary for the tree to be struck down – it could not 'not happen'. It is only by taking a partial view of the event that it appears not to be necessary; and partial views, according to the dialectical method itself, are always false. Consequently, as one author puts the criticism: in dialectical materialism "'contingency' alone cannot help us to escape from the domain of strict necessity."[116] Contingency, understood in the Marxist–Leninist sense, cannot put a dent in necessity to make room for freedom; it is precisely the existence of freedom itself which alone can limit necessity.

However, it would be unfair to Soviet philosophy not to mention that there are various interpretations of the categories of determinism, law, causality, necessity, and contingency, which differ from the presentation of the *Osnovy*. A recent Soviet article distinguishes, for example, six different understandings of causality and three different understandings of law among Soviet dialectical materialists.[117] It is not within the scope of this work to discuss the divergent opinions in this very large area,[118] but some consideration must be given to the different views of contingency, the particular category which is called on to play an important role in the Soviet discussion of the ontological presuppositions of freedom.

Three variations on the above doctrine of contingency are fairly widespread. The *first* takes issue with the view that contingency is the product of exclusively external causes.[119] It claims that many contingencies are conditioned by the action of internal and essential causes as well. One author even divides contingencies into internal contingencies and external contingencies. The internal ones flow from the nature of the thing itself, from the necessity of its process, as one of its manifestations; an example would be the chance appearance of a variation within a biological organism.[120] The insufficiency of such a position, however, is apparent; it discards the former grounds for distinguishing between necessity and contingency without providing any other basis for doing so. The *second* variation is a converse of the first: it states that not only can contingency be internal, but necessity can be external.[121] A necessary phenomenon can be one engendered by a combination of external circumstances. As is evident, this external necessity is actually identical to what was previously defined as contingency. Consequently, the criticism that the Soviet doctrine of contingency in no way allows for a weakening of the determinist principle is confirmed by this interpretation: contingency equals external necessity. And the Soviets still must explain how it is that some phenomena "can occur, and also can not occur, can happen in one way or in another."[122] A *third* variation does not, as the first two do, lead contingency back to necessity, but it presents contingency as a very remote and tenuous reality. Contingency is the chance coordination of events at different levels of reality which have nothing to do with each other.[123] The fact that a comet appeared in the sky just before Napoleon's invasion of Russia would be such a contingency. It is pure coincidence. The weakness of this view is obvious: all it states is that some events in the universe are not manifestly causally relevant to some others, although they are found together in temporal or spatial co-ordination; in this sense all events are contingent, and in practically innumerable ways. But it leaves unanswered the question whether each event, in relation to the factors which are in fact causally relevant to it, is necessary or not. And this contingency of remote detachedness hardly serves to explain the possibility of freedom, except perhaps to point out that the whole universe does not come to bear on every human act – for example, that human acts are not determined by the positions of the stars.

Besides these various attempts to account for contingency, mainly it seems by juggling the relevant ontological categories back and forth, there is another approach, based on a reflection on the data of science: that the indeterminacy principle of quantum physics reveals to us a new kind of regularity in micro-objects, different from that of the macro-world, and that the behavior of these micro-objects thus has a contingent character.[124] To put the matter differently: it is pointed out that there is only a probable connection operative between micro-phenomena, so that after a given state of a material system several different states can follow; that these states are not determined by strict 'dynamic laws' but only by statistical laws.[125] Although the Soviets maintain that this does not entail philosophical indeterminism, at least some insist that the probability relation is an aspect of reality and not merely a consequence of our imperfect knowledge of it. It indicates that not everything happens necessarily.

Whatever consequences this may entail for the explanation of human freedom the Soviets assess very cautiously. B. M. Kedrov is openly skeptical in judging the philosophical implications of modern physical theory. He admits that the limits of description of micro-objects indicates that there is a new type of regularity (zakonomer'nost') here, different from any other. But this does not entail for him a rejection of the principle of determinism or that of causality. It only shows that there are forms of causal connection other than the mechanical ones, and it points to a determinism of a higher and more complex character than in LaPlacian mechanism. Kedrov also questions the explanation of free decisions as a consequence of the indeterminacy of the micro-particles which make up man: as if, because the behavior of the microparticles remains undetermined, so also would the behavior of the whole individual be undetermined, and thus there would allegedly remain a "place for complete feedom of will."[126] Kedrov cannot accept that view. His argument is that in order to explain spiritual processes, including human acts, one should not look for explanatory factors in the physical organization of the individual but rather in his psychic and social life.[127] As each sphere of reality is different and irreducible, one should seek causes for phenomena in factors which pertain to the same order. This "applies fully to the spiritual and social life of man, where events are primarily determined not by the micro-particles which make up the human body, but by regularities which lie in the plane of these mental and social phenomena."[128]

Another leading Soviet philosopher, I. S. Narskij, sees the new anti-mechanist understanding of the micro-world as more relevant to the problem of freedom than does Kedrov. He states that "the interaction of macro- and micro-contingencies can account for the fact of relative *human freedom*."[129] However, this is not done by directly reducing macro-contingencies to micro-contingencies. Nor does the probable character of the micro-world have a serious effect on the physiological basis of human 'macro-decisions', since billions of micro-particles are involved here.[130] Actually, Narskij does not explain exactly how the contingency of the micro-world makes freedom possible, and says that further study on this point is needed. All he does is to insist that the possibility of freedom be explained both from the social *and* from the natural scientific point of view, and to give some hint as to how they are related: "Processes which lead to the growth of the level of 'freedom' in the micro-world are not without *indirect* consequences for the social macro-world. In social processes freedom is possible as actively realized and 'expanding' internal necessity, and the limits of its realization are determined by the limits of the given material possibilities."[131] Apparently he considers that micro-contingencies somehow contribute to the scope of these 'material possibilities', thereby expanding the limits of social freedom. Exactly why they do this is not explained.

4.2. *The Objective Possibilities Inherent in Reality*

The discussion of necessity and contingency is, in recent works on free-dom, increasingly supplemented by a brief consideration of the categories 'possibility' and 'actuality'. This also has the intention of qualifying diamat's ontological determinism in order to allow for freedom. It seeks to show that reality is an open rather than a closed system and, in particular how it is that the necessary laws of nature and society can to some extent fall under the influence of human decisions.

The general thesis that the category of possibility is universally applicable means that all types of reality, all things and phenomena can under certain conditions change into something else. They all carry an 'objective possibility' for becoming something different.[132] Moreover, and this is the relevant point here, there is always more than one objective possibility which can become real.[133] Although each process is governed by necessary laws, it can develop in various different ways, depending on its nature and conditions.[134] This is not to say that any conceivable result may follow; a distinction is made between formal (logically possible but actually remote) possibilities and real possibilities, those for which the general conditions are present. But there is at all times a plurality of objective possibilities out of which actuality emerges. One author goes so far as to say: "All that exists in reality is the result of the selection of possibilities."[135] This conception of objective possibili-ties is seen as another counter-point to mechanistic determinism, which pretends to read the future in the present. In the Soviet view, not only can the exact character of future events not be read in the present – because it contains many objective possibilities – but in the future the possibilities themselves will be different; the possibilities themselves develop.

This conception of the relationship of possibility and actuality helps to explain how freedom can be based on an understanding of necessity, and how man can be a cause in the world at all. Human freedom consists in the knowledge of the objective possibilities of a process gov-erned by necessary laws and the choice of that possibility which best corresponds to the person's needs. He then acts in a way in which his action becomes the final condition which actually brings that possibil-ity into being. His action "intervenes in the natural flow of the process'[136] to realize a possibility.

The passage from possibility to actuality does not usually occur in the same way in both nature and society. In nature it is for the most part spontaneous. That is, it occurs without the intervention of man (unless, of course, he is intervening). In society however, it is *always* necessary for men to actively realize the inherent possibilities. For example, the socialist revolution was an objective possibility which was inevitably to come about at some time, but it could do so only when all the conditions for it were present, and these included both objective and subjective factors (the revolutionary will of the CP).[136a] This distinction between the two kinds of transformation from possibility to reality is significant in two respects: it gives a kind of an ontological basis for distinguishing the character of social laws from that of natural laws; and it implies that human behavior itself – always classified as social being – does not arise spontaneously, naturally out of objective factors, whether these be the physiological make-up or environmental influences of the individual.

However, the main function of this discussion in explaining freedom is to show that the nexus of reality on which human agency acts is such that it allows man himself to be a causal agent. No state of affairs is closed to the extent that it can lead to only one future condition. Also, the existence of a plurality of objective possibilities which can be known gives the agent a set of alternatives on which he can exercise his decision. Such a choice is not arbitrary, since the possibilities are clearly delimited, but it is still free, since there are several of them.

This explanation seems to be a significant contribution to the formulation of a viable theory of freedom. It certainly demonstrates in a more clear fashion how determinism and freedom can be reconciled than did the appeals to 'contingency'. However, two considerations might suggest that the notion of a plurality of objective possibilities be regarded cautiously. First of all, the categories of possibility and actuality are more general than those of necessity and contingency; they do not really specify the structure of causal connections, as the latter do. The question must still be posed: why is it and how can it be that there are really several objective possibilities in something that has a fully determinate set of causes and conditions? To answer this, one has to make recourse again to the categories of necessity, causality, etc., and face the same problems over again. Secondly, if the knowledge of objective laws on the basis of which free judgments are made is in fact a knowledge of the possibilities (plural) of development of some reality, then the notion of law acquires a very special meaning. A law in this context can be no more than a general tendency of a process which can work itself out in different ways. In fact, the *Osnovy* states that "every law in nature and society appears not in pure form, but as a tendency."[137] But apart from the fact that Soviet philosophers do not understand this to mean that a law is nothing but a tendency, it is clear that there are laws, for example in physics, which do not allow for a plurality of possible outcomes. Again a question presents itself: how can a law or set of laws operate so as to produce a relatively undetermined outcome?

4.3. *Causality and Choice in Self-Regulating Systems*

It is manifest that the Soviet discussions of the two sets of ontological categories – necessity and contingency, actuality and possibility – leave many important questions unanswered. The primary concern of these discussions seems to be to explain how the world in which man lives and upon which he must act is structured so that it is at least possible for him to insert his free act into it. It is a discussion of the context, the objective field of reference of acts – the world as acted upon. A main problem, however, which is generally overlooked in this discussion, pertains to the way in which the world acts upon the agent. How is it that the agent can act freely if his acts are under the influence of external causes, as is everything in the world? The universal scope of the causal principle accepted by diamat entails that every phenomenon, although it may be a cause from one point of view, is an effect from another; there is always something other than itself which is its cause. How then can free acts, in particular the acts of choice, be anything other than links in a causal chain of events?

This problem has not received much attention in Soviet discussions of freedom and necessity. In fact, it is often summarily dismissed as a 'metaphysical' problem. However, some interesting work relating to the problem has recently appeared, which examines the relation between external causality and the activity of self-regulating systems. This work concerns more than just 'human systems' – its scope includes all living systems and cybernetical mechanisms – and does not address itself directly to the problem of human freedom, but its conclusions are directly relevant, as will be seen.

B. S. Ukraincev seeks to answer the question: how is it that a system chooses its behavior under the influence of external causes?[138] In physical interactions the reaction of an object to an external influence is just that – a re-action; it is an activity, but does not go beyond the limits of reciprocal response. The character of the reaction does depend on the nature of the thing reacting as well as on the peculiarities of that type of reaction, but nevertheless it "is compelled by the external cause and is the only effect which can follow it in the given conditions."[139] This is a fact which has its basis in the laws of physical reality. But besides these physical reactions there are also acts *(postupky)* which are "a result of a choice by man of his behavior".[140] How is this to be explained? In what sense could a reaction to external impulses be a choice (for man as well as for other analogous systems)?

Rejecting the 'idealist' solution that it derives from the priority of spirit over matter, Ukraincev asserts that the materialist explanation of choice bases itself upon the recognition of the universality of the causal principle and the existence of objective laws of the process of choice. That is, the very act of choice must be considered as a special type of phenomenon, more complex than the physical dynamism of reaction; it is the activity of a "system interacting with its environment".[141] There are at least three conditions for the realization of such an interaction: First, there must be a plurality of possibilities all of which bear some meaning for the choice as its result. Secondly, there must be a system which is able to turn any of those possibilities into reality. And thirdly, there must be a kind of inner necessity for the realization of the choice.[142]

The first condition is a crucial one. In the previous section, it was mentioned that the Soviets understand reality to have various inherent possibilities, leaving the future open in some way. Ukraincev makes this more precise by examining a specific type of cause-effect relation which holds when self-regulating systems are involved. The main point is that given the same external cause acting on the system, there can be several *different effects*. This is schematized as follows.

$$C \rightarrow S \rightarrow E_1 \quad (C = \text{cause}, \ S = \text{system}, \ E = \text{effect})$$
$$C \rightarrow S \rightarrow E_2$$
$$\cdot \quad \cdot \quad \cdot$$
$$C \rightarrow S \rightarrow E_n$$

He is very much aware of the fact that this contradicts the principle of causality as it operates in the physical world – where one cause cannot produce different effects – but maintains that here a different and more complex type of interaction is operating. And this is absolutely necessary for choice. The choice of behavior presupposess that in the presence of one cause and given set of conditions, different effects can follow. A more complicated, higher type of cause-effect relationship is necessary.

The second condition is the existence of the unique type of reality which is the 'self-regulating system', the thing which can direct the influence of the cause in different directions. Ukraincev points to several characteristics of a self-regulating system: (1) It is an open, functioning, complex system, operating with energy extracted from the surroundings and maintaining an active equilibrium with the latter.[143] (2) It is able to reverse its states; that is, its physical entropy can not only not increase, but insofar as it is capable of self-perfection *(samosoveršenstvovanie)*, it can actually diminish (this does not entail a refutation of the second law of thermodynamics, since the entropy of the self-regulating system dimishes at the expense of the increase in entropy of the surroundings). (3) It has a certain stability *(ustojčivost')*, due to the ability to adjust its elements and behavior as a whole. The element of the system which makes this possible is its 'functional constant' or 'inner purpose'.[144] To sum up, a self-regulating system is open, self-perfecting, and held together by an inner purpose.

Now the behavior of these systems differs from physical things in that the system chooses its behavior. Something arises in its behavior which cannot be explained by physical laws or even by the composite elements of this system. How does this new factor (the choice) arise? Ukraincev explains this by pointing out that such systems produce information by reflection, accumulation and transformation of the external world. The result is a special kind of cause, an 'inner informational cause' which acts differently from physical causes.[145] In the choice of behavior, this informational cause leads to the selection of a course of action to accomplish the inner purpose, the goal of the system. The whole process is thus seen as the choice of a means to attain a goal. The goal is, at least for non-human systems, given. But the means to accomplish this goal is chosen, for although physical causes exert themselves on the system in a univocal fashion, the whole informational content of the system is interposed, and the relation of external causes to the resultant behavior is not a predictably determined one. In the words of the author: "the informational causes model, as it were, the external causes, 'displace' their effect in a direction needed by the self-regulating system, and thus give rise to a cause-effect relation different from that of physical phenomena, in which a choice is made of any of the many possible effects."[146]

This position is an attempt to explain the characteristic structure of the behavior of one whole region of reality – informational systems – including all living things and cybernetical devices. For this reason, it is difficult to understand the use of the term 'choice', which usually applies only to human agents. There is no doubt that the model here for the understanding of informational systems is man; for example, Ukraincev mentions that the process of choice always has an axiological aspect. It is, in fact, only by analogy to human behavior that one can speak about the axiological behavior of cats and computers as well as of man. Thus, nothing is really explained by this view until one knows how human choice is possible. Further, the mere fact that informational factors work with a different kind of causality does not immediately entail that real choice can occur. Since the informational content of a system is a determinate, and not an indeterminate content, it would seem that the behavior of the system could be sufficiently explained by saying that the external causes plus the informational content produces the behavior. Why speak of choice?

Ukraincev's position would be rejected by most Soviet philosophers dealing with the problem of freedom – not because his analysis is wrong, but because its scope is too large. What he attributes to all living systems, namely purposeful activity, would be attributed by most only to man. It is precisely this that is seen as distinguishing human behavior from all other behavior and which permits the attribution of freedom to human behavior. To put it differently, his analysis of the choice of behavior by informational systems reflects fairly well the way in which Soviet philosophers of man understand human choice – except that they would restrict it solely to man, because of their refusal to accept the reality of goals or purposes in any being which does not possess consciousness.

5. THE STRUCTURE OF FREE ACTIVITY

Man is the only being in the universe that is free. The Soviets generally consider the use of the word 'free' to describe the behavior of elementary particles or cybernetical systems to be ultimately an anthropomorphic usage and thus not valid. In their own mind, freedom is a social category, pertaining only to society and the social beings, namely men, that make it up. Now is it held that freedom is a quality of all men, living in any society, or does it belong only to a few, to men at a high stage of social development? Although the latter is suggested by older studies and especially in works of a general ideological rather than strictly philosophical nature such as one finds in *Kommunist,* recent studies analyzing the properly philosophical aspects of freedom have clearly stated that freedom is not *just* a product of socio-historical development, but is *also* a basic trait of man as such.[147] Increasingly, reference is made to the early statement by Marx that free activity is man's properly generic activity which distinguishes him from the animals.[148] This is found also in his analysis in *Kapital* of the difference between human labor activity and the constructive activity of animals. According to one author. Marx "includes the notion of freedom in his characterization of human activity".[149] Further support is found in Lenin, who distinguishes between human purposeful activity and the action of non-human causes, and relates freedom directly to purposeful activity. Thus freedom becomes a characteristic of "every purposeful human activity".[150] It is always mentioned that the measure of freedom attained by any individual depends upon the society in which he lives, but the exercise of free conscious activity is seen to be a *generic* human trait.[151] As one author puts it, freedom is "deeply rooted in man; it is connected with the very essence of man as a creatively-active being."[152]

5.1. *Preliminary Delimitations*

Before presenting the analysis of the elements of free activity, it will be useful to discuss some of the more general considerations which enter into the Soviet discussions.

First of all, it is always emphasized that the primary sense of 'freedom' is not freedom *from* but freedom *for* something. What is important is not that human activity be seen as in some way detached from a set of causes, but that it be understood as a unique type of determinism which itself functions in an efficacious way. Negative freedom is called 'formal', and 'abstract', "having nothing in common with the active, creative manifestation of the human being."[153] A free act is always directed towards the transformation of some possibility into reality by striving for the realization of some goal.[154]

Secondly, it is nevertheless maintained that free acts are in fact not exhaustively determined by external factors. Tugarinov defines freedom as "the possibility for man to think or act, not from external compulsion, but in accordance with his own will."[155] Here the negative point is made, that this human activity is not univocally determined from without. In spite of the fact that Soviet philosophy does not oppose freedom and determinism, it does assert that there is a relative autonomy of human activity in relation to the totality of natural and social influences which impinge upon it.[156] Especially important in this regard is the understanding of the role of social factors. Although it is often said that the Marxist position asserts that human actions are mere products of social forces, many Marxist–Leninists do not understand social determinism in this fashion. Economic factors determine human actions only in a remote and average fashion; as one author puts it, there is always a "certain range for individual decision".[157] Individuals can actually act so as to oppose the necessary laws of economic and social development, although these laws will, in the end, produce their inevitable effects in society.

Thirdly, freedom is always relative, never absolute.[158] It is conditioned by several objective factors. The two most often mentioned are: First, insofar as free acts must be based on knowledge, their level of perfection depends upon the degree of knowledge attained by the individual and the society in which he lives. Secondly, the object of a person's choice is always a very restricted range of possibilities; the alternatives among which he chooses are given, are set for him by the natural and social conditions of his life.[159] Man may not do or even choose to do whatever he wishes. The range of his activity is very much restricted by factors beyond his control.

5.2. *Analysis of the Elements of Free Activity*

The definitions of freedom given by various Soviet authors are very similar, and differ mainly insofar as they may emphasize different aspects. The following five definitions are representative: "Freedom can be characterized as the goal-setting, choosing activity of social man, accomplished on the basis of the cognition of objective necessity"[160]; "freedom is conscious goal-directed activity in accordance with known necessity, basing itself upon and utilizing the knowledge of the objective laws of nature and society"[161]; "freedom consists in the knowledge of necessity, the activity of man in accordance with this knowledge, and the possibility and capability of choice in his actions"[162]; "freedom is the practical mastery of necessity, the conscious and purposive realization of necessity in a form which corresponds to the interests of man"[163]; "freedom presupposes the knowledge of necessity, the freedom of choice of the desired possibility, the proposing of a goal on this basis, the choice of the means for its realization, and especially the practical realization – freedom of action, the concluding step in the formation of freedom."[164] In all of these definitions, freedom is presented as a special type of human activity of a relatively complex structure. It is comprised not only of the knowledge of necessity, or of choice alone, but it is a chain of activity including these and other elements.

Several aspects of freedom contained in these definitions can be considered essential.

First of all, the general structure of free activity is *finalistic.* Referring to Lenin's connection of the notions of freedom and 'goal, consciousness, striving', Soviet authors maintain that freedom is possible only where a subject is oriented towards the realization of consciously entertained future goals.[165] Free activity is always described as 'goal-positing' *(celepolagajuščaja),* 'goal-directed' *(celeustremljajuščaja)* or 'purposive' *(celesoobraznaja).* This marks it off as a unique form of activity, for although in the higher organisms there is an adaptability to the conditions of their life, most Soviet philosophers would maintain that this can be explained in terms of a consequent deterministic interpretation of nature; there is allegedly no need to assume the existence of goals outside of man.[166] And in man this goal-directed activity is an irreducible type of determination. The key factor here is the goal as an 'ideal form of the future', which is constructed by consciousness in accordance with the person's needs and interests.[167] It is important to note the main idea here: since the goal is a product of consciousness, it functions as a cause in a different way than natural factors. It does not automatically bring about some effect, whether this be the decision of the agent to choose it or the implementation of it through a particular means. This does not mean that goals are arbitrarily conceived. Lenin's point is always well taken, i.e., that the concrete goals are engendered by the conditions of life. They arise from the situation as a reponse to man's actual needs. But insofar as they are 'ideal' entities they have no real efficacy all by themselves. They exert their effect precisely by being chosen and implemented by the agent; that is what is unique about this finalistic type of determination. To reinforce this point, it is almost always emphasized that there is a multitude of goals conceived by man, presenting to him different alternatives.[168] He formulates these himself but then must choose one of them; the goals themselves exert a force upon him that is not sufficient to necessitate his decision. Further, the perception of the means-end relationship and the ability of man to select means to implement this ideally conceived goal represents a uniquely human way of functioning as a cause of some real change in the world. To sum up, the finalistic chain of activity which the Soviets designate as 'free activity' begins with the formulation (which occurs more or less spontaneously) of a variety of goals, proceeds to the choice of one, the selection of the means of implementing it, and finally the concrete action, the 'practice' itself which actually alters reality in some way.

Secondly, as has been often mentioned above, an indispensable component of this activity is the *knowledge* of necessity. Before the individual can choose any goals or set about to realize them, he must have perceived the conditions of his milieu (external necessity) to know what possibilities might be open to him,[169] and he must have gained some knowledge of the laws of reality (internal necessity) in order to determine how his goals are to be achieved. It is important to note again that knowledge is not the culmination of free activity but merely one of its early stages; it is never sufficient by itself (as was explained at length above). Apart from the fact that freedom is aimed ultimately at action rather than at contemplation, it is also recognized that not all acts which are based upon the knowledge of necessity are free acts. For example, a decision which appears to be free (insofar as it is based on knowledge, deliberation, etc.) may in reality be unfree if it contradicts the inner convictions of the subject.[170] It can be based on knowledge but actually compelled by some extrinsic force, and to this extent it is not free.

Further, it is in an act of knowledge in which goals are formed. Although goals are engendered by the real conditions, they are not simple reflections of reality. They cannot be, since they are 'ideal forms of the future'. As such they must be to a certain extent creative products of the mind.[171] This is closely related to the main point of the work of I. V. Byčko considered above, that knowledge plays a liberating, humanizing role in practical activity because it can do more than just copy reality: "The process of arriving at truth, insofar as this is carried out as the cognitive activity of the *real* man,..., is first and foremost an active, creative process, and not a simple 'demonstration of truth' determined univocally by natural necessity. In the process of knowledge, man does not simply follow the prescriptions of this or that logical schema reflecting the demands of that particular necessity, but *freely chooses* its way."[172] The act of formulating goals, as well as the deliberation of the mind to determine their means of implementation, is such an active, creative process.

Thirdly, free acts always involve, in some manner, a *choice.* The importance of choice as an element of free activity is given different weight by various Soviet authors; while all of them recognize that there is no freedom without choice, some go further in stating that the choice is precisely the element for which the activity is termed 'free'. But apart from Byčko, Soviet philosophers do not usually place choice in the act of knowledge itself; they understand it to follow upon knowledge. It follows upon the cognitive apprehension of goals because there is always a multitude of possible goals which arise, and only one of them can be pursued; thus one has to be chosen.[73] It is also stated in many Soviet discussions that the person also freely chooses the means of realizing the goal. Unfortunately, there is no explanation of the difference, if any, between the two choices. One author points out that the end determines to a large extent the means[174], but he does not draw the implications this seems to have for the choice involved. There is in general very little discussion of the structure of the act of choice by Soviet philosophers writing on freedom. Some of the contributions in this area, coming mostly from psychologists or moral philosophers, will be treated briefly in the next chapter. What is, however, always made clear is that the act of choice is not just an apparent, merely phenomenal reality. It is a "manifestation of the human will", the "result of internal, subjective, active work" of the person.[175] It does not represent any kind of absolute freedom, as is claimed by the existentialists, but it is also not just an adaptation to circumstances[176]. It is a relatively autonomous, real act of the will (note that the phrases 'freedom of will' and 'act of the will' do not indicate an acceptance of a faculty psychology which assumes the will to be a separate power). Perhaps in response to the frequent Western condemnation of the Marxist–Leninist position as deterministic, the point is always made that free choice is not ruled out by historical determinism. The laws of history, although they determine the general development of society, do not, to speak metaphorically, pre-select the goals which the individuals adopt. There is always a "conscious choice of a definite position", i.e., one of the possible goals "in relation to the conflicting classes and parties."[177]

Fourthly, since free activity is finalistic insofar as it strives to realize some goal, and this goal has been formulated as a way of satisfying man's real needs and interests, the chain of activity must not stop with choice. It must pass from the inner realm of the psychic over into *practical activity.* Soviet philosophy insists that if the finalistic process remains enclosed within the sphere of subjectivity there is no real freedom, but it remains abstract, ideal, illusory, etc.: "only by means of practical activity is freedom attained in reality *(na dele)*"[178]. One author describes this final stage of freedom in the following way: "man, finding himself impelled by an inner need to realize his choice, his very self, acts, creates and thereby overcomes his own subjectivity. It is the realization of the transition from internal to external activity, from the subjective into the objective."[179] Thus, the Soviet position rejects the traditional separation of freedom of choice from freedom of external action; the two form a natural unity. And insofar as free activity terminates in an actual incursion into the world – as practice – it is itself a special type of objective determination in this world. As one author puts it, man comes forward as a "'co-author' and 'rival' of nature".[180]

CHAPTER VII

THE DIFFERENT TYPES AND ASPECTS OF FREEDOM

At the beginning of the last chapter, it was pointed out that in the Marxist–Leninist tradition there are four distinguishable, although not unrelated notions of freedom: freedom as self-realization, historico-social freedom, the freedom of human activity, and freedom of will. The third type receives the greatest amount of consideration which can be regarded as genuinely philosophical. And in the last chapter the principles of the Soviet position which were presented, although they apply in a general way to all four types, were understood to be directed, as they are in the Soviet discussions, to an explanation of freedom of activity – how man can act as a cause in the world in a relatively autonomous fashion. Now in the present chapter this must be supplemented with a brief presentation of the other types of freedom and the special aspects of the problems – such as the role of values in free acts and the special case of moral freedom – to complete the picture of the Soviet situation.

1. CERTAIN ASPECTS OF FINALISTIC ACTIVITY

In view of the fact that freedom is almost always explained as a consequence of the finalistic structure of human activity, it seems necessary to present, before going on to the other types of freedom, certain particular aspects of human finality that have been clarified in recent discussions and which seem relevant to the explanation of freedom. The most important of these are: the origin and nature of a goal, the character of finalistic causality and the role of values in the determination of goals.

1.1. *The Origin and Nature of Goals*

First of all, as N. N. Trubnikov points out, the discussion of 'goals' understands by that term something very specific. One meaning of the term 'goal' is that which indicates the final good of man. It is expressed in the phrase 'the goal of life'.[1] It is closely connected with the notions of welfare *(blago)* and happiness, and can be taken as the end of human striving *('predel stremlenie' čeloveka)*. This is not the meaning usually given to the term in the discussions of goal-directed activity. It is the proximate goal rather than the ultimate goal which is normally meant. That is, a goal is understood as a limited and immediately given subjective idea which precedes some real occurrence and is the latter's precondition and ideal form.[2] Goals are things that arise and disappear, are realized or frustrated, are formed and altered in man's every-day activity. With this particular understanding of goals, the Soviets bypass the question, although apparently not in a conscious way, of whether or not man freely chooses his ultimate goal. The whole question of the ultimate goal does not arise in the discussion of free activity or freedom of will but only in the context of the Marxian 'freedom as self-realization'.

Now in what way do goals arise? Certainly their origin is not, for Marxist–Leninists, purely a matter of human invention. As Lenin says, goals are engendered by the objective world. And he seems to express approval of Hegel's statement that man is frequently subject to nature with regard to his goals.[3] The starting point of goal-formation is seen to be the fact that reality, as it is, does not satisfy man's needs; there is a 'contradiction' between reality and human needs. Out of this grows "an idea of how reality *ought to be* in order to satisfy man".[4] Once this goal is realized, there is a new situation which also does not satisfy man, because his needs develop; he forms new goals, and so on. Thus, a goal arises as a response to needs. This is expressed in many definitions: "a goal is a need reflected in consciousness"[5]; "a goal is a need which has been posited as external, as an object".[6] But as several authors point out, it is more than just the reflection of a need. That is the aspect which is basically determined by external necessity. It is not just the reflection of the need as such but also the idea of the object that will satisfy the need. It is, as a matter of fact, these two seen together in 'contradiction'. The achievement of the goal then becomes the resolution of this contradiction.[7] In any case, there are two elements which enter into goal formation: the reflection of real human needs and the construction in consciousness of some future object or condition which will satisfy them. In view of the fact that this latter does not yet exist in reality, the goal is called an 'ideal form' of it. This second element is what allows one to speak of the free choice of goals. Man cannot choose his needs. They are given. But since there are always several ways in which one's needs can be fulfilled, and these arise in the mind as ideal forms of future results, there can be – in fact there must be – a choice.

There is some uncertainty in the Soviet discussions as to actually what the nature of a goal is, i.e., what it encompasses. The distinction is made by one author between the goal as the actual future result of the human activity, and the goal as the mental form of this result which occurs previously in the agent.[8] The same term can be used, he points out, only because the two coincide in content. Another author prefers to distinguish between goal and 'result' since, he says, there is always only a relative coincidence between the intended goal and the actual result of human activity.[9] And the degree of that coincidence depends on the means which are adapted. Although some attempts are made to include the means in the concept of the goal[10], the two are usually distinguished; and, as mentioned before, the question thus comes up in the discussion of freedom as to whether both the goal and the means are freely chosen, or just the former. But whatever differences there might be in the conception of the nature of a goal, there is agreement that it is an ideal form of some future result which is not just a reflection of some present object, that it is a very complex kind of thing, and that it has to be affirmed – chosen, if you will – by man in order for it to function as a cause.

1.2. Goals as Causes

It is not easy to understand how goals *do* function as causes. To assert *that* thy are real causes (irreducible to any set of efficient causes) is in itself a rejection of mechanistic determinism. But, it is held, one also cannot contrast efficient and final causes as totally opposed to each other in nature; this is also an 'error' of the mechanist position.[11] Final causes work in a very complex way, with their main characteristic being "that the co-ordination of a series of causes is subordinated to the task of producing a definite effect, that is, depends upon the latter".[12] The effect, as end, has an influence on the (efficient) causes which produce it. The process operates contrariwise to efficient causality, since the cause depends upon the effect. How is this explained? One author appeals to the 'dialectical' understanding of causality, and says that the possibility of finality lies in the principle of the "reverse influence of the effect on the cause which is producing it"[13] – that is, the two mutually interact. However, that does not fully answer the question, for the end as effect could obviously not be, in the same relation, a cause of that which brings it about. Another author adds that there are two levels of determination here (cause upon effect and effect upon cause), and that where there is finalistic causality the finality takes precedence; it explains the other (efficient) connection. To put it differently, the connection of efficient cause and effect "exists because the system S" within which it occurs "is a finalistic system".[14]

This situation, quite difficult to understand on the general ontological level, becomes somewhat more comprehensible where S is a human system, because, as is pointed out, the goal is an ideal form of the intended result and not that result itself. Thus the goal as an *ideal* brings into operation the (efficient) cause-effect chains which lead to the goal as actual *reality*. Nevertheless, the difficulty remains, to explain how some ideal entity can exert an influence on the concrete world at all. The Soviets account for the real efficacy of the ideal goal by simply asserting that these goals are not only ideal forms; they *also* have a real dimension. Some point out that the ideal is a social category, and "as a characteristic of social process, is fully real, and therefore can be a component of real determination".[15] Others look to its psycho-physical basis in man: it possesses 'material being' in the neurophysiological activities of the brain and through this connection can direct and regulate actual human behavior.[16] This of course completely begs the question, which is: how *can* the ideal exert an effect on the real order? The Marxist–Leninist position seems to want to have it both ways. Finalistic activity as a *unique* form of determination depends upon the goal's *ideal* nature; but as a factor which actually affects the world, it is also *real*.

1.3. *The Dependence of Goals upon Values*

A different and very important dimension of human finality has been brought to light in the context of recent Soviet attempts to develop a theory of value. It is the recognition that all such activity has a value dimension, i.e., involves the consideration and application of values. The neglect of this aspect in one book-length presentation of the structure of human activity prompted severe criticism.[17] The author, N. N. Trubnikov, had ruled out the axiological approach on the assumption that 'abstract goals' (i.e., values) did not enter into the logic of human activity since they were never realized, as concrete goals are.[18] But, a critic points out, since the process of the formation and realization of goals does not come to an end – it continues in a seemingly endless succession – a question arises as to the *hierarchy* of these goals. It is necessary to explain the "correlation and subordination of goals in any particular chain of concrete activity."[19] And he feels that what ultimately specifies this hierarchy is some scheme of values: If the adoption of any goal presupposes a value judgment *(ocenka),* then the person who makes this judgment is assuming a definite position, "which rests upon a definite system of values".[20]

In the previous chapter, the stages of finalistic activity were presented as: knowledge, formation and choice of a goal, and finally action. V. P. Tugarinov, in a book on value theory, rephrases the triad as: knowledge, value judgment, practice. He thereby places the whole process of goal-positing into the framework of the valuational activity of man. The goal itself, he says, arises in consciousness as a mental form of a value.[21] The necessity for a value judgment following upon the act of knowledge is elsewhere explained by O. M. Bakuradze by pointing out that knowledge does no more than establish the facts of an object; it does not express the *relation* of the subject to that object.[22] The latter appears only in a value judgment, in which the object is judged to be useful or harmful, good or bad, etc., for the subject. A goal is set up by a value judgment when what is judged as valuable does not yet exist in fact, or exists and its continued existence is desired. The goal appears to man as "something which ought to be".[23] And that is precisely the definition of value: "Value is not that which is but that which ought to be."[24] It is the 'ought' present in every value judgment constituting a goal which establishes the demand of the goal to be realized.

Now what implications does this have for the explanation of freedom? First of all, it shows that the setting up of goals does not follow some kind of automatic stimulus-response pattern. Earlier it was mentioned that goals arise as responses to human needs. This poses the question: are they only responses? O. I. Džioev distinguishes two kinds of relationship of needs to objects. One is an 'immediate relationship', in which there is no recognition of the value of the object; it is enough for the subject to perceive the object, and he will wish it.[25] The second, on the basis of which goals are constructed, is a 'normative relationship'; it appears when the immediate reaction is approved or disapproved by the subject.[26] To put the point more broadly, on top of the natural relation of need to fulfillment is superimposed a value judgment. The latter is an essential part of the goal-formation. As Džioev puts it elsewhere: 'the goals of people depend upon the kind of values by which they are guided.'[27] Secondly, insofar as values have some objective reality, their role in the subjective process of evaluation can be a liberating role. Besides purely individual values, there are both class values and universal human values (e.g., justice, goodness, beauty). Thus, the subject does not necessarily have to follow his own individual values; he can critically consider them from the point of view of social values (e.g. the value of one's own existence can be suspended in favor of a higher, social value). He can, in turn, compare different class-values and judge them on the basis of the higher criteria, the universal human values.[28] The existence of the two higher levels of values thus allows the subject to be at least relatively free of the context in which he is operating: he can judge his own life on the basis of objective social values, and society (as well as his own life) on the basis of the supreme values. Džioev makes a special point of affirming the unconditional or 'absolute' character of the latter. He asserts unequivocally that they have a certain objective validity, independent of the historical process, for they are rooted in human nature.[29] This is important in view of the fact that Marxist–Leninists have tended to emphasize the social and thus class-bound character of all human activity, including free acts, and have sometimes practically identified social and anthropological categories. Džioev significantly modifies this view by giving these unconditional values a role in the very structure of human action, thus making it at least partially free of class determination. As he argues the point: since free activity involves the setting up of goals on the basis of the person's set of values, "if values were totally determined by the concrete historical conditions, if they would be devoid of any autonomy, freedom would be an illusion."[30]

2. THE EXPLANATION OF FREE WILL

In the discussion of freedom as the goal-directed activity of man pre-sented above, there appears a broad consensus among Soviet philoso-phers. The same thing cannot be said of the treatments of free will *(svoboda voli)*. It was seen that one stage in this goal-directed activity is the choice of a goal. And on that everyone agrees: man makes choices, whenever he is faced with a plurality of alternative courses of action. Further, these choices are not directly determined by the environment, natural or social. However, the question still remains: are these choices themselves free within the structure of psychic activity? This problem, known as the problem of free will, has received little attention in Soviet philosophical literature, and not much more in Soviet psychology. The reason for this can certainly be traced back to the classics. Engels said that free will is 'nothing but' the ability to make a well-informed decision, thereby reducing free will to judgment. And Lenin referred to 'the absurd tale of free will', a remark which is frequently quoted in current literature. Following this line of thinking, very many Soviet philosophers state that 'free will' is just another phrase which means freedom of action or free choice of behavior,[31] and is one to be avoided, since it allegedly carries the 'metaphysical' connotations of 'absolute freedom' or of a purely psychic phenomenon. A further reason, found in the classics, for the neglect of this concept, is the actual position of Engels and Lenin. As was shown in chapters three and four, both seem to be psycho-logical determinists, although their positions are far from being clear. In view of this it might be considered surprising that there is any serious discussion at all of free will.

2.1. *Free Will as Self-Mastery*

A frequently encountered view is that free will consists in mastery over oneself. Engels had said that freedom consists in mastery over nature, over society and over man himself.[32] This third type is sometimes identi-fied as free will. In what does this mastery consist? The broadest explana-tion is that it is a kind of self-reliance, the power to use one's own abilities to accomplish goals. It is thus different in different men and depends upon training, education, personal abilities, and traits of char-acter such as persistence and courage.[33] Such a concept of self-mastery does not pose any problems, but neither does it seem to have much to do with free will. A more relevant interpretation of self-mastery sees it as the subordination of our wishes and feelings to our reason.[34] Being free means to avoid being the slave of one's passions, and to overcome their influence with strong and deliberate rational judgment; in one formulation, "to direct and restrain one's emotions, passions and motives"[35]. This Spinozistic idea is, however, rejected by many authors. One states that human emotions and feelings constitute a real source of wealth of the individual and are to be cultivated rather than suppressed.[36] A more substantive objection is based on a conception of the unity of the rational and affective sides of man. Using a somewhat inappropriate terminology, V. E. Davidovič distinguishes two aspects of volition, the 'objective' and the 'subjective'. The objective side is thought, reason, which grasps the contradictions in reality, formulates goals, etc.; the subjective side is the "dynamism *(energičnost')* of practical activity, its emotivity *(emocional'nost'.)*"[37] In his view, to separate these two sides of will is to mystify the whole process of volition. Thus, the concept of free will as self-mastery, when worked out beyond the superficial meaning of self-reliance and emotional self-control (which might have been all that Engels meant), does not turn out to be a viable concept in dialectical materialism.

In the opinion of Davidovič, the emotions even play a positive role in freedom. He rejects both the intellectualist position of Spinoza which condemns the emotions and ultimately reduces will to intellect, and the Freudian view that men are controlled by their instinctual feelings.[38] Both assess the emotions negatively, and both end up rejecting free will. Davidovič admits that the emotional side of man is less under control than the rational side, but does not see how the latter can operate without the former. Lenin had said: "Without 'human emotions' there would never have been, nor would there be any human *searching* for the truth."[39] The emotions give a kind of push that the intellect does not supply. A recent attempt to account for the emotions in terms of information theory explains them as a "compensatory mechanism, making up for a deficiency of information, and necessary for the attainment of goals, the satisfaction of needs."[40] The emotions come into play where there is a lack of a fully reasoned basis for acting, especially in complicated situations; they supply the force which moves the person into action.[41] Thus not only does free will not lie in the independence of the intellect from the emotions, since such independence is impossible; but the emotions often necessarily come into play. And since they can either strengthen the will or paralyze it, it is important for the well-functioning of free will that one develop his positive emotions and, in general try to bring the rational and emotional aspects of his activity into a harmonious balance.[42]

What does not come out very clearly in this discussion is the difference between emotion and will. Davidovič sometimes seems to let the emotions do the work of the will, i.e., in acting upon the information supplied by the intellect; but at other times he states that the emotions move the will (and are thus something different). The reason for this problem, and for the general ambiguity and vagueness which surrounds all of these discussions is the lack of any clearly articulated conception of the will. Without a satisfactory understanding of the nature of the will (or of 'volition', if the faculty term is to be avoided), it can hardly be explained how the volitional functions are free.

2.2. The Nature of the Will

The state of the Soviet discussions on the will is certainly not a happy one. In the philosophical literature there is almost no consideration of the nature of the will. It is practically non-existent, in contrast to the very extensive work on the cognitive functions. Even in discussions of freedom there is very little attempt to explain the nature of will or volition. The situation is only moderately better in Soviet psychology. It is openly admitted that in older textbooks it is hard to find any serious treatment of the will, and that recent attempts to arrive at a 'scientific' position have not succeeded.[43] However, in the opinion of V. I. Selivanov, a leading Soviet psychologist, the picture is not totally dark. He finds numerous accomplishments in the Soviet work, and has devoted several articles to a survey of the situation, at the same time trying to formulate the common core of opinion on the nature of the will to which most Soviet psychologists adhere.

A fundamental question is: what kind of a psychic entity, *generically*, is the will? According to Selivanov, Soviet psychologists do not commit the error of reducing it to the intellect or emotions. What must be avoided however is the conception of the will as a separate faculty, as in the faculty psychology of Christian Wolff. Some Soviets define the will very narrowly as a 'psychic process' or a 'property of the person'. But Selivanov finds, in Rubinštejn as well as in many others, a kind of middle ground: the genus of 'will' is 'capacity' *(sposobnost')*, which is defined as "a system of associated psychic functions anchored in the individual"[44]. Thus, generically the will is comparable, as a part of the psyche, to the intellect *(um)*. They are parallel capacities.

It is more difficult to state the *specific* properties of the will. Selivanov lists several typical conceptions: will is the conscious (as opposed to the unconscious and instinctual) effort of the person in response to certain motives; its essence is expressed in selective goal-directed behavior; it is the exercise of certain selective acts, namely those in which the individual is actively struggling to overcome some obstacle; it is the conscious self-regulation by man of his behavior; it is the self-regulation in which there is a struggle for the attainment of goals; it is the power of man over his passions and lower motives; it is not only the power of the higher motives over the lower, but all conscious control of man's behavior; etc.[45] These characterizations are somewhat imprecise, and tend to state not so much what the will is or does, but rather how the being who has a will behaves. Selivanov introduces some clarity into the situation by reducing the above-mentioned qualities of the will to three: (a) "the dynamism *(aktivnost')* of motivation and the volitional force connected with it"; (b) "the deliberative character of behavior and the capacity for purposefully overcoming obstacles"; (c) "the conscious regulation of one's behavior and the consciousness of one's own power over it."[46] Two of these three points refer to behavior. This is in keeping with the view that all psychic functions are connected with the real external life of the person. The will, like the intellect, does not exercise its function in a separate, atomic kind of fashion, but is a link in a larger chain of activity. The same point is made by claiming that there is no absolute separation of the internal from the external in volitional processes; will cannot exercise any functions outside of the context of the interaction of man with the external world.[47] However, the act of the will is itself, as A. N. Leont'ev states, an 'intra-psychic' process; it is exercised within the person.[48] Now, insofar as the will is an 'intra-psychic' capacity, it is seen as activity, force, effort. One author defines will as "the active side of the human psyche, its inner dynamism, its tendency".[49] This basic idea is a very traditional one. If one asks further, however, on what does this dynamism immediately operate, no simple answer is available. What is said is that the will directs or acts upon motives, goals, and behavior. Ruling out behavior as a mediate rather than immediate object, we end up with the view that the will is a conscious force which acts upon (i.e., selects or rejects) motives and goals, the result of which is the control over one's own behavior.

The relation between the intellect and the will poses special problems in Marxism–Leninism. The claim for the genetic primacy of practice over thought creates this difficulty. If, as Engels said, there was no thinking before practice, then thought does not seem able to be a precondition of it (or of will). On the other hand, Marx had said that the productive activity of man differs from that of animals in that man first has an idea of what he is going to do before he does it. In the face of this inconsistency, a characteristic double solution is given: thought *first* arose only as an aspect of practice, but then *later* acquired a certain autonomy, although it can never be fully divorced from practice.[50] Given this solution, Davodovič can state the relationship of intellect and will: In all human behavior which is not just reflex activity, 'goal-positing thought' precedes the behavior; there must be an 'ideal prototype' of the activity.[51] But in order for the thought to become a reality, will must come into play. The will then decides, sanctioning or rejecting the goal presented in consciousness, and the actual behavior follows.

An important dimension of the will, as of any psychic activity, is its connection with the physiological mechanisms of higher neural activity. This is particularly important here, because the Pavlovian principles of physiological psychology which are broadly adopted by Soviet psychologists are often seen as implying a denial of free will. Pavlov himself had stated that "the mechanism of volitional motion is a conditioned, associated process which is governed by all the laws of higher neural activity."[52] And according to Selivanov, present-day Soviet psychologists accept this determinist interpretation of the volitional act[53]: "Having discarded the idealist understanding of motives and aspirations as primary causal acts, Soviet psychologists consider these phenomena to be secondary formations, which are formed as a result of external material influences, as a reflection of the needs of man and his relations to reality."[54] And even though they would generally accept Rubinštejn's principle that external influences are not the sole determinants, since they must be 'refracted' through subjective factors, this would not seem to alter the position significantly, since the subjective factors (those that are acquired) must themselves be a result of a causal, conditioned-reflex process.

It is beyond the scope of the present work to consider at length the physiology of the conditioned-reflex process or to judge to what extent Soviet psychology is Pavlovian. Let us just make two remarks in this regard. First of all, it is noteworthy that the Soviet philosophers themselves who have written on the notion of freedom during the past decade or so only rarely mention and never really discuss the problems posed by Pavlovian psychology. And this is only slightly less true regarding their attitude towards the whole of their psychology. References to psychological works are, with the exception of a few cases, practically negligible. The reasons for this are not evident, but one factor might be the apprehension on the part of the philosophers who wish to affirm the real freedom of man, to face up to a psychology which is, at least on the surface, decidedly deterministic. Secondly, in several of the cases where reference is made to the physiological basis of volition, Pavlov's physiology is considered to be inferior in its capacity to account for volitional processes to that of N. A. Bernštejn, who "goes beyond the narrow limits of classical reflex theory".[55] Bernštejn considers Pavlov's theory to be 'atomistic' and incapable of explaining the integral activity of the organism; he proposes as an alternative to determinism a 'physiology of activity'.[56] The extent of Bernštejn's following in the Soviet union may or may not be large. There is certainly opposition to his position by some psychologists.[57] But it is significant that some philosophers are appealing to him rather than to Pavlov, because they are unwilling to accept a deterministic physiological psychology. Perhaps the whole attitude of the philosophers towards this problem, which includes both unconcern for and some disappointment with Pavlovian physiology, is best explained by a remark by one author, that in his opinion, because of the complexity and very deep inwardness of volitional acts, no "sufficiently convincing theoretical model of their operation" has yet been presented.[58]

2.3. *The Free Character of the Will*

However, to state that one type of physiological determinism which entails a denial of free will is not advocated by all philosophers does not mean that there are not other reasons, of a general philosophical character, adduced against the freedom of will. One such position, familiar enough in Western philosophy, is that free will is a fiction which arises in our minds: it appears to us that we are free because the process of volition is so complex that we are not able to perceive all of the intermediate causal links.[59] This, as well as other similar positions, is an attempt to apply the principle of determinism, without qualification, to volitional phenomena. And as mentioned above, there is certainly a basis for such a position to be found in the classics – in Engels and in Lenin, both of whom are quoted.[60] The response to this view by the defenders of free will is twofold. First of all, it is claimed that Lenin was speaking out against the subjectivist thesis of the absolute freedom of the will, and did not in fact deny that there is relative freedom. But secondly, and more importantly, an argument for free will is constructed on the basis of our experience of freedom.[61] The argument proceeds as follows: It is a fact that we consider our volitional acts to be free. There seems to arise in us a kind of force, which is experienced by us and is corroborated by our actions. Now, given that the experience or feeling of freedom is a fact, can it be denied that freedom is an objective reality? No it cannot, for Marxism–Leninism affirms the principle of the unity of the subjective and objective. There is no basis for saying that free volition is just a subjective fantasy, so "is it not more true to affirm that our subjective experience of free volition also has an objective foundation?"[62] The reality of free will thus follows from a consequent application of this principle of dialectical materialism.

Another type of consideration which questions the free character of the will refers to the role of *motives* in choice. T. I. Ojzerman criticizes the position that the will is autonomous vis-à-vis its motives.[63] If the will is able to overcome the influence of some motives, he says, it is only because this will is determined, in its act, by other motives. Thus, "the will is not self-caused, nor is it master of its own acts."[64] And Ojzerman consequently prefers to speak not of 'free will' but of the 'freedom of the person'. This view is far from being universally accepted or even widely followed. V. P. Tugarinov considers it to be characteristic only of *mechanistic* determinism to assert that the will is determined by a struggle of motives in which the strongest one prevails.[65] In his own view, the subject can exert an influence on this struggle of motives; he does not just passively accept its result. This is possible because, as a matter of fact, there are two kinds of motives – natural motives and purposive *(celevye)* motives. The subject can oppose his purposive motives, his conscious goals, to the natural motives, and since the purposive motives can be stronger than the latter, the subject can thereby triumph in the struggle. Tugarinov goes even further and says that the ability to influence and direct our motivation is just what is meant by 'will'.[66] A third position on this problem is offered by R. Gal'ceva, who rejects the whole approach. In her view the attempt to solve the problem of free will by an analysis of motivation is unsound, because it stays within the bounds of the mechanism of the will.[67]

These conflicting views concern the question of whether the will can be free or is in some respect free. Davidovič, who stands on the libertarian rather than the determinist side of the field, goes a step further in developing the thesis that the will is *necessarily* free, of its very nature. The will, for him, is rooted in the 'center' of man as the force of the conscious regulation of his own behavior.[68] Consequently, if the subject is not relatively autonomous in his choice of goals, then he cannot exercise the function of the volition. Although other philosophers claim that the freedom of the will is a fiction, for Davidovič the conception of a will *without* freedom is the fiction. To deny the freedom of will is to deny the very inner nature of volition, and it is ultimately to deny the very nature of the person; a subject without volition is not a person, but a mere 'mechanical agent'.[69]

However, it is one thing to assert that the will is free, but quite another to explain how it is that there can be an act which is somehow its own beginning; or, to put the question simply, if the free act is not the result of other causes, then from what source does it come? Davidovič tries to answer this question by appealing to the dialectical understanding of the formation of new qualities in which there is a development from simple to complex or part to whole. Free will is a quality of the whole person; it is not a quality of the brain or of the organism. Now the person can be described, in the terms of cybernetical systems theory, as a 'unique, complex, dynamic system'.[70] Such systems have the specific trait of emergence; they are able to exhibit properties which separately do not belong to any one of their component parts. This is in accord with the Leninist assertion of the whole's predominance over and irreducibility to its parts. Consequently, freedom of will can be understood as a new property which emerges from the complex and interrelated functions of the person as a whole. Davidovič's view here is an interesting attempt to give an ontological substantiation for the possibility of freedom. But there seems to be a difficulty in it which he does not perceive. If the wholist approach is adopted, then it would be questionable to ascribe freedom in a special way to the will, as he does. Certainly the will, or volitional function, is not the whole man. It would seem, and is even indicated in his own previously given statements, that the whole person is declared free in virtue of the freedom of his will and not the other way around. In a sense, that begs the whole question, which is: how can a person perform a free act of the will?

2.4. *The Value-Orientation of Volition*

A very special and highly interesting approach to the understanding of volition and its free character has been developed by S. N. Čxartišvili, a Soviet psychologist. He tries to explain the nature of genuine volition, as opposed to impulsive behavior, by referring to its special type of value-orientation. Although his position certainly does not stand in the mainstream of Soviet psychology, it deserves attention here both because of its own inherent merit and because it is a variant which, due to the rapid growth of value theory in philosophy, may soon become more widely appreciated.

Čxartišvili finds the state of Soviet psychology deplorable for two reasons. First of all, it presents a picture of the person which is radically different from the real person we meet in everyday life.[71] For example the person as deterministically conceived by the psychologists is not able, theoretically, to place the good of society over his own, or to follow ethical norms, as is in fact demanded of him. The 'person' of psychology lacks any ability for autonomous activity (free choice) since "in every case he is determined by such factors, the presence or absence of which is completely independent of him."[72] He is understood by the majority of psychologists to be motivated and ruled only by his needs. If this is true, then moral responsibility disappears and evil deeds become mere unlucky accidents, for it certainly does not depend on the subject what needs arise in him or how strong they are. But this whole position seems to be contradicted by everyday experience, which indicates that persons have the ability to rise above their immediate needs and to pursue goals which in no way correspond to these present needs.[73] How is this to be explained? The lack of a valid concept of the will – this is Čxartišvili's point – in Soviet psychology leaves us without an answer. The standard characterizations of the will single out properties, such as the conscious character of behavior or the force of overcoming obstacles, which can be explained without recourse to a notion of will.[74] Is there then any genuine volition which is free and whose essence is irreducible to other psychic functions?

Observation indicates to Čxartišvili that there are two essentially different types of behavior. One kind, *impulsive behavior*, is directed by an immediate need towards whose satisfaction the acts of the subject are directed. There is here no objective evaluation of a goal or of its consequences; the value of the goal is purely subjective, arising and disappearing wholly in accordance with the subjective condition of the need. Expressed more simply: "Impulsive behavior has only one goal: to satisfy in the fullest and quickest way the need which is motivating it."[75] A second kind of behavior, *volitonal behavior*, is of an essentially different nature. As others have pointed out, it depends upon the development of a high level of consciousness and utilizes the many functions of the intellect. But it is not for this reason that it is called 'volitional'. The reason is that what initiates and directs the behavior is not a need, but the person himself as subject of the will. That is, the "source, impeller *(pobuditelem)* and directing principle" of the behavior is the act of will itself, and not a need as in impulsive behavior.[76] In everyday experience we definitely feel that we ourselves are directing our behavior, often in opposition to the satisfaction of a need. Will is, if anything at all, the reality of this experience. There is another important difference between the two types of behavior: not only are their sources different, but so are their goals. Volition is always directed toward the "objective values of the possible results of the behavior".[77] There are two aspects to this. One is that while impulsive action aims for the immediate satisfaction of a need which is the behavior itself, volition aims at realizing results which remain after and are extrinsic to the act. The other feature is that in volition the goal is seen, not just as fulfilling subjective needs, but as possessing objective value.

This is the important point of Čxartišvili's analysis: the real motive of willing is the *objective value* of the goal. This motive, which appears in the form of a value judgment, is a phenomenon which is "independent of the condition of the individual".[78] The subject of volition perceives in reality a system of things all of which have a definite value. There is a hierarchy of values. And when he is confronted with a decision, he can choose as the motive of his behavior a value which is objectively higher than some other value, even though the latter may be subjectively more important to him – as, for example, when people sacrifice their lives for their country.[79] Čxartišvili does not mean to say, however, that since in volitional behavior objective values are the motives, that needs play no role here. On the contrary, values are understood as that which satisfies human needs. But in volition, as opposed to impulsive behavior, needs are only remotely involved – as an ideal component of the meaning of the value – and have no force to stimulate behavior.[80] The act of volition, in selecting an objective value, manifests its independence from the forces and demands of its own subjective condition, and that is why it can be called free.

Čxartišvili's position is, as should be apparent, somewhat unique in Soviet psychology. He not only moves beyond a physiological determinism, but also restricts the scope of the 'need-response' model by introducing an essentially different type of psychic activity: that which has as its source the subject itself, and as its motive an objective value, which unlike a subjective need does not compel the subject in moving it to make its decision. Certainly the introduction of such an objective value dimension into psychology could have far-reaching consequences beyond its role in explaining the freedom of volition.

3. THE MORAL ASPECT: FREEDOM AND RESPONSIBILITY

The problem of determinism and freedom has often arisen in connection with a reflection on the moral life of man, because the fact of moral responsibility seems to demand, in order for it to be real, that man be possessed of some kind of freedom. Soviet ethicians have not been remiss in confronting this issue, and there is a considerable literature devoted to it. This literature is important not because there is much in the way of theoretical articulation of the concept of freedom, but because it indicates the extent of acceptance and to some degree the official approval of an understanding of freedom which does not differ substantially from what has already been presented above. Although the general textbooks in dialectical materialism say very little on freedom, each of the general works in ethics devotes a chapter to it[81]; they thus serve as the means of transmission and of popularization of the Soviet theory of freedom. Another reason for considering the discussion of freedom and responsibility is that much of the Western misunderstanding of the Soviet view – in particular that freedom for the Marxist–Leninist allegedly consists in the understanding of and adaptation to necessity – is based upon a generalization of just one dimension of the ethical discussion.

First of all, a good part of the discussion of freedom by ethicians is a presentation and affirmation of the general principles with which we have already dealt: that freedom must be understood within the context of the practical activity of man; that both voluntarists and mechanists err in their extremes, not seeing that freedom and determinism must be somehow combined; that not all events in the universe are necessary; that knowledge is a precondition and component part of freedom but not its culmination; that human activity is restricted by but not univocally determined by the objective social conditions; that, in general, human actions arise from an interplay of the subjective and objective, inner and outer; and that man's finalistic activity is a unique kind of causality in which he is the author of new lines of determination.[82] There points have already been discussed, and it is sufficient to note that they are also affirmed by the ethicians.

The question that is peculiar to the ethical discussion is: in what sense is freedom, or free will, a presupposition of moral responsibility? In answering this question much confusion has been created by an unfortunate faithfulness to Engels' remarks about free will in *Anti-Dühring*. He had said that free will is nothing but the ability to make well-founded judgments which would lead to the control over nature and society. That is, acts of free will are those based on the *correct* knowledge of necessary laws. This is a far cry from what is normally meant by free will, especially in the context of the moral problem. And it forces Engels' Soviet followers to state that since every moral act is not necessarily one that is a morally correct judgment, therefore free will cannot be a prerequisite of moral responsibility.[83] Now does this mean that the Soviets construct their ethics on the basis of a deterministic interpretation of moral decisions?

A distinction is always made between two different types of freedom – freedom of choice and freedom of the will.

Freedom of choice is always considered to be a necessary precondition of moral responsibility. It is asserted that every moral position starts with the fact that an individual can, in the same circumstances, "act differently according to his own choice".[84] He possesses this ability because of the "objective possibility of different variants of behavior".[85] Even in extremely difficult situations he can choose from among the possible variants the one which best corresponds to his own moral convictions. It is admitted that the surrounding social milieu has an enormous influence on the consciousness and behavior of the individual, but this does not mean that the class will and the individual will are the same. The individual can, in his choices, not only deviate from the needs of his class; he can even contradict them.[86] And this holds true for all times, i.e., it is to some extent independent of the historical dialectic. A. F. Šiškin, the dean of Soviet ethics, says: "there is some measure of freedom in the choice of an action in every society, even where the people are not masters of their fate."[87] Without this measure of freedom, there can be no kind of moral responsibility; or to express the point more positively, it is precisely the existence of a real possibility of choice which 'creates the responsibility' of man for his actions.[88]

The reasons brought forward in support of this position are the standard ones. It is recalled that necessity is not a universal category: although everything is causally conditioned, not everything is necessary. If this were not the case – i.e. if all events were necessary – then all human actions including crimes would be justified, which is of course unacceptable.[89] In fact, the manner in which necessity functions in relation to moral decisions is to determine the boundaries of possible behavior: "the sphere of necessity is the 'spectrum of possibilities' for the freedom of the individual."[90] This understanding of necessity applies to social laws as well. The latter are seen as general tendencies determining the total outcome of history, but which by no means determine "the content of all the events in the lives of individual persons".[91] Again, what the necessary (here social) laws do is to set boundaries to the activities of the people, and within these men can act either in accordance with or against moral norms.[92]

Now although freedom of choice is considered a condition of all moral responsibility, a second type of freedom is not – what is, curiously, designated as 'freedom of will'. A man is always free to choose, but this alone is only formal freedom; he is genuinely free only when his decision is in conformity with the laws of necessity (as apprehended) and especially with the moral demands imposed by the needs of society.[93] That is, freedom of will is present only when there is a correct or morally good choice. The distinction that is being made here is similar to the traditional distinction between freedom of will and license. Freedom of will is the capacity to choose the good, not just to choose (either the good or the evil). One author explains moral freedom as the regulation of one's actions which is based upon an acceptance of duty and the transformation of this acceptance into the main motive for behavior.[94] This higher type of freedom also differs from freedom of choice in that it includes activity – actual behavior – as one of its component parts. This point follows naturally from Soviet moral theory, which maintains that there is no sharp separation between the inner and outer aspects of the moral act; for example, a person is held morally responsible not only for his good or bad intentions but also for the actual results of his moral decision and behavior.[95]

Due to the almost exclusively social content of Soviet morality, freedom of will thus becomes the capacity to act in accordance with the demands of society. The truly free man is the one who perceives the current needs of social development and then seeks to make these the goal of his actions.[96] These needs often become expressed in laws, and freedom of will can be described as "the conscious, voluntary submission of one's own energies, actions and behavior to the demands of the prevailing set of laws."[97] An exception to this view is presented by A. P. Čermenina, who states that moral freedom involves not only one's relation to society, but also his relation to himself, especially to the development of his potentialities.[98] However, that is an exception; the rule is to understand moral good as the adaptation of the person to the needs of society. Now does this demand to submit oneself to society actually involve a denial of personal freedom, as some critics have pointed out? It certainly does this insofar as it rules out an egocentric pattern of life. A person who pursues egocentric goals is by definition immoral and unfree. However, if one asks what is the *relation* of the person to the social laws which he should follow, the anwer is that it must be a free one. Compelled submission is not genuine moral submission. It is always stated that it is voluntary submission; that is, freedom in the first sense – freedom of choice – is preserved as a part of this second – moral freedom. Šiškin asserts that although Marxism demands an unconditional surrender of one's own wishes to social duty, yet it does not affirm "that duty be fulfilled unwillingly; it does not demand inner constraint".[99] What happens is that the submission of one's behavior to moral rules becomes the following of one's own personal conscience. The mere observance of social regulations becomes in moral activity a realization of moral principles on the basis of personal decision.[100] And yet this is still not the highest level of freedom, for such decisions can be made with the feeling on the part of the subject that there is some tension between his own needs and those of society, even though he chooses the latter. The supreme state of freedom is that in which moral duty becomes 'an inner need of man', a 'moral disposition', so that the interests of society appear as inseparable from one's own.[101] Duty does not disappear but becomes totally internalized, and the person, in acting always for the good of society, is at the same time following his own inner law.

To recapitulate: Two types of freedom are distinguished, freedom of choice and 'freedom of will'. It is only the first which is a necessary condition of moral responsibility. The second, which itself presupposes freedom of choice, is characterized by *right* choice insofar as it follows the moral good. It is in this sense the highest attainment of man.

4. SOCIO-HISTORICAL FREEDOM

The recent Soviet discussions of socio-historical freedom, numerous as they are, add very little to what was previously offered by the classics.

The familiar picture is constantly re-drawn: primitive man was powerless in relation to nature, a slave of natural conditions; as he began to conquer nature, his advance in this kind of freedom produced a much more serious decline in his social freedom, during the three stages of exploitative society; finally the socialist revolution eliminates the social slavery and fosters both the increasing domination by man of nature and the control by him of his own social relations.[102] This is merely a restatement of Karl Marx's understanding of the historical process. But in addition to this, the Soviets also embrace Engels' and Lenin's additions. According to the former, man progressed in freedom to the extent that he acquired a knowledge of necessary laws and utilized these in his actions, first the laws of nature and then the laws of society. E. Arab-Ogly sums up the position of the classical authors by saying that the degree of social freedom depends upon three things: the level of development of the productive forces, the social structure of the particular society, and the level of our knowledge of natural and social processes.[103] Further, Lenin had made the point, by action as much as by argument, that history (at least in its final stages) needs the active participation of human will and conscious activity. This is often reaffirmed in statements that social freedom increases to the extent that man more consciously and actively governs his own social relations. A familiar pair of categories in histomat used to characterize the relation between human activity and historical necessity is 'spontaneity and conscious activity' *(stixijnost' i soznatel'nost')*. What happens spontaneously does so as a natural process and often frustrates the goals of men. This is characteristic of pre-socialist societies. As society progresses, men substitute for the natural historical process a conscious transformation of reality according to plan, directing social reality towards a realization of their goals.[104] It is in this exchange of planned development for spontaneous processes that the social activity of the people becomes genuinely free.[105] And of course the society in which conscious planning reaches its highest stage, and thus produces the highest form of social freedom, is communism.

In order to examine this conception adequately, it would be necessary to introduce historical and sociological as well as philosophical considerations, which is beyond the scope of the present work. Let it suffice to make two remarks on the implications this conception has for the other types of freedom. First of all, it seems to weaken any deterministic conception of historical law. Quite apart from the fact that many Marxist-Leninists characterize historical laws as only general tendencies, it is also very significant that they distinguish the two ways in which these laws operate: before they are known they operate spontaneously, more or less like laws of nature; but after they become tools in the hands of men who themselves reconstruct social reality. This implies at least that the act of consciously planning society is itself not an instance of a spontaneously acting law. The situation is not analogous to the utilization of natural laws (which hold without exception even in things that have been constructed for man's use), because of the self-reference of social laws. In other words, it is significant that these laws, at least at one stage in history, do not themselves fully determine social action (for if they did, the above distinction would be meaningless). Secondly, the whole doctrine of socio-historical freedom, to the extent that it includes a view of the essential culmination of man's control over reality, immediately raises the question of the end of man. Control over nature and society – yes, but for what? Marx had pointed out that communism itself is not the final ideal but is only the movement towards achieving it. The Soviets have long been silent on this question and are only gradually beginning to discuss the problem of the end of man. Some indication of this will be offered in the next section, in connection with their appraisal of Marx's notion of freedom as self-realization.

5. FREEDOM AS THE SELF-REALIZATION OF THE PERSON

It is evident from some of the foregoing discussions that although freedom is characterized as a social category, this does not mean that it applies only to society as a whole; it applies also to individuals. And one can ask the question: what does the 'leap into the realm of freedom', which for society is the establishment of communism, mean for the individual person? Marx had conceived the personal realm of freedom to be a condition in which the individual was engaged in the developing and perfecting of his human capacities through activities freely chosen and pursued for their own sake. This was designated in an earlier chapter as his 'anthropological' (as opposed to social) concept of freedom. Now what is the stance of Soviet philosophy in regard to such a position?

Perhaps the most important consideration here is whether the meaning and fulfillment of human life has any *raison d'etre* other than as a part of the realization of the good of society. There seems to be a near identification in some Marxist–Leninist authors of the respective goals of the individual and society. For example, P. M. Egides maintains that the meaning of individual lives depends upon the meaning of the life of humanity as a whole. He says further that the final significance of individual existence lies "in serving the needs of the world process."[105a] As was pointed out above, Soviet morality is almost exclusively a social morality; what is moral is that which furthers the progressive development of society. Now according to Egides, to be moral and to realize the meaning of life is the same thing. Thus the meaning of life lies exclusively in the service of society'[106] However, this position is far from being representative of Soviet philosophy as a whole. Many refuse to set individual and society in any relation of subordination. They maintain that just as the collective must be the main interest of the individual, so also the individual good of each person is the goal of the collective.[107] The two are parallel, or as Šiškin puts it, the development of the autonomy of the person is proportional to his solidarity with society.[108] The foundation of this position is the belief that in a truly humane socialist society, the interests of the individuals 'coincide' *(sovpadaet)* with the interests of society as a whole.[109] Other philosophers such as G. K. Gumnickij go further in rejecting the type of view put forward by Egides, which reduces the meaning of individual life to that of society. Gumnickij bluntly states that 'humanity', the 'world process', has no meaning at all. It is only the people, pursuing their goals, whose lives have any kind of meaning; humanity has no ultimate purpose of its own.[110] Individuals have to seek to further the immediate needs of society, but they do this because they could not otherwise survive and develop as individuals: "in the end the goal is the good of the individuals".[111] The society does not have its own good which is not connected with the good of the people. Thus the meaning of human life lies not ultimately in the service to society but in "the achievement of personal happiness".[112] This does not mean that one does not have to fulfull his moral duty to society, but, Gummickij maintains, a distinction must be made between the content and the form of moral activity. The content includes the service of the individual to society – he must act for the welfare of others. The form of this however is always personal satisfaction, personal good. The final goal is the good of the individuals themselves.

The attitude of Soviet philosophers towards Marx's notion of personal freedom confirms this latter position. Although it is generally believed that dialectical materialists are hostile to the 'humanism' of Marx, this does not apply here. They continually affirm that the goal of communism is the full and all-round development of the person as an end in himself (samocel').[113] Šiškin, a very representative thinker, interprets the demand of the party program to do 'everything in the name of man and for the good of man', as meaning that the goal of society is to make possible the development of human powers. And he quotes with approval Marx's idea of the true realm of freedom: that it lies in "the absolute revelation of the creative talents of man", "the wholeness of development" of man, "the development of all human powers as such without reference to any previously established standard".[114] The same point is made in different ways by other authors as well, by claiming that socialism means for the person the overcoming of the alienation of his essential powers[115], by pointing to the goal of eliminating the split between the intellectual and physical work of man,[115a] and by placing very strong emphasis on the free choice of one's profession as a condition for personal fulfillment.[116] All of these seem to be aimed at achieving what Marx understood as human self-realization. There does not seem to be any major difference between the stated Soviet view and that of Marx (abstracting, of course, from the idealist categories in which his early work was sometimes framed) on the basic meaning of the freedom of the person. It may be disputed whether or not the Soviets mean precisely the same thing as Marx did or whether they can consistently incorporate the views of the early Marx with dialectical materialism, but this does not belie the fact that they constantly and almost religiously repeat that true freedom for the person lies ultimately in his creative, harmonious and all-round self-development.

CHAPTER VIII

CONCLUSION

In the introduction to this study it was noted that although very little research had previously been done on the Marxist-Leninist understanding of freedom and determinism, nevertheless many Western authors criticized it on several accounts as one which clearly denies personal freedom. This evaluation, categorizing Marxism–Leninism as strongly deterministic, has proved to be untrue in several respects. In general one can say that both the classics and the Soviets strive to find a middle ground between strong determinism on the one hand and libertarianism on the other; they present a reconciliationist position, one which admits both the determinateness of events and the unique, partially irreducible character of free activity.

Because of the length and complexity of the six chapters which present this view in detail, it will be useful to summarize their main conclusions in order to gain a picture of the whole and perhaps to see how the various elements are related.

1. SUMMARY

First, perhaps the most important question concerns the ontology of the *person.* Is the person a mere complex of relations, and thus deprived of any substantiality? In particular, is he defined as a mere product of social relations? Marx explicitly rejected the Hegelian dialectical ontology in an early work, and continued to emphasize that it is the real individuals that make history and that there is no supra-human subject. There is no doubt that he understood the person to be very closely related to his environment, but there is little evidence to indicate that he considered the person to be reducible to this, after the manner of a relational ontology. The sixth thesis on Feuerbach, which refers to the human essence as the ensemble of social relations, must be seen in its context as directed against both Hegelian ontology and Feurbachian anthropology, and not as an affirmation of the dialectical theory of the individual. Soviet Marxists fail to clarify the situation in their own ontology, in which three positions are evident: a substantialist view, a relationist view, and, most widespread, a sort of almalgam of the two. It can only be said that a clearly relationist view is not taken as the definitive position. And those philosophers writing on the nature of man seem to lean more towards substantialism. In questions concerning the nature of man and his relation to the historical development of society, the Soviets express a moderate view of social determinism. It is admitted by many that human nature does not totally change in history; there is an essential core. Although the person cannot exist outside of society, he is not just its product; he is the substantial basis of it. Although social factors form the character, opinions, etc. of the person, they do not exhaustively or even immediately form the person. In sum, an explicit and widespread attempt is made to moderate the social orientation of the Marxist philosophy of man in favor of the autonomy of the person and his nature.

Secondly, the principle of universal *determinism* – that all phenomena are connected with other phenomena which are their causes – is considered to be balanced by several other principles. One is the affirmation that on each level of reality there is a categoreally unique form of process irreducible to any other; an event is never determined by causal factors of a lower order, although it may be to some extent conditioned by them. Further, events are not *pre*-determined, as LaPlace thought, by remote causes; there is no pre-set chain of events stretching back into the past and forward into the future. These two qualifications go a long way in removing obstacles to a viable concept of freedom. Especially the first: the principle of categoreal pluralism makes the materialism of diamat a very unorthodox type of materialism, one for which there are essential qualitative differences in reality. Everything is not reduced to some primordial material stuff, especially man's psychic and social life. But the Soviets want to qualify their determinism even further. And they try to do this by dividing events (or aspects of events) into two types, necessary and contingent. A contingent event is one which could have happened or could not have happened, because although it is caused, it is not necessarily caused. By making this distinction they seek to avoid having to say that everything in the universe has to happen just the way it does, in an iron-clad fashion, and thereby they hope to make room in some general way for freedom. A few authors even point to recent discoveries in micro-physics; the contingency (probable character) of the micro-world allegedly also supports the possibility of freedom. Finally, an analysis of the categories of possibility and actuality leads to the claim that for every circumstance there are a multitude of possible outcomes. Reality is to a certain extent open onto the future; it is for this reason that man can operate as a cause in the flow of events – by acting he determines which of the possibilities will be realized. In all of these points, it is obvious that Soviet philosophers *themselves* see their position as a moderate and highly differentiated determinism, one which poses no special obstacles to the reality of freedom. However, it can be questioned whether they are consistently and consequently adhering to the basic principle of causal determinism by qualifying it in the above ways.

Thirdly, the affirmation of *historical determinism,* according to which society evolves according to certain laws of history, does not seem to entail, in any of the formulations (by Marx, Engels, Lenin or the Soviets), that individuals are fully determined in their actions by social and economic factors. Marx and Engels pointed out that individuals can escape the influences of their class position. They can be, in their conceptions as well as their actions, both ahead of or behind the general course of social development. As a matter of fact most individuals are children of their times and conditions; this is clear. But this does not mean that the influence is absolute; it is a matter of degree. Nor is it permanent: the domination of social circumstances over individuals is supposed to cease with the advent of communism, after which the relation is to be reversed. Consequently, Marx cannot be called a historical determinist if this means that human actions are univocally determined by historical laws and social circumstances. The 'iron necessity' of historical development applies in Marx primarily to socio-economic formations, not to individuals. Engels, in separately published statements, comes closer to a historical determination of individuals by stating that the laws of history operate *through* men, insofar as economic factors determine the motivation of the many individuals whose interaction produces the historical events. But he also makes it clear that he is talking about groups of men (not every individual) and the broad historical developments (not every-day happenings). And later in life Engels explicitly states that he and Marx never meant that economic factors were the *only* determinants of history. Lenin further developed this idea by emphasizing the importance of conscious activity in the transformation of history, and showed by his own actions just how malleable the laws of history and social circumstances really are. The Soviets, finally, introduce several other relevant notions. Historical laws are reduced to the status of statistical (as opposed to dynamic) laws, which apply only in an average fashion; thus the relation between individual acts and historical trends, whatever it is, becomes even more indeterminate. And it is consistently pointed out that social circumstances do not directly affect the person, but only as mediated by, 'refracted through' his own consciousness and inner life. In sum, these positions seem to assert that socio-economic factors determine the general outcome of history and have a very strong influence on human activity, but do not set the specific form of either. There is always a plurality of real possibilities of social development and individual action in any situation.

Fourthly, the understanding of the relation of *'freedom and necessity'* insofar as it applies to individuals departs significantly from the more Hegelian Plekhanovite formulation, which has often been wrongly attributed to Marxism–Leninism. Freedom does not consist in the knowledge of and aquiescence to necessity, in some kind of identification with necessity. A proper reading of the Engels text – which is taken as definitive by both Lenin and the Soviets – clearly shows that the knowledge of necessity is just a precondition for free acts, the latter being realized in some kind of control over nature and society. Freedom is the ability of man to act in a way in which his goals are attained. Lenin's restatement of Engels' position is capable of being interpreted in either a passivist or an activist sense, but the Soviets clearly adopt the second. They develop the idea found in Lenin's *Philosophical Notebooks* that there are two kinds of process – natural and teleological. Man is seen as free because his activity is teleological. The structure of this activity includes numerous elements: the formation of goals, the evaluation of goals, the knowledge of the laws and circumstances necessary for the realization of goals, the choice of the goal and the means to attain it, and the actual exertion of some real act to bring it about. Although it is usually stated that freedom is a characteristic of the whole process, the most significant part is the choice of the goal. The person always stands before a multitude of possible goals which arise in him as ideal forms of the future; he must choose one, and this choice is made according to his own inner needs or convictions – it is not a mere product of the circumstances. If this choice is also based upon knowledge of the situation, it will successfully result in the actual attainment of the goal; free activity thus culminates in 'practice'. Such a position goes far beyond the statement that freedom is the insight into necessity. Furthermore, it cannot be described as 'determinist' in the strong sense of the word. The Soviets understand that human activity is severely delimited by real external and internal causal factors, but they consistently assert that there is an irreducible element of freedom present. To use their words: there is no absolute freedom, but man *is*, in his activity, at least *relatively* free.

A *fifth* set of problems concerns the *freedom of the will*. Are acts of choice genuinely free, or are they themselves mere effects of other causal factors such as needs or motives? Neither the classics nor recent Soviet philosophers provide a consistent or clear point of view on this matter. Marx does not seem even to have presented a philosophical opinion on free will. Engels on the other hand explained the volitional process in a way in which it would be difficult to make room for genuine freedom of choice; he seems to be a determinist in this regard. Lenin then explicitly denies that there is any free will, in view of the 'necessity of human actions', and calls free will an idealist concept. Soviet philosophers and psychologists, however, do not often follow the determinism of Engels and Lenin. The latter's explicit statements are explained by some as a rejection of absolute freedom of will and not of a relatively free will. There is also a difference of opinion concerning whether choices are or are not the immediate product of a struggle of motives. However, these discussions are not very extensive. Most philosophers writing on freedom simply assert that there *is* freedom of choice, without explaining anything at all about the structure of volition. Soviet psychologists appear to be much more consistently deterministic in their explanations than the philosophers. Perhaps this is the reason that the philosphers refer only rarely to psychological discussions. But also in this area there are wide differences of opinion: Pavlov's physiology, the basis for the deterministic explanation of volition, is considered by some as inferior to that of N. A. Bernštejn, which, it is alleged, can better explain human activity. And the standard explanation of decisions as responses to needs has been challenged by one leading psychologist, who explains the freedom of volition by referring to the role of values in the decision.

Sixthly, the discussions of *freedom and responsibility* adopt a very special terminology, mainly due to their reliance on Engels, which allows them to say that moral responsibility presupposes freedom of choice but not 'free will'. This distinction, not used in the general discussions of freedom, means that although all moral acts presuppose choices that could have been other than they are, not all of these choices are good and therefore 'genuinely' free ones. Freedom of will in this special sense means the ability to choose that which is morally good. And since Soviet morality is almost exlusively social morality, the almost paradoxical position results, that freedom of will is the ability to submit one's own desires to the demands of society. This position has given rise to Western criticism of the Soviet view as one which denies personal autonomy vis-à-vis society. However, it must not be overlooked that Soviet ethicians require that this submission itself be a voluntary one: freedom of will goes beyond but still includes free choice.

Finally, it is very interesting that Soviet authors have recently been turning more and more to the writings of the young Marx, and seem to have no argument with his conception of human nature and the *freedom of self-realization*. Treatments of what is often called 'the freedom of the person' abound with references to the goal of communism as being the full and free development of human potentialities. Although this position is contradicted by actual political realities – the real goal of communist states appears to be the increase of state power at the expense of personal self-realization – nevertheless, it does seem to fit in very well in a philosophy which denies any salvation beyond this life. There is no doubt that for Soviet philosophers the full perfection of man – and they do mean individual men, not humanity or society – is the ultimate goal of all human striving. However, they have yet to face up to the fact, so well described by the existentialists, that human life, in the temporal order at least, never seems to achieve it.

2. FINAL REMARKS

The primary purpose of this study has been to investigate and describe the theory of freedom in the Marxist tradition. As a consequence it has become evident that a good part of the Western critique is based on a lack of information or understanding of the relevant texts. This phenomenon itself is interesting: the tendency to characterize the Marxist view as deterministic may very well have been influenced by broader ideological considerations. The fault for this lies of course partially with the Soviets. Freedom is a political concept as well as a philosophical one. And their doctrine of the unity of theory and practice would imply at least that the two would correspond in some way. But this does not prove to be generally the case; only with regard to the socio-historical concept of freedom might any significant connection be drawn between theory and practice.

Although the critique of the Marxist view as one which denies human freedom does not hold up to an investigation of the texts, this does not mean that the position is philosophically sound. Virtually all the discussions suffer from a lack of conceptual clarity which is so great that it is necessary to extrapolate from and interpret even the best statements to be able to see what the genuinely philosophical point is. There is a constant confusion of different types of freedom, often referred to by the same term. And some of the most fundamental issues relevant to a theory of freedom are still unresolved: whether individual being is substantial or relational, what the nature of the will is, how the consistent application of the principle of determinism can leave room for non-necessary events, etc. These important *lacunae* have been discussed in previous chapters, and there is no need to repeat them here. It was mentioned in the introduction that philosophical anthropology was in 1959 one of the 'empty domains' in Soviet philosophy. While that no longer strictly holds – certain general conceptions have been worked out – nevertheless it still remains far behind other areas of philosophy, such as ontology or the philosophy of science, both in quantity and in quality. It is significant that among the very numerous philosophical conferences that have been held, not one, to the knowledge of the present author, has been devoted to the concept of freedom. Thus although the area is no longer an empty domain, it is still very thinly settled.

What has become clear, as we mentioned before, is that the Soviet position is neither a hard determinism nor kind of libertarianism; it is a *reconciliationist* view. It tries to reconcile both determinism and freedom. In conclusion, some reasons might be offered why this view is appropriate to the general tenor of Soviet philosophy and therefore will not very likely be replaced by one of the others even if there is a significant development of Soviet philosophical anthropology in future years.

There are several characteristics of Soviet philosophy which help to explain its position on freedom: First of all, it is not an 'either-or' philosophy but one which constantly asserts 'both... and'. No matter what the area of consideration, it tries to include everything – the ideal as well as the real, intellectual knowledge as well as sense knowledge, the objective as well as the subjective, etc. And it very often tries to reconcile positions which traditionally have been opposed to each other, similar to the opposition between freedom and determinism. Secondly, it is a philosophy whose boundaries often seem to be set by common sense. It resists straying far beyond the limits of common sense in pursuit of the consequent implications of a philosophical conception. A symptom of this attitude is the uncommonly profuse citation of examples, exceeding any explanatory need, which tries to relate the philosophical points to common knowledge or simple facts of life. And what man does not think that he is genuinely free in some way? Thirdly, it is a philosophy for which one common-sense notion in particular functions as an important criterion for evaluating philosophical views – practice. Any view which cannot explain the possibility of practice must be rejected. And both the strong determinist and the indeterminist views fail to explain adequately the way in which man acts in the world: the first cannot account for man's apparently unique type of determination; the second for any efficacious action at all. Fourthly and finally, it has often been noted that Marxism–Leninism tries to combine, in one way or another, two very different philosophical trends – Hegelian dialectics and (implicitly) Aristotelian substantialism. This seems to hold true here as well. The two represent divergent views of the status of the individual. And to the extent that these traditions continue to co-exist in Soviet philosophy, it would seem that there will always have to be a moderated view of both individual autonomy and universal necessity.

ABBREVIATIONS

FE   *Filosofskaja encyklopedija* (Philosophical Encyclopedia), 5 Vols., 1960ff.
FN   *Naucnye doklady vyssej skoly. Filosofskie nauki* (Scientific Reports of the Higher
        Schools. Philosophical Sciences), M.
FS   *Filosofskii slovar'* (Philosophical Dictionary), M., 1963.
izd.   izdanie (edition).
KSPF   *Kratkij slovar' po filosofii* (Concise Dictionary of Philosophy), M., 1966.
L.   Leningrad.
M.   Moscow.
MEW   Marx, K., Engels, F., *Werke,* Berlin, 1962.
OMF   *Osnovy marksistskoj filosofii* (Fundamentals of Marxist Philosophy), M., 1959.
SST   *Studies in Soviet Thought,* Dordrecht, 1961ff.
t.   tom (volume).
VF   *Voprosy filosofii* (Questions of Philosophy), M.
V LGU   *Vestnik leningradskogo universiteta. Ekonomika. Filosofija. Pravo* (Journal of
        Leningrad University. Economics. Philosophy. Law), L.
V MGU   *Vestnik moskovskogo universiteta. Serija VIII. Filosofija* (Journal of Moscow
        University. Series VIII. Philosophy), M.

REFERENCES

CHAPTER I

[1] Quotation marks will be employed according to the following conventions: (1) Double quotation marks will indicate texts taken verbatim from the source given in the reference. (2) Single quotation marks will indicate a special, technical or figurative sense of a term. (3) To refer to the expression itself, a phrase such as "the word ' '" will be used. (4) Italics will be used for emphasis only.

[2] Among the works which evaluate the Soviet system, the following are well known: Friedrich, C. J. and Brzezinski, Z., *Totalitarian Dictatorships and Autocracy*, 2nd ed., Cambridge, 1965; Reshetar, J. S., *The Soviet Polity*, N.Y., 1971; Fainsod, M., *How Russia Is Ruled*, Cambridge, 1965.

[3] Cf. E. Kamenka, 'Philosophers in Moscow', *Survey*. No. 62, Jan., 1967, pp. 15–24.

[4] *Filosofskaja encyklopekija*, t. 4, p. 546; T. I. Ojzerman, *Problemy istoriko-filosofskoj nauki*, M., 1969, p. 219f.

[5] Cf. K. Marko, 'Soviet Ideology and Sovietology', *Soviet Studies* XIX, 4, April, 1968, pp. 465–481; N. Lobkowicz, 'Die Philosophie in der Sowjetforschung', *Moderne Welt*, 1966, 2, pp. 138–148. These authors question the legitimacy of a purely objective and theoretical study of Soviet philosophy and urge research rather into the application of this doctrine in Soviet political and social realities. Apart from the obvious fact that one cannot see how a doctrine is applied before one has determined what the content of the doctrine is, the very complexity of Soviet philosophy would seem to render nearly impossible its comparison with concrete institutions, projects, political procedures, etc. This should be learned from the Soviets' own attempt to make such an application; even in the writings of the more competent philosophers, it turns out to be a highly questionable and at times ridiculous venture.

[6] A. Buchholz, 'Problems of the Ideological East–West Conflict', *SST* I, 1961, p. 130f.

[7] H. Fleischer, *Umrisse einer 'Philosophie des Menschen'*, Berlin, 1967, pp. 3–6; Fleischer, *Philosophie in der Sowjetunion 1964–1965*, Berlin, 1966, pp. 88–105.

[8] The results of the author's bibliographical researches show that while in the 1947–1957 period only two articles dealing expressly with freedom were published, the subsequent period, from 1958 to the present, produced no less than thirty-seven.

[9] Cf. J. M. Bocheński, *Die kommunistische Ideologie und die Würde, Freiheit und Gleichheit der Menschen im Sinne des Grundgesetzes für die Bundesrepublik Deutschland vom 23. Mai 1949, Bonn*, 1963, pp. 46, 56f; Bocheński, *Soviet Russian Dialectical Materialism*, Dordrecht, 1963, pp. 85f, 111, 113; G. A. Wetter, *Der dialektische Materialismus, seine Geschichte und sein System in der Sowjetunion*, Freiburg, 1960, pp. 447–452, 456–458; Wetter, *Soviet Ideology Today*, London, 1966, pp. 74–78; H. Falk, *Die ideologischen Grundlagen des Kommunismus*, Munich, 1961, pp. 54–59, 61–65; H. Fleischer, *Die Ontologie im dialektischen Materialismus*, Berlin, 1964, pp. 206–210; Fleischer, *Umrisse einer 'Philosophie des Menschen'*, pp. 43–49; Lieber, H.-J., *Individuum und Gesellschaft in der Sowjetunion*, Wolfenbüttel, 1964.

[10] Cf. Fleischer's *Umrisse einer 'Philosophie des Menschen'*.

[11] It is difficult to avoid terminological ambiguity when speaking about Marxism, for there are several variants of this doctrine, and the term itself can lead to misunderstandings. For this reason, the following terminological distinctions will be observed whenever possible: (1) The term 'Marxian' will apply only to the teachings of Marx himself. (2) 'Marxist' will usually designate those doctrines developed by Marx and taken over by Engels; it is to be considered a synonym for 'Marxist and Engelsian', indicating a body of thought they held in common. (3) 'Engelsian' will designate only the teachings of Engels himself. (4) 'Leninist', likewise for Lenin. (5) Finally, 'Marxist–Leninist' will apply to that body of doctrine approved by Lenin, which includes: (a) the Marxist and Engelsian views accepted by him, (b) his particular interpretation of these views, and (c) his own original contributions. A somewhat extended use of these terms will also be permitted. For example, Soviet philosophy can be called 'Marxist' insofar as it also contains, among other things, the teachings indicated by this term. In this sense it would be correct to label parts of Soviet historical materialism as 'Marxist', but incorrect to do the same for its epistemology, which would have to be called 'Leninist' or 'Marxist–Leninist'.

[12] Cf. I. Fetscher, *Die Freiheit im Lichte des Marxismus–Leninismus*, Bonn, 1963; F. Neubauer, *Das Verhältnis von Karl Marx und Friedrich Engels, dargestellt an der Bestimmung der menschlichen Freiheit in deren Schriften*, Meisenheim/Glan, 1960; R. Dunayevskaya, *Marxism and Freedom*, N.Y., 1958. The general introductory texts on Communism which contain remarks on the notion of freedom are too many to cite.

[13] The work by Neubauer, *Das Verhältnis von Karl Marx und Friedrich Engels*, attempts to show the basic unity of view of Marx and Engels on the notion of freedom. His method consists primarily in bringing together texts by Marx and Engels where similar thoughts are expressed. Leaving aside for the moment the truth or falsity of his thesis, it is relevant to remark here that his method prevents the bringing-to-light of any views which are characteristically Engelsian.

[14] Cf., for example, E. Fromm, *Marx's Concept of Man*, N.Y., 1961, p. 6.

[15] In the final chapter we hope to make some remarks on this judgment.

[16] The term 'determinist' is meant here in the strong sense as designating the position in which it is maintained: (a) that all phenomena are determined by causal factors, such that once these factors are present then the phenomena must occur in the way in which they do, and (b) that this determinism is incompatible with the acceptance of one or more senses of human freedom.

[17] Falk, *op. cit.*, p. 54.

[18] J. D. Mabbot, 'Free Will', *Encyclopaedia Britannica*, 1965, Vol. 9, p. 747.

[19] *Ibid.* Cf. also S. Hook, *Marx and the Marxists: the Ambiguous Legacy*, Princeton, N.J., 1955, p. 30.

[20] Cff J. Nuttin, *Psychoanalysis and Personality*, N.Y., 1962, p. 95.

[21] G. Marcel, *Les hommes contre l'humain*, Paris, 1951, pp. 22, 24. Quoted in M. I. Petrosjan, *Essay über den Humanismus*, Berlin, 1966, p. 214.

[22] Bocheński, *Die kommunistische Ideologie*, pp. 21–27; Lieber, *op. cit.*, pp. 11–20.

[23] Lieber, *op. cit.*, p. 16.

[24] *Ibid.*

[25] Cf. H. Köhler, *Das Menschenbild des dialektischen Materialismus*, München–Salzburg–Köln, 1957, p. 19.

[26] Cf. Wetter, *Der dialektische Materialismus*, pp. 447–452; G. Hampsch, *The Theory of Communism*, N.Y., 1965, p. 95f.

[27] G. V. Plekhanov, *K voprosy o roli licnosti v istorii, Socinenija*, izd. 2-e, M., 1924–1927, t. 8, p. 277.

[28] Wetter, *Der dialektische Materialismus,* p. 449.

[29] Plekhanov, *op. cit.,* p. 278.

[30] Falk, *op. cit.,* p. 55; cf. also K. Marko, *Sic et non. Kritisches Wörterbuch des sowjet-russischen Marxismus–Leninismus der Gegenwart,* Wiesbaden, 1962, p. 122.

[31] Wetter, *Der dialektische Materialismus,* p. 457.

[32] *Ibid.*

[33] Falk, *op. cit.,* p. 57; Marko, *op. cit.,* pp. 122f.

[34] In Falk the identification is explicit, while Fr. Wetter merely states, "Diese Gedanken Plechanovs über die Freiheit sind bis heute das philosophisch Bedeutsamste, was der russische dialektische Materialismus über diese Probleme hervorgebracht hat", *op. cit.,* p. 450.

[35] Bocheński, *Diamat,* pp. 86, 113; Falk, *op. cit.,* pp. 58, 65; Köhler, *op. cit.,* p. 20; Marko, *op. cit.,* p. 123.

CHAPTER II

[1] A survey of the different interpretations of the relation of Marx to Hegel can be found in Z. A. Jordan, *The Evolution of Dialectical Materialism,* N.Y., 1967, pp. 66–75.

[2] Since Soviet philosophy does consider this a legitimate enterprise, and explicitly bases itself on the 'philosophy' of Marx and Engels, the present work will have to follow this assumption, at least tentatively. In Sections 4.2 and 4.3 of this chapter some critical conclusions are drawn as to the philosophical import of some of Marx's theories.

[3] This seems to be one of the sources of F. Neubauer's erroneous interpretation. He specifies that the first work of Marx which he considers seriously is the *Economic and Philosophical Manuscripts.* Cf. *Das Verhältnis von Karl Marx und Friedrich Engels dargestellt an der Bestimmung der menschlichen Freiheit in deren Schriften,* Meisenheim/Glan, 1960, p. 9. As a consequence, he conceives the 'formal' notion of freedom in an all too narrow manner.

[4] K. Marx, *Über die Differenz der demokratischen und epikureischen Naturphilosophie, Marx–Engels Werke* (henceforth *MEW*), Berlin, 1958–1968; *Ergänzungsband: Schriften, Manuskripte, Briefe bis 1844, erster Teil,* p. 304. Unless otherwise specified, the remaining references in the present chapter will be to writings by Karl Marx.

[5] *Ibid.,* p. 281.

[6] *Ibid.,* p. 277.

[7] *Ibid.,* p. 301.

[8] *Hefte zur epikureischen, stoischen und skeptischen Philosophie, MEW, Ergänzungsband,* p. 100.

[9] For example, Epicurus' affirmation of indetermination is seen as an advance over Democritus' mechanically conceived physical necessity, but it is not explicitly taken over by Marx himself.

[10] *Über die Differenz der demokratischen und epikureischen Naturphilosophie,* p. 304.

[11] *Ibid.,* p. 262.

[12] Cf. H. P. Adams, *Karl Marx in His Earlier Writings,* London, 1965, p. 38f.

[13] "... die Freiheit ist doch wohl das Gattungswesen des ganzen geistigen Daseins." *Aus der 'Rheinische Zeitung', MEW,* Bd. 1, p. 54. In this chapter, as well as in the following chapters on Engels and Lenin, substantial portions of key texts are reproduced in the notes. The reason for this is twofold: in many cases the text itself is being analyzed;

and often differences of interpretation require that the text be cited as support.

[14] "... ein Staat, der nicht die Verwirklichung der vernünftigen Freiheit ist, ist ein schlechter Staat." *Ibid.*, p. 103.

[15] *Ibid.*, p. 94.

[16] "Jede bestimmte Sphäre der Freiheit ist die Freiheit einer bestimmten Sphäre, wie jede bestimmte Weise des Lebens die Lebensweise einer bestimmten Natur ist." *Ibid.*, p. 69.

[17] "Allein wie ganz irrig ist es nun, ... *eine bestimmte Art* zum Mass, zur Norm, zur Sphäre der anderen Arten zu machen. Es ist die Intoleranz einer Art der Freiheit...". *Ibid.*

[18] *Ibid.*, p. 50.

[19] *Bemerkungen über die neueste preussische Zensurinstruktion, MEW*, Bd. 1, p. 13.

[20] *Aus der 'Rheinische Zeitung'*, p. 103.

[21] *Ibid.*, p. 94.

[22] Cf. Adams, *op. cit.*, p. 66.

[23] *Aus der 'Rheinische Zeitung'*, p. 104.

[24] *Ibid.*, p. 51.

[25] "Die Freiheit ist so sehr das Wesen des Menschen, dass sogar ihre Gegner sie realisieren, indem sie ihre Realität bekämpfen; dass sie als kostbarsten Schmuck sich aneignen wollen, was sie als Schmuck der menschlichen Natur verwarfen." *Ibid.*

[26] "Dann aber gehört zur Freiheit nicht nur *was*, sondern ebensosehr, *wie* ich lebe, nicht nur, dass ich das Freie tue, sondern auch, dass ich es frei tue. Was unterschiede sonst den Baumeister vom Biber, wenn nicht, dass der Biber ein Baumeister mit einem Fell, und der Baumeister ein Biber ohne Fell wäre?" *Ibid.*, p. 62f.

[27] "Die Lebensgefahr für jedes Wesen besteht darin, sich selbst zu verlieren. Die Unfreiheit ist daher die eigentlichen Todesgefahr für den Menschen." *Ibid.*, p. 60.

[28] Cf., for example, *Aus der 'Rheinische Zeitung'*, pp. 58f., 65, 69.

[29] *Kritik des Hegelschen Staatrechts, MEW*, Bd. 1, p. 206.

[30] *Ibid.*, p. 207.

[31] "Der *subjektive* Freiheit erscheint bei Hegel als *formelle* Freiheit..., eben weil er die objektive Freiheit nicht als Verwirklichung, als Betätigung der subjektiven hingestellt hat." *Ibid.*, p. 265.

[32] "Die Existenz der Prädikate ist das Subjekt: also das Subjekt die Existenz der Subjektivität, etc. Hegel verselbständigt die Prädikate, die Objekte, aber er verselbständigt sie getrennt von ihrer wirklichen Selbständigkeit, ihrem Subjekt." *Ibid.*, p. 224.

[33] *Ibid.*, p. 228.

[34] "Eben weil Hegel von den Prädikaten der allgemeinen Bestimmung statt von dem reelen Ens (ὑποχείμενον, Subjekt) ausgeht, und doch ein Träger dieser Bestimmung da sein muss, wird die mystische Idee dieser Träger." *Ibid.*, p. 224.

[35] "... er [Hegel] vergisst... dass die Staatsgeschäfte etc. nichts als Daseins-und Wirkungsweisen der sozialen Qualitäten des Menschen sind. Es versteht sich also, dass die Individuen, insofern sie die Träger der Staatsgegeschäfte und Gewalten sind, ihrer sozialen und nicht ihrer privaten Qualität nach betrachtet werden." *Ibid.*, p. 222.

[36] "... der politische Staat kann nicht sein ohne die natürliche Basis der Familie und die künstliche Basis der bürgerlichen Gesellschaft; sie sind für ihn eine *conditio sine qua non*..." *Ibid.*, p. 207. And Marx continues further on, "... das Faktum ist, dass der Staat aus der Menge, wie sie als Familienglieder und Glieder der bürgerlichen Gesellschaft existiere, hervorgehe..." *Ibid.*

[37] "Die Subjekte bedürfen nicht der 'allgemeinen Angelegenheit' als ihrer wahren Angele-

genheit, sondern die allgemeine Angelegenheit bedarf der Subjekte zu ihrer *formellen* Existenz." *Ibid.,* p. 264.

[38] Cf. reference No. 37.

[39] Cf. *supra,* Chapter I, Section 4.

[40] For a competent discussion of this point, see I. Fetscher, 'Marx's Concretization of the Concept of Freedom', in *Socialist Humanism,* ed. by E. Fromm, London, 1967, pp. 238–249.

[41] Describing the liberal concept of Freedom, Marx writes, "Die Freiheit ist also das Recht, alles zu tun und zu treiben, was keinem anderen schadet." *Zur Judenfrage, MEW,* Bd. 1, p. 364. Cf. also *Ibid.,* p. 369.

[42] *Ibid.,* p. 364.

[43] "Es handelt sich [in liberal theory] um die Freiheit des Menschen als isolierter auf sich zurückgezogener Monade." *Ibid.*

[44] "Erst wenn der wirkliche individuelle Mensch den abstrakten Staatsbürger in sich zurücknimmt und als individueller Mensch in seinem empirischen Leben, in seiner individueller Arbeit, in seinen individuellen Verhältnissen, *Gattungswesen* geworden ist, erst wenn der Mensch seine "forces propres' als gesellschaftliche Kräfte erkannt und organisiert hat und daher die gesellschaftliche Kraft nicht mehr in der Gestalt der *politischen* Kraft von sich trennt, erst dann ist die menschliche Emanzipation vollbracht." *Ibid.,* p. 370.

[45] Cf. Sections 1.1 and 1.2 of this chapter.

[46] Later on, in *Die heilige Familie,* Marx makes essentially the same point. He states that, according to the materialist philosophy, with which he is in sympathy, man is free "nicht durch die negative Kraft, dies und jenes zu meiden, sondern durch die positive Macht, seine wahre Individualität geltend zu machen". And this positive freedom is achieved only insofar as man "entwickelt... seine wahre Natur... in der Gesellschaft". *MEW,* Bd. 2, p. 138.

[47] Cf., for example, R. T. DeGeorge, 'The Soviet Concept of Man', *Studies in Soviet Thought,* 1946, 4, p. 261f.; G. Kline, 'Was Marx an Ethical Humanist?', *Ibid.,* 1969, 2, p. 99f.

[48] For example: "... das Verhältnis des Mannes zum Weib ist das *natürlichste* Verhältnis des Menschen zum Menschen. In ihm zeigt sich also, inwieweit das *natürliche* Verhalten *menschlich* oder inwieweit das *menschliche* Wesen ihm zum *natürlichen* Wesen, inwieweit seine *menschliche Natur* ihm zur *Natur* geworden ist." *Ökonomisch-Philosophische Manuskripte* (henceforth, *Manuskripte*), *MEW, Ergänzungsband,* p. 535. "Der *Kommunismus* als *positive* Aufhebung des *Privateigentums* als *menschlicher Selbstentfremdung* und darum als wirkliche *Aneignung* des *menschlichen* Wesens durch und für den Menschen." *Ibid.,* p. 536. "Der Mensch ist ein Gattungswesen...". *Ibid.,* p. 515. "Wenn der Mensch von Natur erst in der Gesellschaft...". *Die heilige Familie,* p. 138.

[49] Arguing against Bentham's utilitarianism, Marx writes: "Diese Natur selbst ist nicht aus dem Nützlichkeitsprinzip zu konstruieren. Auf den Menschen angewandt, wenn man alle menschliche Tat, Bewegung, Verhältnisse usw. nach dem Nützlichkeitsprinzip beurteilen will, handelt es sich erst um die menschliche Natur im allgemeinen und dann um die in jeder Epoche historisch modifizierte Menschennatur." *Kapital,* Bd. I, *MEW,* Bd. 23, p. 637.

[50] For an attempt to argue this point, cf. E. Fromm, *Marx's Concept of Man,* N.Y., 1961, pp. 24–26. An opposing view is expressed by S. Hook in *Marx and the Marxists: the Ambiguous Legacy,* Princeton, 1955, p. 23. Jean Calvez describis the Marxian concept of the human essence in the following way: "... l'essence étant chez Marx ce qui au terme du développement doit devenir parfaitement adéquat à l'apparence ou à l'existence."

La pensée de Karl Marx, Paris, 1956, p. 147.

[51] *Die deutsche Ideologie, MEW*, Bd. 3, p. 21.

[52] "In der Art der Lebenstätigkeit liegt der ganze Charakter einer species, ihr Gattungs-charakter...". *Manuskripte*, p. 516.

[53] *Ibid.*, p. 578f.

[54] *Die deutsche Ideologie*, p. 21.

[55] *Ibid.*

[56] *Kapital*, Bd. I, p. 194.

[57] *Manuskripte*, p. 546.

[58] *Kapital*, Bd. I, p. 192.

[59] Marx points out that an animal "produziert einseitig, während der Mensch universell produziert". *Manuskripte*, p. 517.

[60] *Ibid.*, p. 546.

[61] Marx distinguishes two senses of human nature: (1) human nature 'in general', and (2) human nature 'as modified in each historical epoch'. Cf. *Kapital*, Bd. I, p. 637; the text is reproduced in reference No. 49. Human nature in the first sense is 'produced' only insofar as it is actualized. In the *Manuscripts* Marx writes that industry is to be conceived as the "exoterische Enthüllung der menschlichen Wesenskräfte". *Manuskripte*, p. 543. And in *Capital* he states that as man, through the employment of his faculties in work, "auf die Natur ausser ihm wirkt und sie verändert, verändert er zugleich seine eigne Natur. Er entwickelt die in ihr schlummernden Potenzen und unterwirft das Spiel ihrer Kräfte seiner eigenen Botmässigkeit". *Kapital*, p. 192. The powers are there 'slumbering', due to human nature 'in general'; they do not spring up *ex nihilo* at the commencement of certain concrete activity. On the other hand, these powers can be developed, perfected, oriented in one direction or another. It is more than just the specification of the individual actions which changes; the real disposition of the human faculties changes, and it is *this* which is the human nature as modified in each historical epoch. This distinction of two senses of human nature' is also indicated in a passage in *The Holy Family*, where Marx speaks of "die *menschlichen Wesenseigenschaften*, so entfremdet sie auch erscheinen mögen," which bond together the members of civil society. *Die heilige Familie*, p. 128.

[62] "Das Tier ist unmittelbar eins mit seiner Lebenstätigkeit. Es unterscheidet sich nicht von ihr. Es ist *sie*. Der Mensch macht seine Lebenstätigkeit selbst zum Gegenstand seines Wollens und seines Bewusstseins. Er hat bewusste Lebenstätigkeit. Es ist nicht eine Bestimmtheit, mit der er unmittelbar zusammenfliesst." *Manuskripte*, p. 516.

[63] *Ibid.*

[64] *Ibid.*, p. 536.

[65] *Kapital*, Bd. III, *MEW*, Bd. 25, p. 828.

[66] The latter two aspects will be treated here in an order contrary to that of the famous passage on alienation in the *Manuscripts*. Actually, the remarks on the alienation of man from his species-being sum up the three other concrete aspects of alienation (from the product, the labor activity, and one's fellow-man) and thus seem to be placed more appropriately at the end. In our opinion, this alienation from man's species-being does not present a fourth concrete aspect of alienation, but *is* the resulting state of affairs – if you will, the entire situation seen from the point of view of its non-correspondance to what man is according to his human species.

[67] *Manuskripte*, p. 511.

[68] *Ibid.*, p. 512.

[69] The theme of the alienation of the worker from the object of his work, first articulated in the *Manuscripts*, appears later in the analysis of the power of money (in *Grundrisse*

der Kritik der politischen Ökonomie) and in the theory of the fetishization of commodities *(Kapital)*. Cf. I. Fetscher, *op. cit.*, pp. 19–39.

[70] Cf. *Manuskripte*, p. 514f.

[71] *Ibid.*

[72] *Ibid.*, p. 518.

[73] *Ibid.*, p. 519.

[74] Cf. Section 1.4 of this chapter.

[75] *Ibid.*, p. 515f.

[76] "Eben in der Bearbeitung der gegenständlichen Welt bewährt sich der Mensch daher erst wirklich als ein *Gattungswesen*. Diese Produktion ist sein werktätiges Gattungsleben. Durch sie erscheint die Natur als *sein* Werk und seine Wirklichkeit." *Ibid.*, p. 517.

[77] *Ibid.*

[78] "In der Art der Lebenstätigkeit liegt der ganze Charakter einer species, ihr Gattungscharakter, und die freie bewusste Tätigkeit ist der Gattungscharakter des Menschen." *Ibid.*, p. 516.

[79] *Ibid.* Cf. also *Die deutsche Ideologie*, p. 67.

[80] *Ibid.*, p. 517.

[81] Cf. reference No. 27.

[82] *Ibid.*, p. 546.

[83] *Die deutsche Ideologie*, p. 35. For an interesting discussion of the various meanings of the term 'communism' in Marx's writings, cf. G. Petrović, *Marx in the Mid-Twentieth Century*, Garden City, N.Y., 1967, pp. 154–169.

[84] *Ibid.*, pp. 34f, 67f.

[85] *Kapital*, Bd. III, p. 828.

[86] *Kritik des Gothaer Programms*, MEW, Bd. 19, p. 21.

[87] Cf. I. Fetscher, *Die Freiheit im Lichte des Marxismus–Leninismus*, Bonn, 1963, p. 33.

[88] *Die deutsche Ideologie*, p. 33.

[89] *Ibid.*, p. 74f.

[90] Quoted by I. Fetscher, 'Marx's Concretization of the Concept of Freedom', p. 347. Taken from *Marx–Engels-Gesamtausgabe*, I/iii, p. 546.

[91] *Ibid.*

[92] "Wie der Wilde mit der Natur ringen muss, um seine Bedürfnisse zu befriedigen, um sein Leben zu erhalten und zu reproduzieren, so muss es der Zivilisierte, und er muss es in allen Gesellschaftsformen und unter allen möglichen Produktionsweisen." *Kapital*, Bd. III, p. 828.

[93] *Ibid.*

[94] "Das Reich der Freiheit beginnt in der Tat erst da, wo das Arbeiten, das durch Not und äussere Zweckmässigkeit bestimmt ist, aufhört; es liegt also der Natur der Sache nach jenseits der Sphäre der eigentlichen materiellen Produktion." *Ibid.*

[95] *Ibid.*

[96] "Jenseits desselben [the realm of necessity] beginnt die menschliche Kraftentwicklung, die sich als Selbstzweck gilt, das wahre Reich der Freiheit, das aber nur auf jenem Reich der Notwendigkeit als seiner Basis aufblühen kann. Die Verkürzung des Arbeitstags ist die Grundbedingung." *Ibid.*

[97] Quoted by I. Fetscher, *Die Freiheit im Lichte des Marxismus–Leninismus*, p. 37. Taken from *Grundrisse der Kritik der politischen Ökonomie, Rohentwurf*, Berlin, 1953, p. 599.

[98] *Ibid.*

[99] Cf. S. Hook, *op. cit.*, p. 18.

[100] *Zur Kritik der politischen Ökonomie, MEW*, Bd. 13, p. 8f.

[101] "Auch wenn eine Gesellschaft dem Naturgesetz ihrer Bewegung auf die Spur gekommen ist– und es ist der letzte Endzweck dieses Werks, das ökonomische Bewegungsgesetz der modernen Gesellschaft zu enthüllen – , kann naturgemässe Entwicklungsphasen weder überspringen noch wegdekretieren." *Kapital*, Bd. I, p. 15f.

[102] "Es handelt sich um diese Gesetzte selbst, um diese mit eherner Notwendigkeit wirkenden und sich durchsetzenden Tendenzen." *Ibid.*, p. 12.

[103] *Die deutsche Ideologie*, p. 34.

[104] *Kapital*, p. 16.

[105] Letter, 'Marx an P. W. Annenkow, 28, Dezember 1846', *MEW*, Bd. 27, p. 452.

[106] *Zur Kritik der politischen Ökonomie*, p. 8f.

[107] Cf. esp. the letters, 'Engels an J. Bloch, 21/22. September 1890', *MEW*, Bd. p. 463, and 'Engels an W. Borgius, 25. Januar 1894' *MEW*, Bd. 39, p. 205f.

[108] *Zur Kritik der politischen Ökonomie*, p. 9. Cf. also *Manifest der kommunistischen Partei, MEW*, Bd. 4, p. 480.

[109] *Das Elend der Philosophie, MEW*, Bd. 4, p. 130. Cf. also *Die deutsche Ideologie*, p. 26.

[110] *Manifest der kommunistischen Partei*, p. 462.

[111] "Wie daher früher ein Teil des Adels zur Bourgeoisie überging, so geht jetzt ein Teil der Bourgeoisie zum Proletariat über, und namentlich ein Teil der Bourgeoisideologen, welche zum theoretischen Verständnis der ganzen geschichtlichen Bewegung sich hinaufgearbeitet haben." *Ibid.*, p. 472.

[112] *Der Achtzehnte Brumaire des Louis Bonaparte*, in *Ausgewählte Schriften*, Berlin, 1966, Band 1, p. 276.

[113] The letter 'Marx an P. W. Annenkow, 28. Dezember 1846', p. 452.

[114] *Das Elend der Philosophie*, p. 75.

[115] Die deutsche Ideologie, p. 424.

[116] *Ibid.*, p. 417.

[117] *Ibid.*, p. 424.

[118] *Ibid.*

[119] "Die Freiheit ist von den Philosophen bisher in doppelter Weise bestimmt worden; einerseits als Macht, als Herrschaft über die Umstände und Verhältnisse, in denen ein Individuum lebt – von allen Materialisten…" This passage is crossed out in the manuscript, but the following pages (pp. 282–295) confirm that it is a true expression of Marx and Engels' position.

[120] *Ibid.*, p. 285.

[121] *Ibid.*

[122] *Manifest der kommunistischen Partei*, p. 463.

[123] "In der Wirklichkeit trug sich die Sache natürlich so zu, dass die Menschen sich jedesmal so weit befreiten, als nicht nur ihr Ideal vom Menschen, sondern die existierenden Produktivkräfte ihnen vorschreiben und erlauben." *Die deutsche Ideologie*, p. 417.

[124] *Ibid.*

[125] *Ibid.*

[126] *Zur Kritik der politischen Ökonomie*, p. 8f.

[127] Previous revolutionary classes had claimed to represent all of humanity, but these were all false claims; they represented only a larger proportion of humanity than previous progressive classes. Cf. *Die deutsche Ideologie*, p. 47f.

[128] Cf. *Zur Kritik der Hegelschen Rechtsphilosophie. Einleitung. MEW*, Bd. 1, p. 390f.

[129] "Die *allseitige* Abhängigkeit, diese naturwüchsige Form des *welt-geschichtlichen*

Zusammenwirkens der Individuen, wird durch diese kommunistische Revolution verwandelt in die Kontrolle und bewusste Beherrschung dieser Mächte, die, aus dem Aufeinanderwirken der Menschen erzeugt, ihnen bisher als durchaus fremde Mächte imponiert und sie beherrscht haben." *Die deutsche Ideologie*, p. 37.

[130] Cf. *ibid.*, pp. 70f. and 74f.

[131] *Ibid.*, p. 74.

[132] *Ibid.*, p. 75.

[133] This view is widely attributed to Marx. Cf., for example: V. Venable, *Human Nature: the Marxian View*, N.Y., 1945, p. 191; F. Neubauer, *op. cit.*, p. 41; C. Rossiter, *Marxism: the View From America*, N.Y., 1960, p. 83; T. Dobzhansky, *The Biological Basis of Human Freedom*, N.Y., 1956, p. 134.

[134] Cf. *Die heilige Familie*, p. 100, and Marx's marginal notes to *Die deutsche Ideologie*, published as part of the English translation. *The German Ideology*, M., 1964, p. 53f.

[135] This is the position taken by Soviet philosophers.

[136] *Kritik des Hegelschen Staatrechts*, pp. 204, 258f.

[137] *Kapital*, B.I., p. 12.

[138] *Ibid.*, p. 16.

[139] *Kapital*, Bd. III, p. 828.

[140] Both the idea of alienation and the ideal of the final self-fulfillment of man depend upon the assumption of a human nature. If man had no human nature, he would not be alienated in any particular condition, but only different than before. Likewise, the human self-realization of the future man is only conceivable as the fulfillment of what man always was potentially, i.e., by the nature that was always his.

[141] Cf., for example, the article on 'free will' by J. D. Mabbot, in *Encyclopedia Britannica*, 1960, Vol. 9, p. 747.

[142] "Bei der Untersuchung *staatlicher* Zustände ist man allzu leicht versucht, die *sachliche Natur der Verhältnisse* zu übersehen und alles aus dem *Willen* der handelnden Personen zu erklären." *Rechtfertigung des **-Korrespondenten von der Model, MEW*, Bd. 1, p. 177.

[143] *Das Elend der Philosophie*, p. 75.

[144] "Allerdings, der Arbeiter, der Kartoffeln kauft, und die ausgehaltene Mätresse, die Spitzen kauft, folgen beide nur ihrer respektiven Meinung; aber die Verschiedenheit der Stellung, die sie in der Welt einnehmen und die selbst wiederum ein Produkt der sozialen Organisation ist." *Ibid*.

[145] "Die soziale Macht, d.h. die vervielfachte Produktionskraft, die durch das in der Teilung der Arbeit bedingte Zusammenwirken der verschiedenen Individuen entsteht, erscheint diesen Individuen, weil das Zusammenwirken selbst nicht freiwillig, sondern naturwüchsig ist, nicht als ihre eigne, vereinte Macht, sondern als eine fremde, ausser ihnen stehende Gewalt, von der sie nicht wissen woher und wohin, die sie also nicht mehr beherrschen können, die im Gegenteil nun eine eigentümliche, vom Wollen und Laufen der Menschen unabhängige, ja dies Wollen und Laufen erst dirigierende Reihenfolge von Phasen und Entwicklungsstufen durchläuft." *Die deutsche Ideologie*, p. 34.

[146] *Ibid.*, p. 293f.

[147] Cf. Section 4 of Chapter I and 1.3 of this chapter.

[148] Cf. Section 1.3 of this chapter.

[149] "Feuerbach löst das religiöse Wesen in das *menschliche* Wesen auf. Aber das menschliche Wesen ist kein dem einzelnen Individuum innewohnendes Abstraktum. In seiner Wirklichkeit ist es das Ensemble der gesellschaftlichen Verhältnisse.

Feuerbach, der auf die Kritik dieses wirklichen Wesens nicht eingeht, ist daher gezwungen:

(1) von dem geschichtlichen Verlauf zu abstrahieren und das religöse Gemüt für sich zu fixieren, und ein abstrakt-*isoliert*-menschliches Individuum vorauszusetzen." *Thesen über Feuerbach, MEW*, 3, p. 6.

[150] *Die heilige Familie*, p. 60.

[151] *Ibid.*, p. 79.

[152] *Ibid.*, p. 59.

[153] *Thesen über Feuerbach*, p. 6.

[154] It is in this direction that the 6th thesis is interpreted by Jean Calvez. Cf. *La pensée de Karl Marx*, p. 147.

[155] Marx rejects the position of B. Bauer, which he descibes as follows: "*Die Geschichte wird daher, wie die Wahrheit,* zu einer aparten Person, einem metaphysischen Subjekt, dessen blosse Träger die wirklichen menschlichen Individuen sind." *Ibid.*, p. 83.

[156] Cf., for example, *Die deutsche Ideologie*, pp. 20, 25f, 67, 74f.

[157] Cf. reference No. 62.

[158] "Sie [the proletarian class] ist, um einen Ausdruck von Hegel zu gebrauchen, in der Verworfenheit die *Empörung* über diese Verworfenheit, eine Empörung, zu der sie notwendig durch den Widerspruch ihrer menschlichen *Natur* mit ihrer Lebenssituation, welche die offenherzige, entschiedene, umfassende Verneinung dieser Natur ist, getrieben wird." *Die heilige Familie*, p. 37.

[159] Cf. reference No. 62.

CHAPTER III

[1] The authoritative biography of Engels, which reveals the details of his close relation to Marx, was written by G. Mayer, *Friedrich Engels: Eine Biographie*, 2 Bd., The Hague, 1934.

[2] For example, Marx was responsible for writing Section 10, Part II, of *Anti-Dühring*, and Engels often wrote articles for the *New York Herald Tribune* which were published under Marx's name.

[3] Cf. Z. A. Jordan, *The Evolution of Dialectical Materialism*, N.Y., 1967, pp. 3–6.

[4] For treatments of the classics which do distinguish clearly between the thought of Marx and Engels, cf. G. A. Wetter, *Der dialektische Materialismus*, Freiburg, 1960, Ch. 2; J. M. Bocheński, *Soviet Russian Dialectical Materialism*, Dordrecht, 1963, p. 18f; Jordan, *op. cit.*, Ch. 5 and 10; R. T. De George, *Patterns of Soviet Thought*, Ann Arbor, 1966, Ch. 5.

[5] F. Neubauer attempts to show the identity of the views of Marx and Engels on such early Marxian concepts as human alienation and man's species-being. Unfortunately, in order to do so, he is forced into taking statements out of context and relying on merely verbal comparisons. An indication of the weakness of his hypothesis is suggested by the type of evidence he brings forward: he cites, as supporting their alleged identity of view, the fact that Engels did not substantially alter the text of the *Capital* in later editions! Cf. *Das Verhältnis von Karl Marx und Friedrich Engels dargestellt an der Bestimmung der menschlichen Freiheit in deren Schriften*, Meisenheim/Glan, 1960, p. 100.

[6] In the preface to the second edition of *Anti-Dühring*, Engels tells us that he had read the whole manuscript to Marx. This seems to indicate only that Marx did not object to its contents, and it can hardly be inferred from this remark that the book is an expression of Marx's own views.

[7] Plekhanov was the first to describe the views of Marx and Engels by the term 'dialectical materialism'. Cf. *Izbrannye filosofskie proizvedenija* (Selected Philosophical Works), t.1, pp. 443–445.

[8] K. Marx and F. Engels, *Die deutsche Ideologie, MEW*, Bd. 3, pp. 282–295 (Engl.: *The German Ideology*, London, 1965, pp. 326–341).

[9] F. Engels, *Herrn Eugen Dührings Umwälzung der Wissenschaft ("Anti-Dühring")* (Henceforth *Anti-Dühring*), MEW, Bd. 20, p. 106. (Engl.: *Anti-Dühring, Herr Eugen Dühring's Revolution in Science*, Moscow, 1962, p. 156.) Unless otherwise specified, all further references in this chapter will be to works by Engels.

[10] *Dialektik der Natur, MEW*, Bd. 20, p. 452. (Engl: *Dialectics of Nature*, Moscow, 1964, p. 182.)

[11] *Anti-Dühring*, p. 106. (Engl., p. 157.)

[12] *Ibid.*, p. 107. (Engl., p. 158.)

[13] *Ibid.*

[14] *Ibid.*, p. 253. (Engl., p. 372.)

[15] *Ibid.*, p. 255 (Engl., p. 374.)

[16] *Ibid.*, p. 264. (Engl., p. 388.)

[17] Cf. Sections 2.3 and 3.3 of Chapter II.

[18] *Anti-Dühring*, p. 264. (Engl., p. 388f.)

[19] *Die Entwicklung des Sozialismus von der Utopie zur Wissenschaft, MEW*, Bd. 19, p. 228. (Engl.: *Socialism: Utopian and Scientific*, in Marx/Engels, *Selected Works*, Moscow, 1962, Vol. 2. p. 155.)

[20] Cf. Section 2.3 of Chapter II.

[21] *Dialektik der Natur*, p. 322f, 447f. (Engl., pp. 34, 176f.)

[22] *Ibid.*

[23] Cf. Sections 2 and 4 of the present chapter.

[24] *Anti-Dühring*, p. 273f. (Engl., p. 404.)

[25] Cf. Section 2.3 of Chapter II.

[26] *Anti-Dühring*, pp. 105–110. (Engl., pp. 155–163.)

[27] Cf. Chapter VI, especially Sections 2 and 5.

[28] "Hegel war der erste, der das Verhältnis von Freiheit und Notwendigkeit richtig darstellte. Für ihn ist die Freiheit die Einsicht in die Notwendigkeit. 'Blind ist die Notwendigkeit nur, *insofern dieselbe nicht begriffen* wird'". *Anti-Dühring*, p. 106. (Engl., p. 157.)

[28a] It is interesting to note that Marx, in his *Kritik des Hegelschen Staatsrechts*, ridiculed Hegel for wanting to present the state as a realization of freedom but in fact solving all conflicts through a "natural necessity which stands in opposition to freedom". *MEW*, Bd. 1, p. 2. Marx's enthusiasm for the Hegelian solution to the problem of freedom and necessity was considerably cooler than Engels'.

[29] G. V. Plekhanov, *K. voprosu o roli ličnosti v istorii*, in *Sočinenija*, 2nd ed., Moscow, 1924–1927, Vol. 8, p. 277f. (Engl.: *The Role of the Individual in History*, N.Y., 1940, p. 16.)

[30] "... indem sich der subjektive Wille des Menschen den Gesetzen unterwirft, verschwindet der Gegensatz von Freiheit und Notwendigkeit. Notwendig is das Vernünftige als das Substantielle, und frei sind wir, indem wir es als Gesetz anerkennen und ihm als der Substanz unseres eigenen Wesens folgen: der objektive und der subjektive Wille sind dann ausgesöhnt und ein und dasselbe ungetrübte Ganze". G. F. W. Hegel, *Philosophie der Geschichte*, in *Werke*, Jubiläumsausgabe, Stuttgart, 1927–1939, Bd. 11, p. 71.

[31] In logic "... ist der Geist rein bei sich selbst und hiermit frei, denn die Freiheit ist

eben dies, in seinem Anderen bei sich selbst zu sein". And "Freiheit ist nur da wo kein Anderes für mich ist, das ich nicht selbst bin". G. W. F. Hegel, *System der Philosophie, Werke,* Bd. 8, p. 87.

[32] G. F. W. Hegel, *Philosophie der Geschichte, Werke,* Bd. XI, p. 44–45.

[33] "Nicht in der geträumten Unabhängigkeit von den Naturgesetzen liegt die Freiheit, sondern in der Erkenntnis dieser Gesetze, und in der damit gegebenen Möglichkeit, sie planmässig zu bestimmten Zwecken wirken zu lassen." *Anti-Dühring,* p. 106. (Engl., p. 157.)

[34] "Freiheit des Willens heisst daher nichts anderes als die Fähigkeit, mit Sachkenntnis entscheiden zu können. Je *freier* also das Urteil eines Menschen in Beziehung auf einen bestimmten Fragepunkt ist, mit desto grösserer *Notwendigkeit* wird der Inhalt dieses Urteils bestimmt sein; während die auf Unkenntnis beruhende Unsicherheit, die zwischen vielen verschiedenen und widersprechenden Entscheidungsmöglichkeiten scheinbar willkürlich wählt, eben dadurch ihre Unfreiheit beweist, ihr Beherrschtsein von dem Gegenstande, den sie gerade beherrschen sollte." *Ibid.*

[35] "Freiheit besteht also in der auf Erkenntnis der Naturnotwendigkeiten gegründeten Herrschaft über uns selbst und über die äussere Natur; sie ist damit notwendig ein Produkt der geschichtlichen Entwicklung." *Ibid.*

[36] Cf. Section 3.4 of Chapter II.

[37] *Anti-Dühring,* p. 264. (Engl., p. 388.)

[38] *Ibid.*

[39] *Ludwig Feuerbach und der Ausgang der klassischen deutschen Philosophie,* MEW, Bd. 21. p. 296. (Engl.: Marx/Engels, *Selected Works,* Vol. 2, p. 390f.)

[40] *Ibid.* (Engl., p. 391).

[41] *Ibid.*

[42] *Ibid.*

[43] *Ibid.,* p. 297. (Engl., p. 391.)

[44] *Ibid.*

[45] *Ibid.* (Engl., p. 392.)

[46] *Ibid.,* p. 298. (Engl., p. 393.)

[47] *Ibid.,* p. 300. (Engl., p. 395.)

[48] *Ibid.,* p. 298. (Engl., p. 392.)

[49] *Ibid.,* p. 299. (Engl., p. 393.)

[50] Letter of Engels to J. Bloch, Sept. 21, 1890, *MEW,* Bd. 37, p. 463. (Engl.: *Karl Marx and Friedrich Engels: Selected Correspondance,* Moscow, no date, p. 498.)

[51] *Ludwig Feuerbach und der Ausgang der klassischen deutschen Philosophie,* p. 300. (Engl., p. 395.)

[52] *Ibid.,* p. 297. (Engl., p. 391.)

[53] *Ibid.,* p. 281f. (Engl., p. 377.)

[54] Letter of Engels to J. Bloch, p. 464. (Engl., p. 499.)

[55] *Anti-Dühring,* p. 105. (Engl., p. 155.)

[56] *Ibid.,* p. 106. (Engl., p. 157.)

[57] While Neubauer finds no difficulty in presenting a synoptic view of the whole of Marx's and Engels' statements on freedom, certain Neo-Marxists take Engels to task, esp. in connection with the relation between freedom and necessity, for distorting the Marxian position. Cf. G. Petrović, *Marx in the Mid-Twentieth Century,* N.Y., 1967, pp. 115–134.

CHAPTER IV

[1] Cf., for example, V. I. Lenin, *Polnoe sobranie sočinenij* (henceforth *Sočineij*), izd. 5-e, Moscow, 1958ff, t. 39, p. 281, t. 38, p. 349, t. 41, p. 425. Please note that, unless specified otherwise, all further references in this chapter will refer to works by Lenin.

[2] *Sočinenij*, t. 14, p. 108, t. 23, p. 150.

[3] *Sočinenij*, t. 1, p. 158.

[4] "Determinizm ne tol'ko ne predpolagaet fatalizma, a naprotiv, imenno i daet počvu dlja razumnogo dejstvovanija." *Ibid.*, p. 440.

[5] Z. A. Jordan, in *The Evolution of Dialectical Materialism*, London, 1967, interprets the text in this way; cf. p. 354f.

[6] "Ideja determinizma, ustanavlivaja neobxodimost' čelovečeskix postupkov, otvergaja vzdornuju pobasenku o svobode voli, nimalo ne uničtožaet ni razuma, ni sovesti čeloveka, ni ocenka ego dejstvij. Sovsem naprotiv, tol'ko pri determinist. českom vzglade i vozmožna strogaja i pravil'naja ocenka, a ne svalivanie čego ugodno na svobodnuju volju." *Ibid.*, p. 157.

[7] *Ibid.*, p. 440.

[8] In reply to Bogdanov's assertion that Mach's philosophy has no room for the ideas of God, free will and immortality, Lenin writes: "'Ne možet byt' mesta' dlja etix idej isključitel'no v filosofii, kotoraja učit, čto suščestvuet tol'ko čuvstvennoe bytie..., t.e. v filosofii materializma." *Sočinenij*, t. 18, *Materializm i empiriokriticizm* (henceforth *Materializm*, p. 230; *Materialism and Empiriocriticism*, Moscow, 1964, p. 202f).

[9] "Dejstvitel'nyj vopros, voznikajuščij pri ocenka obščestvennoj dejatel'nosti ličnosti, sostoit v tom, pri kakix uslovijax etoj dejatel'nosti obespečen uspex? v čem sostojat garantii togo, čto dejatel'nost' eta ne ostanetsja odinočnym aktom, tonuščim v more aktov protivopoložnyx? *Sočninenij*, t. 1, p. 159.

[9a] Cf. *Sočinenij*, t. 1, p. 440; *Materializm*, p. 195f. (Engl., p. 172); *Sočinenij*, t. 26, p. 53. (Engl.: *The Teachings of Karl Marx*, N.Y., 1964, p. 15f.)

[10] *Materializm*, pp. 195–201. (Engl., pp. 172–177.)

[11] For a discussion of the epistemological significance of Lenin's treatment of freedom and necessity, cf. N. N. Pospelov, 'V. I. Lenin o svobode i neobxodimost' (V. I. Lenin On Freedom and Necessity), in *Kniga V. I. Lenina 'Materializm i Empiriocriticizm'*, Moscow, 1959.

[12] "V osobennosti nado otmetit' vzgljad Marksa na otnošenie svobody k neobxodimosti: 'slepa neobxodimost', poka ona ne soznana. Svoboda est' soznanie neobxodimosti' (Engels v "Anti-Djuringe")". *Sočinenij*, t. 26, p. 53. (Engl., *The Teachings of Karl Marx*, p. 15.)

[13] Cf. also *Materializm*, p. 198f. (Engl., p. 175), where Lenin lumps together 'Hegel and Marx' as the discoverers of the (Engelsian) solution to the problem of freedom and necessity.

[14] Cf. *supra*, Ch. 3, Section 2.

[15] "Engel's beret poznanie i volju čeloveka – s odnoj storony, neobxodimost' prirody – s drugoj, i vmesto vsjakogo opredelenija, vsjakoj definicii, prosto govorit, čto neobxodimost' prirody est' pervičnoe, a volja i soznanie čeloveka – vtoričnoe. Poslednie dolžny, neizbežno i neobxodimo dolžny, prisposobljat'sja k pervoj..." *Materializm*, p. 196. (Engl., p. 173.)

[16] After quoting Engels' statement, Lenin writes: "... = priznanie ob'ektivnoj zakonomernosti prirody i dialektičeskogo prevraščenija neobxodimosti v svobodu (naravne s prevraščeniem nepoznannoj, no poznavaemoj, 'vešči v sebe' v 'vešči dlja nas', 'suščnosti veščej' v 'javlenija')". *Sočinenij*, t. 26, p. 53. (Engl., *The Teachings of Karl Marx*, p. 16.)

[17] *Materializm*, p. 197. (Engl., p. 173f.)

[18] "... poka my ne znaem zakona prirody, on, syščestvuja i dejstvuja pomino, vne našego poznanija, delaet nas rabami 'slepoj neobxodimosti'. Raz my uznali etot zakon, dejstvu-juščij (kak tysjači raz povtorjal Marks) *nezavisimo* ot našej voli i ot našego soznanija – my gospoda prirody. Gospodstvo nad prirodoj, projavljajuščee sebja v praktike čelove - -čestva, est' rezul'tat ob'ektivno-vernogo otraženija v golove čeloveka javlenij i processov prirody..." *Ibid.*, p. 198. (Engl., p. 174.)

[19] *Sočinenij*, t. 29 *(Filosofskie tetrady*, henceforth *Tetrady)*, p. 195. (Engl.: V. I. Lenin, *Collected Works*, Vol. 38, *Philosophical Notebooks*, Moscow, 1961, p. 213.)

[20] "NB Svoboda = sub'ektivnost', ('ili') cel', soznanie, stremlenie NB". *Tetrady*, p. 148. (Engl., p. 164.)

[20a] Cf. L. V. Nikolaeva, *Svoboda – neoboxodimyj produkt istoričeskogo razvitija*, M., 1964, p. 4; T. A. Kazakevič, 'Cel' i svobody', *V LGU* 1968, 23, p. 55; V. E. Davidovič, *Problemy celovečeskoj svobody*, L'vov', 1967, p. 10.

[21] "2 formy *ob'ektivnogo* processa: priroda... i *cele* polagajuščaja dejatel'nost' čeloveka." *Ibid.*, p. 170. (Engl., p. 188.)

[22] *Ibid.*

[23] *Ibid.*, p. 171. (Engl., p. 189).

[24] *Ibid.*

[25] *Ibid.*, p. 172. (Engl., p. 189). Cf. Hegel, *Werke*.

[26] Cf., for example, Jordan, *op. cit.*, pp. 354–357; J. M. Bocheński, *Soviet Russian Dialectical Materialism*, Dordrecht, 1963, p. 30; S. Hook, *Marx and the Marxists: the Ambiguous Legacy*, Princeton, N.J., 1955.

[27] Jordan, *op. cit.*, p. 355; Bocheński, *op. cit.*, p. 30.

[27a] Cf. Chapter II, Section 3.1 and Chapter III, Section 3.

[28] *Sočinenij*, t. 1, pp. 136–138; t. 26, pp. 55–58. (Engl., *The Teachings of Karl Marx*, pp. 18–20.)

[29] It cannot be said that Lenin's two above-mentioned revisions were cut of whole cloth. Marx himself had been careful not to deny that Russia might take a different road to communism than would the Western European countries. Cf. the letter of Marx to V. Zasulich of March 8, 1881, *MEW* Bd. 35, p. 166f. And his own activity in the Communist League and the International Working Mens Association showed that he did not reject political activity as a means of promoting the proletarian revolution. Both Marx and Lenin were revolutionaries; but while Marx sought primarily to enlighten the *minds* of the slumbering proletariat, Lenin concentrated on compensating for their lack of practical *will*.

CHAPTER V

[1] T. I. Ojzerman, 'Nekotorye aspekty marksistsko–leninskogo ponimanija svobody', *V MGU* 1966, 3, p. 32.

[2] *Ibid.*, p. 32f.

[3] G. E. Glezerman, 'Obščestvo, kollektiv, ličnost'', in *Kollektiv i ličnost'*, M., 1968, p. 4f., 7f.

[4] Cf. V. P. Tugarinov, *Ličnost' i obščestvo*, M., 1965, p. 30, and the leading article in *VF* 1963, 2.

[5] Tugarinov also mentions this as one determining factor, and adds that Marxism's

emphasis on the role of the masses (in contrast to that of the individual) was a natural reaction to the other extreme, prevalent in 'idealist' philosophy. *Ibid.*

[6] M. I. Petrosjan, *Gumanizm,* M., 1964, p. 12f.

[7] *Ibid.,* pp. 13–15.

[8] *Osnovy marksistskoj filosofii,* M., 1963, p. 110; Tugarinov, *op. cit.,* p. 7.

[9] J. M. Bocheński, 'The Great Split', *Studies in Soviet Thought* 1968, 1, p. 7.

[10] V. P. Tugarinov, *Sootnošenie kategorij dialektičeskogo materializma,* L., 1956, p. 23. The Russian term *'predmet'* will be translated here as 'thing' rather than as 'object', since it is clear that it is being used in an ontological, rather than in an epistemological sense.

[11] *Ibid.,* p. 26.

[12] *Ibid.,* p. 30. Tugarinov also tries to show that the affirmation of a substantial support of properties is a necessary pre-supposition of logic. Cf. 'Gegen den Idealismus in der mathematischen Logik', in *Über formale Logik und Dialektik,* Berlin, 1952, p. 102f.

[13] Tugarinov, *Sootnošenie,* p. 30.

[14] *Ibid.,* p. 29.

[15] *Ibid.,* p. 27.

[16] *Ibid.,* pp. 28, 33.

[17] *Ibid.,* p. 40.

[18] *Ibid.,* p. 41.

[19] A. I. Uemov, *Vešči, svojstva i otnošenija,* M., 1963.

[20] *FE,* t. 4, the entries *'predmet'* and *'svojstvo'.*

[21] Uemov, *Vešči,* p. 9.

[22] *Ibid.,* p. 13f.

[23] *Ibid.,* p. 19.

[24] *Ibid.,* p. 21.

[25] *Ibid.,* p. 64.

[26] *Ibid.,* p. 66.

[27] *Ibid.,* p. 67.

[28] *Ibid.,* pp. 71, 79.

[29] *Ibid.,* p. 36.

[30] *Ibid.,* p. 52.

[31] *Ibid.,* p. 72.

[32] A. I. Uemov, 'Ontologičeskie predposylki logiki', *VF* 1969, 1, p. 77.

[33] Uemov, *Vešči,* p. 77f.

[34] *Ibid.,* pp. 74–86.

[35] Uemov, 'Ontologičeskie predposylki', p. 77.

[36] *FS,* p. 69.

[36a] *Ibid.,* pp. 69, 331.

[37] *Ibid.,* pp. 331, 339.

[38] *OMF,* p. 184f.

[39] *FE,* t.4, p. 183.

[40] I. B. Novik, 'O kategorijax "vešč" i "otnošenie"', *VF* 1957, 4, p. 219.

[41] *Ibid.*

[42] *FE,* t. 1, p. 251, the entry 'inter-connection' (vzaimosvjaz) by E. Il'enkov, G. Davydova, and V. Lektorskij.

[43] V. S. Bibler, *O sisteme kategorij dialektičeskoj logiki,* Dušanbe, 1958, pp. 50, 155. Quoted in: F. Rapp, *Gesetz und Determination in der Sowjetphilosophie,* Dordrecht, 1968, p. 40.

[44] *Ibid.*, p. 49.

[45] Cf. S. T. Meljuxin, *Materija v ee edinstve, beskonečnosti i razvitii*, M., 1966, p. 47.

[46] *FS*, p. 261.

[47] Cf. the articles in the *Voprosy filosofii*, 1967, Nos. 3 and 6; 1968, 4; 1969, 10; also Meljuxin, *op. cit.*, Ch. 3, Sections 4 and 5. In the recent East German textbook, *Marxistische Philosophie* (Berlin, 1967), a whole chapter is devoted to 'The System-Character of Objective Reality'.

[48] It must be noted here that the terms 'social' and 'society' are used in Soviet writings in the most diverse senses, and often to the detriment of clarity. For example, when something is described as 'social', this can mean as little as 'somehow connected with society' (analogous in its vagueness to the use of the term 'material'); it can also mean 'proper only to social life', such as language; or in the strictest senses, 'an element of society' and 'proper to the society as a whole'. Further, the term is used, often without specification, in descriptive, genetic and normative senses; that is, it can mean either 'actually social', 'social in origin', or 'sanctioned by society'. In view of the fact that Marxist philosophers feel compelled, by their tradition, to describe virtually every phenomenon which extends beyond the material or biological world as 'social', this terminological confusion is one of the basic obstacles to the development of a clearly articulated philosophical position.

[49] *KSF*, p. 330.

[50] G. D. Balyčeva, 'Voprosy socialističeskogo gumanizma v trudax V. I. Lenina', *FN* 1969, 5, p. 14f.

[51] I. S. Narskij, 'O probleme "celovečeskoj prirody" v rannix trudax K. Marksa', *V MGU*, 1967, 6, pp. 16, 19; N. M. Berežnoj, 'Obosnovanie K. Marksom naučnoj koncepcii čeloveka v "Kapitale"', in *Filosofskie problemy "Kapitala" K. Marksa*, M., 1968, p. 134.

[52] Narskij, *op. cit.*, p. 16.

[53] Berežnoj, *op. cit.*, p. 134.

[54] *Ibid.*, p. 139.

[55] *Ibid.*, p. 140. According to L. V. Bueva, at an all-union symposium on the problems of the person held in Moscow, a majority of the participants expressed disagreement with the "one-sided consideration of man as only a social being". L. V. Bueva, *Social'naja sreda i soznanie ličnosti*, M., 1968, p. 25.

[56] Berežnoj, *op. cit.*, p. 140.

[57] Narskij, *op. cit.*, p. 16.

[58] Drozdov, *Čelovek i obščestvennye otnošenija*, L., 1966, p. 9.

[59] *Ibid.*, p. 8.

[60] *Ibid.*, p. 10.

[61] *Ibid.*

[62] *Ibid.*, p. 28.

[63] Ojzerman, *op. cit.*, p. 32.

[64] *Ibid.*

[65] I. S. Kon, *Sociologija ličnosti*, M., 1967, p. 9.

[66] Ojzerman, *op. cit.*, p. 32.

[67] Tugarinov, *Ličnost'*, p. 14.

[68] *Ibid.*

[69] V. I. Lenin, *Sočinenij*, t. 29, p. 318, emphasis mine.

[70] Tugarinov, *op. cit.*, p. 12.

[71] *Ibid.*, p. 13.

[72] Drozdov, *op. cit.*, p. 6.

⁷³ *Ibid.*, p. 23.

⁷⁴ *Ibid.*, p. 26.

⁷⁵ *Ibid.*, p. 23.

⁷⁶ *Ibid.*, p. 26.

⁷⁷ G. L. Smirnov, *Formirovanie kommunističeskix obščestvennyx otnošenij*, M., 1962, p. 7.

⁷⁸ Drozdov, *op. cit.*, p. 26.

⁷⁹ *Ibid.*, p. 28.

⁸⁰ *Ibid.*, p. 29.

⁸¹ *Ibid.*

⁸² *Ibid.*, p. 27.

⁸³ *Ibid.*, p. 28.

⁸⁴ Tugarinov, *Ličnost'*, p. 25.

⁸⁵ V. I. Lenin, *Sočinenij*, t. 1, p. 424.

⁸⁶ Kon, *op. cit.*, p. 11.

⁸⁷ Cf. Sections 2.1 and 4.3 of Chapter II.

⁸⁸ S. Rodriges, 'Problema čeloveka i kategorija "otčuždennyj trud" v "ekonomičesko-filosofskix rukopisjax 1844 goda" K. Marksa', *V MGU*, 1969, 5, p. 73.

⁸⁹ *Ibid.*, p. 72.

⁹⁰ T. I. Ojzerman, *Formirovanie filosofii marksizma*, M., 1962; E. V. Il'enkov, 'From a Marxist–Leninist Point of View', in N. Lobkowicz, *Marx and the Western World*, Notre Dame, 1967; I. S. Narskij, *op. cit.*

⁹¹ M. B. Mitin, 'V. I. Lenin i problema čeloveka', *VF* 1967, 8, p. 22.

⁹² *Ibid.*, p. 24.

⁹³ *Ibid.*, p. 26.

⁹⁴ Narskij, *op. cit.*, p. 15.

⁹⁵ *Ibid.*, p. 16.

⁹⁶ *Ibid.*

⁹⁷ *Ibid.*, p. 17.

⁹⁸ *Ibid.*, p. 18.

⁹⁹ *Ibid.*, p. 19.

¹⁰⁰ Cf. H. Fleischer, 'The Limits of "Party-Mindedness"', *Studies in Soviet Thought* 1962, 2, p. 123.

¹⁰¹ *Kratkij slovar' po etike*, M., 1965, p. 287.

¹⁰² O. I. Džioev, 'Cennost' i istoričeskaja neobxodimost'', *FN* 1966, 6, p. 35f.

¹⁰³ Tugarinov, *Sootnošenie*, p. 86.

¹⁰⁴ Tugarinov, *Ličnost'*, p. 35.

¹⁰⁵ *Ibid.*, p. 40.

¹⁰⁶ K. N. Ljubutin, 'Starye idei v novoj odežde', *VF* 1965, 7, pp. 126–136.

¹⁰⁷ Džioev, *op. cit.*, p. 35.

¹⁰⁸ Z. M. Orudžev, '"Kapital" K. Marksa – neisčerpaemyj ob'ekt filosofskix issledovanij', *V MGU* 1969, 5, pp. 89–94; T. V. Samsonova, 'K analizu problemy ličnosti v "Kapitale" K. Marksa', in *Filosofskie problemy "Kapitale" K. Marksa*, M., 1968, pp. 157–178.

¹⁰⁹ Orudžev, p. 93.

¹¹⁰ T. I. Ojzerman, *Problemy istoriko-filosofskoj nauki*, M., 1969, p. 220.

¹¹¹ *FE*, t. 3, p. 196. Cf. also V. E. Davidovič, *Problemy čelovečeskoj svobody*, p. 43f.

¹¹² V. P. Tugarinov, 'Kommunizm i ličnost'', *VF* 1962, 6, pp. 14–23.

¹¹³ Note that when the term 'ličnost'' is used in philosophical texts in this second sense, it does not carry the connotation it often has in English, indicating the emotional type of the person (which is the object of characterology); rather it includes everything which

belongs to being a person, e.g., skills, knowledge, intelligence, etc.

[114] *Ibid.*, p. 16.

[115] *Ibid.*

[116] *Kommunizm i ličnost'*, M., 1964, p. 9.

[117] *Ibid.*, p. 10. An interesting definition of the person by S. L. Rubinštejn (*Bytie i soznanie*, M., 1957, p. 312) is also criticized along similar lines.

[118] R. T. DeGeorge, 'The Soviet Concept of Man', *Iris Hibernia* 1964, p. 20, *The New Marxism*, N.Y., 1968, p. 64. DeGeorge presents Tugarinov's position as the general Soviet view; but the fact that numerous Soviet authors have criticized Tugarinov precisely in this point indicates that this judgment must be modified.

[119] *Ibid.*, pp. 20, 25.

[120] Tugarinov, *Ličnost'*, p. 40.

[121] *Ibid.*, p. 41.

[122] *Ibid.*

[123] Nevertheless, this would seem to involve Tugarinov in serious difficulties. For even if a young child has not yet achieved the use of reason or a sense of moral responsibility, he would be considered to be due certain rights and to possess personal worth.

[124] *Ibid.*, p. 42.

[125] *FS*, p. 234; *FE*, t. 3, p. 196; *Čelovek v socialističeskom i buržuaznom obščestve (materialy simpoziuma po problemam ličnosti i obščestva v Institute filosofii A.N. S.S.S.R.)*, M., 1966, p. 307.

[126] G. M. Gak, *Dialektika kollektivnosti i individual'nosti*, M., 1967, p. 14; V. Afanes'ev, 'O celostnosti ličnosti', in *Kollektiv i ličnost'*, M., 1968, p. 30.

[127] Gak, *op. cit.*, p. 14.

[128] Tugarinov, *Ličnost'*, p. 128.

[129] Gak, *op. cit.*, p. 14.

[130] *Čelovek v socialističeskom i buržuaznom obščestve*, pp. 50, 328.

[131] Gak, *op. cit.*, p. 14.

[132] *Die deutsche MEW*, Bd. 3, p.

[133] This is the position represented by Gak, the authors of the sbornik, *Kommunizm i ličnost'*, I. S. Kon, V. P. Tugarinov (with certain qualifications) and many others.

[134] Tugarinov, *Ličnost'*, p. 93.

[135] Cf. also V. E. Davidovič, *op. cit.*, p. 46f.

[136] *Kommunizm i ličnost'*, p. 15.

[137] Gak, *op. cit.*, p. 20.

[138] Cf. the opening definition of the term 'person' in the *FE*, t. 3, p. 196; Tugarinov, *Ličnost'*, p. 43; L. V. Bueva, *Social'naja sreda i soznanie ličnosti*, M., 1968, p. 43.

[139] Tugarinov, *Ličnost'*, p. 43.

[140] *FE*, t. 3, p. 196.

[141] *Ibid.* Kon sometimes expresses himself as if he would include non-social characteristics in his conception of the person; but he does not carry this through in his discussion.

[142] B. D. Parygin, *Social'naja psixologija kak nauka*, L., 1965, p. 114.

[143] *Ibid.*

[144] K. K. Platonov, 'Psixologija ličnosti', in *Čelovek v socialističeskom i buržuaznom obščestve*, p. 310.

[145] S. L. Rubinštejn, *Bytie i soznanie*, M., 1957, p. 312. For a Soviet critique of Rubinštejn's definition of the person, see *Kommunizm i ličnost'*, p. 9f.

[146] Cf. T. R. Payne, *S. L. Rubinštejn and the Philosophical Foundations of Soviet Psychology*, Dordrecht, 1968, p. 137f.

[147] E. A. Budilova, K. A. Slavskaja, 'Problema ličnosti v trudax S. L. Rubinštejna', *Voprosy psixologii*, 1969, 5, 137–144.
[148] Tugarinov, *Ličnost'*, p. 45.
[149] *Ibid.*, p. 52.
[150] *Ibid.*, p. 61f.
[151] Gak, *op. cit.*, p. 18f.
[152] Tugarinov, *op. cit.*, p. 72f.
[153] Cf. the texts quoted by H. Fleischer, *Umrisse einer Philosophie des Menschen*, pp. 35–37: M. I. Petrosjan, *Gumanizm*, M., 1964, p. 188f; F. V. Konstantinov, 'Celovek i obščestvo', in *Celovek i epoxa*, M., 1964, p. 100; *et al.*
[154] V. P. Tugarinov, *Kommunizm i ličnost'* M., 1966, p. 31. Quoted in Fleischer, *op. cit.*, p. 36.
[155] A. F. Šiškin, 'Čelovek kak vysšaja cennost'', *VF* 1965, pp. 1, 3–15.
[156] *Ibid.*, p. 9.
[157] Cf. *Die deutsche Ideologie*, *MEW*, Bd. 3, pp.
[158] Afanas'ev, *op. cit.*, p. 27.
[159] Cf. A. G. Myslivčenko, 'Kritika ekzistencialistskogo ponimanija svobody', *VF* 1963, 10, 91–101; M. B. Mitin, 'Nesostojatel'nost' ekzistencialistskogo ponimanie ličnosti', *Ko* 1965, 8, 101–111; V. V. Lazarev, 'Ekzistencialistskaja koncepcija čeloveka v SŠA', *VF* 1967, 3, 160–169; R. A. Bozik, 'Kritika nekotoryx buržuaznyx koncepcij ličnosti v zapadno-germanskoj filosofii', *V LGU* 1966, 5, 74–82.
[160] Tugarinov, *Ličnost'*, p. 21.
[161] Afanas'ev, *op. cit.*, p. 31.
[162] *Ibid.*, p. 32.
[163] *Ibid.*
[164] *Ibid.*, p. 33.
[165] *Ibid.*, p. 34; Tugarinov, *Ličnost'*, p. 22.
[166] *Ibid.*
[167] *Ibid.*, p. 38.
[168] Tugarinov, *Ličnost'*, p. 21.
[169] Bueva, *op. cit.*, p. 73.
[170] *Ibid.*
[171] Tugarinov, *Ličnost'*, p. 20.
[172] V. I. Lenin, *Sočinenij*, t. 29, p. 194.
[173] Tugarinov, *Ličnost'*, p. 21.
[174] Bueva, *op. cit.*, pp. 67–69.
[175] *Ibid.*, p. 64. Cf. A. Schaff, 'Die Marxistische Auffassung vom Menschen', *Deutsche Zeitschrift für Philosophie*, 1965, 5.
[176] Bueva, *op. cit.*, p. 64.

CHAPTER VI

[1] The title of the book by L. V. Nikolaeva is: *Svoboda – neobxodimyj produkt istoričeskogo razvitija*, M., 1964.
[2] *FE*, t. 4, pp. 559–563.
[3] Cf. *ibid.*, pp. 564–567 (the entry 'free will').
[4] Such problems as immortality and the meaning of human life are among those now

being considered. Cf. I. D. Pancxava, *Čelovek, ego žiz'ni bessmertie*, M., 1967: V. I. Šinkaruk, 'Marksistskij gumanizm i problema smysla čelovečeskogo bytija', *VF* 1969, 6, 59–64.

[5] Cf. T. I. Ojzerman, 'Nekotorye aspekty marksistsko–leninskogo ponimanija svobody', *V MGU* 1966, 3, pp. 25–34.

[6] Cf., for example the above-quoted work by Nikolaeva.

[7] D. T. Axmedli, *Svoboda i neobxodimost'*, Baku, 1960, pp. 11–17. R. Gal'ceva uses a similar double-principled methodology in her article in the *Filosofskaja encyklopedija* *(op. cit.)*.

[8] *FS*, p. 397.

[9] V. E. Davidovič, *Problemy čelovečeskoj svobody*, L'vov, 1967, pp. 184–202.

[10] A. G. Myslivčenko, 'O vnutrennej svobody čeloveka', in *Problema čeloveka v sovremennoj filosofii*, M., 1969, pp. 248–268.

[11] S. N. Čxartišvili, 'Problema voli v psixologii', *Voprosy psixologii* 1967, 4, pp. 72–81.

[12] Cf., for example, Ojzerman, 'Nekotorye aspekty', p. 28. For the argument that the whole psychological problem should be placed in the sociological context, see N. N. Pospelov, 'V. I. Lenin o svobode i neobxodimosti', in *Kniga V. I. Lenin 'Materializm i empiriokriticizm'*, M., 1959, p. 280f.

[13] Cf. above, Ch. III, Section 2.2.

[14] S. L. Rubenštejn, *Grundlagen der allgemeinen Psychologie*, Berlin, 1962, p. 625f. (Unfortunately, the Russian original of this work was not available to the author.)

[15] I. S. Narskij points to this ambiguity and urges that the two senses be distinguished. Cf. 'Istolkovanie kategorii "slučajnost'"', *FN* 1970, 1, p. 52.

[15a] For a more extensive discussion of these alternative positions, see *Free Will and Determinism*, ed. by B. Berofsky, N.Y., 1966, especially the Preface and Introduction.

[16] *FE*, t. 1, p. 283.

[17] *Ibid.;* Davidovič, *op. cit.*, pp. 21–24; *KSPF*, p. 39f.

[18] Tugarinov, *Ličnost' i obščestvo*, M., 1965, p. 62.

[19] Davidovič, *op. cit.*, p. 15.

[20] Tugarinov, *Ličnost'*, p. 62.

[21] Ojzerman, 'Nekotorye aspekty', p. 28.

[22] Davidovič, *op. cit.*, pp. 28–30.

[23] Ojzerman, 'Nekotorye aspekty', p. 32.

[24] Besides the criticism of existentialism which is found in the articles on freedom, several special studies have been written on the existentialist notion of freedom: M. L. Čalin, 'Problema svobody v ekzistencializma', in *Kritika sovremennoj burzuaznoj filosofii i sociologii*, M., 1963; A. G. Myslivčenko, 'Kritika ekzistencialistskogo ponimanija svobody', *VF* 1963, 10, pp. 91–101; M. A. Kissel, 'Ontologija Žan-pol' Sartra – kritičeskij analiz', *V LGU* 1966, 17, pp. 53–65; V. Mixeev, 'Kritik an der existentialistischen Auffassung der Freiheit', in *Das Problem der Freiheit im Lichte des wissenschaftlichen Sozialismus*, Berlin, 1956, pp. 454–462.

[25] Mixeev, *op. cit.*, p. 455.

[26] T. A. Sakarova, 'Problema čeloveka v koncepcijax francuzskix ekzistencialistov', in *Sovremennyj ekzistencializm*, M., 1966, p. 302; Čalin, *op. cit.*, p. 188.

[27] Čalin, *op. cit.*, p. 189.

[28] Mixeev, *op. cit.*, p. 456f.

[29] A. Schaff, in his collection of essays, *A Philosophy of Man* (London, 1963), recognizes this gad-fly function of existentialism, but he denies the possible rapprochement of the existentialist and Marxist positions; they are, for him, essentially incompatible. Cf. p. 30.

[30] *KSPF*, p. 61.

[31] *FS*, p. 121.

[32] G. L. Andreev, *Xristianstvo i problema svoboda*, M., 1965, pp. 33–39; Ju. D. Krasovskij, 'Illjuzija svobody v ideologii baptizma', FN 1967, 4, pp. 109–115; Davidovič, *op. cit.*, p. 20.

[33] *FE*, t. 4, p. 564f.; cf. also Axmedli, *op. cit.*, pp. 18–20.

[34] Andreev, *op. cit.*, p. 17.

[35] *Ibid.*

[36] *Ibid.*, p. 78.

[37] *Ibid.*

[38] V. Afanas'ev, *Marxist Philosophy*, M., 1963, p. 146.

[39] *FE*, t. 4, p. 564.

[40] *Ibid.*; cf. also Nikolaeva, *op. cit.*, p. 14.

[41] Nikolaeva, *op. cit.*, p. 15, Axmedli, *op. cit.*, pp. 36–44.

[42] *FS*, p. 121.

[43] Davidovič, *op. cit.*, p. 19.

[44] G. A. Svečnikov, in *Filosofija i sovremennoe estestvoznanie*, M., 1968, p. 125.

[45] *FS*, p. 121; *KSPF*, p. 61.

[46] Davidovič, *op. cit.*, p. 18.

[47] *Ibid.*

[48] *Geschichte der Philosophie* (translation of *Istorija filosofii*, M., 1967), Berlin, 1962, Vol. 1, pp. 371–384; Afanas'ev, *op. cit.*, p. 28.

[49] *KSPF*, p. 258.

[50] *Geschichte der Philosophie*, p. 381; Axmedli, *op. cit.*, p. 35.

[51] Axmedli, *op. cit.*, p. 32.

[52] *Geschichte der Philosophie*, p. 378; Axmedli, p. 31.

[53] *KSPF*, p. 258; *Geschichte der Philosophie*, p. 381.

[54] Axmedli, *op. cit.*, p. 21.

[55] M. Dynnik, 'Das Problem der Notwendigkeit und Freiheit in der Geschichte der Philosophie der vormarxschen Epoche', in *Das Problem der Freiheit*, p. 114.

[56] Axmedli, *op. cit.*, p. 52.

[57] *Ibid.*, p. 53.

[58] *Ibid.*, p. 54.

[59] *Ibid.*

[60] *Ibid.*

[61] T. I. Ojzerman, 'Marksistsko-leninskoe rešenie problemy svobody i neobxodimosti', *VF* 1954, 2, p. 19.

[62] *Ibid.*

[63] Axmedli, *op. cit.*, p. 58.

[64] Ojzerman, 'Marksistsko–leninskoe rešenie', p. 20.

[65] Cf. I. V. Byčko, *Poznanie i svoboda*, M., 1969, p. 7.

[66] *Geschichte der Philosophie*, p. 99; Ojzerman, 'Marksistsko–leninskoe rešenie', p. 20.

[67] *KSPF*, p. 258.

[68] Ojzerman, 'Nekotorye aspekty', p. 25; Ojzerman, 'Marksistsko–leninskoe rešenie', p. 20.

[69] Ojzerman, 'Nekotorye aspekty', p. 26.

[70] Myslivčenko, *op. cit.*, p. 256.

[71] G. A. Wetter, *Der dialektische Materialismus*, Freiburg, 1960, pp. 447–451; G. Hampsch, *The Theory of Communism*, N.Y., pp. 94–99.

[72] G. V. Plekhanov, *Sočinenija,* izd. 2e, M., 1924–1927, t. VIII, p. 278 (italics mine).
[73] *Ibid.*
[74] *Ibid.*
[75] Byčko, *op. cit.,* p. 8.
[76] Pospelov, *op. cit.,* p. 276.
[77] Axmedli, *op. cit.,* p. 64.
[78] Pospelov, *op. cit.,* p. 277.
[79] *Ibid.,* p. 279.
[80] Pospelov leans toward this interpretation.
[81] Nikolaeva, *op. cit.,* p. 28; Axmedli, *op. cit.,* pp. 66–69; Pospelov, *op. cit.,* p. 282.
[82] Pospelov, *op. cit.,* p. 282.
[83] Axmedli, *op. cit.,* p. 68; Pospelov, *op. cit.,* p. 283.
[84] Pospelov, *op. cit.,* p. 283.
[85] Axmedli, *op. cit.,* p. 69.
[86] *Ibid.;* Nikolaeva, *op. cit.,* p. 38; Pospelov, *op. cit.,* p. 284.
[87] Pospelov, *op. cit.,* p. 285.
[88] Byčko, *op. cit.,* p. 155.
[89] *Ibid.,* p. 155.
[90] *Ibid.,* p. 154.
[91] *Ibid.*
[92] *Ibid.,* p. 6.
[93] *Ibid.,* p. 15, p. 30.
[94] *Ibid.,* p. 29.
[95] *Ibid.,* p. 31.
[96] *Ibid.*
[97] *Ibid.,* p. 34.
[98] *Ibid.,* p. 127f.
[99] *Ibid.,* p. 147.
[100] *Ibid.,* p. 149.
[101] *Ibid.,* p. 190.
[102] *Ibid.,* p. 193.
[103] *Ibid.,* p. 149.
[104] *Ibid.*
[105] *Ibid.,* p. 150.
[106] Ojzerman, 'Marksistsko–leninskoe rešenie', p. 25f; Davidovič, *op. cit.,* p. 17.
[107] *OMF,* p. 186f.
[108] *OMF,* p. 188.
[109] G. A. Wetter, *Soviet Ideology Today,* London, 1966, p. 72.
[110] *OMF,* p. 207.
[111] *OMF,* p. 210; *Fundamentals of Dialectical Materialism,* ed. by G. Kursanov, M., 1967, p. 220.
[112] A. V. Gulyga, *Čto takoe neobxodimost' i čto takoe slučajnost',* M., 1959, p. 24.
[113] *OMF,* p. 187; cf. also p. 210.
[114] *OMF,* p. 211.
[115] Wetter, *op. cit.,* pp. 86–89.
[116] *Ibid.,* p. 88.
[117] V. I. Kupcov, M. P. Terexov, 'Ponjatie determinizma v marksistskoj filosofii, *FN* 1970, 1, pp. 54–61; M. A. Parnjuk, *Determinizm dialektičeskogo materializma,* Kiev, 1967; I. V. Kuznecov, *Problema pričinnosti v sovremennoj fizike,* M., 1960.

[118] Cf. F. Rapp, *Gesetz und Determination in der Sowjetphilosophie*, Dordrecht, 1968.
[119] N. V. Pilipenko, *Neobxodimost' i slučajnost'*, M., 1965, p. 37f; G. M. Straks, 'O dialektike neobxodimosti i slučajnosti', *V MGU* 1966, 3, pp. 84–86; *Fundamentals*, p. 219.
[120] *Fundamentals*, p. 219.
[121] *Ibid.*, p. 220.
[122] *OMF*, p. 207.
[123] B. M. Kedrov, 'O determinizme', *FN* 1968, 1, p. 43; Gulyga, *op. cit.*, p. 28.
[124] *KSPF*, p. 185.
[125] *Ibid.*, p. 62.
[126] Kedrov, *op. cit.*, p. 47.
[127] *Ibid.*, p. 48.
[128] *Ibid.*
[129] Narskij, *op. cit.*, p. 51.
[130] *Ibid.*
[131] *Ibid.*
[132] *OMF*, p. 212.
[133] Byčko, *op. cit.*, p. 156.
[134] Ojzerman, 'Marksistsko–leninskoe rešenie', p. 26.
[135] *Fundamentals*, p. 230.
[136] Byčko, *op. cit.*, p. 157.
[136a] *OMF*, p. 216.
[137] *OMF*, p. 215.
[138] B. S. Ukraincev, 'Processy samoupravlenija i pričinnost'', *VF* 1968, 4, pp. 36–46.
[139] *Ibid.*, p. 39.
[140] *Ibid.*
[141] *Ibid.*, p. 40.
[142] *Ibid.*
[143] *Ibid.*, p. 41.
[144] *Ibid.*
[145] *Ibid.*
[146] *Ibid.*, p. 44.
[147] Ojzerman, 'Nekotorye aspekty', p. 26; Myslivčenko, *op. cit.*, p. 249; *FE*, t. 4, p. 560.
[148] Myslivčenko, *op. cit.*, p. 249; Byčko, *op. cit.*, p. 16f.
[149] Ojzerman, 'Nekotorye aspekty', p. 26.
[150] *Ibid.*
[151] *FE*, t. 4, p. 560.
[152] Myslivčenko, *op. cit.*, p. 249.
[153] *Ibid.*, p. 253.
[154] Davidovič, *op. cit.*, p. 15.
[155] Tugarinov, *Ličnost'*, p. 61; *FE*, t. 4, p. 559.
[156] Myslivčenko, *op. cit.*, p. 253.
[157] *Ibid.*, p. 251.
[158] Davidovič, *op. cit.*, p. 31.
[159] Myslivčenko, *op. cit.*, p. 254.
[160] Davidovič, *op. cit.*, p. 10.
[161] *KSPF*, p. 258.
[162] *FE*, t. 4, p. 559.

[163] Ojzerman, 'Nekotorye aspekty', p. 26.
[164] T. A. Kazakevič, 'Cel' i svoboda', *V LGU* 1968, 23, p. 53.
[165] Davidovič, *op. cit.*, p. 10.
[166] *Ibid.*, p. 11.
[167] *Ibid.*, p. 10.
[168] *Ibid.*, p. 15.
[169] Myslivčenko, *op. cit.*, p. 256.
[170] *Ibid.*
[171] Byčko, *op. cit.*, p. 34f.
[172] *Ibid.*, p. 202.
[173] *FE*, t. 4, p. 559.
[174] Davidovič, *op. cit.*, p. 15.
[175] Myslivčenko, *op. cit.*, p. 259.
[176] *Ibid.*, p. 260.
[177] *Ibid.*, p. 264.
[178] *Ibid.*
[179] *Ibid.*
[180] Davidovič, *op. cit.*, p. 71.

CHAPTER VII

[1] N. N. Trubnikov, 'Otnošenie celi, sredstva i resultata dejatel'nosti čeloveka', *VF* 1964, 6, p. 60.
[2] *Ibid.*
[3] Lenin, *Tetrady*, p. 171.
[4] I. V. Byčko, *Poznanie i svoboda*, M., 1969, p. 33.
[5] A. Spirkin, *Kurs marksistskoj filosofii*, M., 1966, p. 102.
[6] M. B. Turovskij, *Trud i myšlenie*, M., 1963, p. 126.
[7] Trubnikov, *op. cit.*, p. 61.
[8] V. N. Kodin, 'K probleme opredelenija ponjatija "cel"', *V MGU* 1968, 1, p. 30.
[9] Trubnikov, *op. cit.*, p. 66.
[10] Kodin, *op. cit.*, p. 31f.
[11] M. G. Makarov, 'Cel', in *Nekotorye voprosy dialektičeskogo materializma*, L., 1962, p. 140.
[12] *Ibid.*, p. 140.
[13] *Ibid.*
[14] O. I. Džioev, *Priroda istoričeskoj neobxodimosti*, Tbilisi, 1967, p. 16.
[15] *Ibid.*, p. 15.
[16] Makarov, *op. cit.*, p. 143.
[17] E. G. Judin, 'Filosofskij analiz struktury dejatel'nosti', *VF* 1968, 9, p. 163f.
[18] N. N. Trubnikov, *O kategorijax 'cel'', 'sredstvo', 'resultat'*, M., 1968.
[19] Judin, p. 163.
[20] *Ibid.*, p. 164.
[21] V. P. Tugarinov, *Teorija cennosti v marksizme*, L., 1968, p. 18.
[22] O. M. Bakuradze, 'Istina i cennost'', *VF* 1966, 7, p. 45.
[23] *Ibid.*, p. 47.
[24] *Ibid.*

[25] Džioev, *op. cit.*, p. 92.

[26] *Ibid.*, p. 93.

[27] O. I. Džioev, 'Cennost' i istoričeskaja neobxodimost'', *FN* 1966, 6, p. 36.

[28] Džioev, *Priroda*, p. 93.

[29] Džioev, 'Cennost'', p. 35.

[30] *Ibid.*, p. 36.

[31] A. I. Santalov, 'Ugolovnaja otvetstvennost' i "svoboda voli"', *V LGU* 1968, 5, p. 120f.

[32] T. I. Ojzerman, 'Nekotorye aspekty marksistsko–leninskogo ponimanija svobody', *V MGU* 1966, 3, p. 25.

[33] *Ibid.*, p. 28.

[34] B. P. Šubnjakov, 'Marksistsko–leninskoe ponimanie svobody voli', in *Naučnya trudy,* Jaroslav. Gos. ped. inst., t. 2, vyp. 2, Jaroslavl', 1963, p. 124.

[35] V. E. Davidovič, *Problemy čelovečeskoj svobody,* L'vov, 1967, p. 194.

[36] Ojzerman, *op. cit.*, p. 28.

[37] Davidovič, *op. cit.*, p. 195.

[38] *Ibid.*, pp. 195–198.

[39] *Ibid.*, p. 199.

[40] P. V. Simonov, *Čto takoe emocija,* M., 1966, p. 36.

[41] Davidovič, *op. cit.*, p. 199.

[42] *Ibid.*

[43] V. I. Selivanov, 'K voprosu o ponjatii voli v psixologii', in *Učennye zapiski,* Rjansk. Gos. ped. inst., t. 59, p. 97.

[44] V. I. Selivanov, 'Ponjatie voli v psixologii', in *Materialy vtoroj mežvuzovskoj naučnoj konferencii po problemam psixologii voli,* Rjazan', 1967, p. 4.

[45] Selivanov, 'K voprosu', p. 97f.

[46] *Ibid.*

[47] V. I. Selivanov, 'Problema voli v sovetskoj psixologii', *Voprosy psixologii,* 1964, 1, p. 84.

[48] A. N. Leont'ev, *Problemy razvitija psixiki,* M., 1965, p. 348.

[49] Davidovič, *op. cit.*, p. 184.

[50] *Ibid.*, p. 185.

[51] *Ibid.*

[52] Quoted in T. Földesi, *The Problem of Free Will,* Budapest, 1966, p. 178.

[53] Cf. E. V. Milerian, 'Involuntary and Voluntary Attention', in *Psychology in the Soviet Union,* Stanford, 1957, p. 90.

[54] Selivanov, 'Problema voli', p. 85.

[55] Byčko, *op. cit.*, pp. 150–152; Davidovič, *op. cit.*, p. 186.

[56] E. V. Šoroxova, 'Princip determinizma v psixologii', in *Metodologičeskie i teoretičeskie problemy psixologii,* M., 1969, p. 23.

[57] *Ibid.*

[58] Davidovič, *op. cit.*, p. 185.

[59] N. M. Amosov, *Modelirovanie myšlenija i psixiki,* Kiev, 1965, p. 220f; quoted in Davidovič, *op. cit.*, p. 190.

[60] Šubnjakov, *op. cit.*, p. 124f; Santalov, *op. cit.*, p. 22.

[61] Davidovič, *op. cit.*, p. 191f.

[62] *Ibid.*

[63] Ojzerman, 'Nekotorye aspekty', p. 28.

[64] *Ibid.*

[65] V. P. Tugarinov, *Sootnošenie kategorij istoričeskogo materializma*, L., 1958, p. 110.

[66] *Ibid.*

[67] *FE*, t. 4, p. 564.

[68] Davidovič, *op. cit.*, p. 187.

[69] *Ibid.*, p. 188.

[70] *Ibid.*, p. 193.

[71] S. N. Čxartišvili, 'Problema voli v psixologii', *Voprosy psixologii* 1967, 4, p. 72.

[72] *Ibid.*

[73] *Ibid.*, p. 73.

[74] *Ibid.*, p. 74.

[75] *Ibid.*, p. 76.

[76] *Ibid.*, p. 77.

[77] *Ibid.*, p. 78.

[78] *Ibid.*, p. 79.

[79] *Ibid.*

[80] *Ibid.*, p. 80.

[81] Cf. A. F. Šiškin, *Osnovy marksistskoj etiki*, M., 1961, and *Osnovy kommunističeskij morali*, M., 1955; N. V. Rybakova, *Očerki marksistko–leninskoj etike*, L., 1963; M. S. Danieljan, *Nekotorye voprosy marksistsko–leninskoj etiki*, Erevan, 1962.

[82] Cf. the above and: A. P. Čermenina, 'Ponimanie svobody v marksistsko–leninskoj etike', *FN*, 1964, 6, pp. 111–118.

[83] D. A. Kerimov, 'Svoboda i pravo', *FN* 1964, 3, p. 20f.

[84] Čermenina, *op. cit.*, p. 112.

[85] V. T. Efimov, 'Problema svobody i neobxodimosti v marksistsko–leninskoj etike', *FN* 1959, 2, p. 68.

[86] *Ibid.*

[87] Šiškin, *Osnovy*, p. 204.

[88] Ivanov, Rybakova, *op. cit.*, p. 147.

[89] N. A. Beljaev, D. A. Kerimov, 'Ličnost' i zakonnost'', in *Čelovek i obščestvo*, L., 1966, p. 131.

[90] Čermenina, *op. cit.*, p. 115.

[91] Ivanov, Rybakova, *op. cit.*, p. 142.

[92] Šiškin, *Osnovy*, p. 171f.

[93] *Ibid.*, p. 173f.; K. A. Švarcman, *Etika bez morali*, M., 1964, p. 164.

[94] Čermenina, *op. cit.*, p. 117.

[95] Šiškin, *Osnovy*, p. 205f.

[96] *Ibid.*, p. 171.

[97] Kerimov, 'Svoboda', p. 20.

[98] Čermenina, *op. cit.*, p. 118.

[99] Šiškin, *Osnovy*, p. 395.

[100] *Kratkij slovar po etike*, M., 1965, p. 398.

[101] *Ibid.*; *Kommunizm i ličnost'*, M., 1964, p. 342.

[102] Cf., for example, D. T. Axmedli, *Svoboda i neobxodimost'*, Baku, 1960, pp. 106–162.

[103] *FE*, t. 4, p. 560.

[104] *FS*, p. 436.

[105] *FE*, t. 4, p. 561.

[105a] P. M. Egides, *Smysl žizni – v čem on?*, M., 1963, p. 33.

[106] *Ibid.*

[107] A. F. Šiškin, 'Čelovek kak vysšaja cennost'', *VF* 1965, 1, p. 12.

[108] *Ibid.*
[109] I. D. Pancxava, *Čelovek, ego žizn' i bessmertie*, M., 1967, p. 92.
[110] G. K. Gumnickij, 'Smysl žizni, sčast'e, moral'', *VF* 1967, 5, p. 102.
[111] *Ibid.*, p. 104.
[112] *Ibid.*, p. 103.
[113] N. M. Berežnoj, 'Obosnovanie K. Marksom naučnoj koncepcii čeloveka v "Kapitale"', in *Filosofskie problemy "Kapitala" K. Marksa*, M., 1968, p. 145.
[114] A. F. Šiškin, 'Socializm i moral'nye cennosti čelovečestva', *VF* 1967, 10, p. 71; cf. also T. V. Samsonova, 'K analizu problemy ličnosti v "Kapitale" K. Marska', in *Filosofskie problemy "Kapitale" K. Marska*, p. 175, p. 179; Byčko, *op. cit.*, p. 26.
[115] M. T. Iovčuk, 'Problema duxovnoj svobody ličnosti', in *Ličnost' pri socializme*, M., 1968, p. 164.
[115a] N. V. Markov, 'Trud umstvennyj i fizičeskij', *VF* 1968, 11, pp. 37–46.
[116] L. A. Margolin, 'Svoboda vybora professii', in *Ličnost' pri socializme*, pp. 179–187.

BIBLIOGRAPHY

(WORKS CITED)

Adams, H. P.: *Karl Marx in His Earlier Writings,* London, 1965.
Afanas'ev, V.:
(1) *Marxist Philosophy,* M., 1963.
(2) 'O celostnosti ličnosti' (On the Integrity of the Person), in *Kollektiv i ličnost'.*
Amosov, N. M.: *Modelirovanie myšlenija i psixiki* (The Modeling of Thought and Psyche), Kiev, 1965.
Andreev, G. L.: *Xristianstvo i problemy svobody* (Christianity and the Problems of Freedom), M., 1965.
Axmedli, D. T.: *Svoboda i neobxodimost'* (Freedom and Necessity), Baku, 1960.
Bakuradze, O. M.: 'Istina i cennost'' (Truth and Value), *VF* 1966, 7, pp. 45–48.
Balyčeva, G. D.: 'Voprosy socialističeskogo gumanizma v trudax V. I. Lenina' (Questions of Socialist Humanism in the works of V. I. Lenin), *FN* 1969, 5, pp. 14–24.
Batiščev, G. S.: 'Obščestvenno-istoričeskaja, dejatel'naja suščnost' čeloveka' (The Historical, Active Essence of Man), *VF* 1967, 3, pp. 20–29.
Bauer, R. A.: *The New Man in Soviet Psychology,* Cambridge, 1952.
Beljaev, N. A. and Kerimov, D. A.: 'Ličnost' i zakonnost'' (Person and Law), in *Čelovek i obščestvo.*
Berežnoj, N. M.: 'Obosnovanie K. Marksom naučnoj koncepcii čeloveka v "Kapitale"' (Marx's Foundation of a Scientific Conception of Man in *Capital*), in *Filosofskie problemy 'Kapitale' K. Marksa.*
Bibler, V. S.: *O sisteme kategorii dialektičeskoj logiki* (On the System of the Categories of Dialectical Logic), Dušanbe, 1958.
Bocheński, J. M.:
(1) *Contemporary European Philosophy,* Berkeley and Los Angeles, 1957.
(2) *Soviet Russian Dialectical Materialism,* Dordrecht, 1963.
(3) *Die kommunistische Ideologie und die Würde, Freiheit und Gleichheit der Menschen im Sinne des Grundgesetzes für die Bundesrepublik vom 23. Mai 1949,* Regensburg, 1963.
(4) 'The Great Split', *SST* 1968, 1, pp. 1–15.
Bozik, R. A.: 'Kritika nekotoryx buržuaznyx koncepcij ličnosti v zapadnogermanskoj filosofii' (Critique of Several Bourgeois Conceptions of the Person in West German Philosophy), *V LGU* 1966, 5, pp. 74–82.
Buchholz, A.: 'Problems of the Ideological East–West Conflict', *SST* I, 1961, pp. 120–132.
Budilova, E. A. and Slavskaja, K. A.: 'Problema ličnosti v trudax S. L. Rubinštejna' (The Problem of the Person in the Works of S. L. Rubinštejn), *Voprosy psixologii* 1969, 5, pp. 137–144.
Bueva, L. V.: *Social'naja sreda i soznanie ličnosti* (The Social Environment and the Consciousness of the Person), M., 1968.
Byčko, I. V.: *Poznanie i svoboda* (Knowledge and Freedom), M., 1969.
Čagin, B. A.: *Sub'ektivnyj faktor. Struktura i zakonomernosti* (The Subjective Factor. Structure and Laws), M., 1968.

Čalin, M. L.: 'Problema svobody v ekzistencializma' (The Problem of Freedom in Existentialism), in *Kritika sovremennoj buržuaznoj filosofii i sociologii.*
Calvez, J.: *La pensée de Karl Marx,* Paris, 1956.
Čelovek i epoxa (Man and the Present Age), M., 1964.
Čelovek i obščestvo (Man and Society), M., 1966.
Čelovek v socialističeskom i buržuaznom obščestve (Man in Socialist and Bourgeois Society), M., 1966.
Čermenina, A. P.: 'Ponimanie svobody v marksistsko–leninskoj etike' (The Conception of Freedom in Marxist–Leninist Ethics), *FN* 1964, 6, pp. 111–118.
Čxartišvili, S. N.: 'Problema voli v psixologii' (The Problem of Will in Psychology), *Voprosy psixologii* 1967, 4, pp. 72–81.
Danieljan, M. S.: *Nekotorye voprosy marksistsko–leninskoj etiki* (Some Questions in Marxist–Leninist Ethics), Erevan, 1962.
Das Problem der Freiheit im Lichte des wissenschaftlichen Sozialismus, Berlin, 1956.
Davidovič, V. E.: *Problemy čeloveceskoj svobody* (Problems of Human Freedom), L'vov, 1967.
DeGeorge, R. T.:
(1) 'The Soviet Concept of Man', *SST* 1964, 4.
(2) *Patterns of Soviet Thought,* Ann Arbor, 1966.
(3) *The New Marxism,* N.Y., 1968.
Dobzhansky, T.: *The Biological Basis of Human Freedom,* N.Y., 1956.
Drozdov, A. V.: *Čelovek i obščestvennye otnošenija* (Man and Social Relations), L., 1966.
Dunayevskaya, R.: *Marxism and Freedom,* N.Y., 1958.
Dynnik, M.: 'Das Problem der Notwendigkeit und Freiheit in der Geschichte der Philosophie der vormarxschen Epoche', in *Das Problem der Freiheit im Lichte des wissenschaftlichen Sozialismus.*
Džioev, O. I.:
(1) 'Cennost' i istoričeskaja neobxodimost'' (Value and Historical Necessity), *FN* 1966, 6, pp. 34–39.
(2) *Priroda istoričeskoj neobxodimosti* (The Nature of Historical Necessity), Tbilisi, 1967.
Efimov, V. T.: 'Problema svobody i neobxodimosti v marksistsko–leninskoj etike' (The Problem of Freedom and Necessity in Marxist–Leninist Ethics), *FN* 1959, 2, pp. 66–76.
Egides, P. M.: *Smysl žizni – v cem on?* (What is the Meaning of Life?), M., 1963.
Fainsod, M.: *How Russia Is Ruled,* Cambridge, 1965.
Falk, H.: *Die ideologischen Grundlagen des Kommunismus,* München, 1961.
Fetscher, I.:
(1) *Die Freiheit im Lichte des Marxismus–Leninismus,* Bonn, 1963.
(2) 'Marx's Concretization of the Concept of Freedom', in *Socialist Humanism,* pp. 238–249.
Filosofija i sovremennoe estestvoznanie (Philosophy and Contemporary Science), M., 1968.
Filosofskaja enciklopedija (Philosophical Encyclopedia), 5 Vols., M., 1960ff.
Filosofskie problemy 'Kapitale' K. Marksa (Philosophical Problems of Marx's *Capital*), M., 1968.
Filosofskij slovar' (Philosophical Dictionary), M., 1963.
Fleischer, H.:
(1) 'The Limits of Party-Mindedness', *SST* 1962, 2, pp. 119–131.
(2) *Die Ontologie im dialektischen Materialismus,* polycopied, Berlin, 1964.
(3) *Philosophie in der Sowjetunion 1964–1965,* Berlin, 1966.

(4) *Umrisse einer 'Philosophie des Menschen'*, Berlin, 1967.
Földesi, T.: *The Problem of Free Will*, Budapest, 1966.
Free Will and Determinism, ed. by B. Berofsky, N.Y., 1966.
Fromm, E.: *Marx's Concept of Man*, N.Y., 1961.
Friedrich, C. J. and Brzezinski, Z.: *Totalitarian Dictatorships and Autocracy*, 2nd ed., Cambridge, 1965.
Fundamentals of Dialectical Materialism, ed. by G. Kursanov, M., 1967.
Gak, G. M.: *Dialektika kollektivnosti i individual'nosti* (The Dialectics of Collectivity and Individuality), M., 1967.
Geschichte der Philosophie (translation of *Istorija filosofii*), Berlin, 1962.
Glezerman, G. E.: 'Obščestvo, kollektiv, ličnost'' (Society, the Collective and the Person), in *Kollektiv i ličnost'*.
Gulyga, A.: *Čto takoe neobxodimost' i čto takoe slučajnost'?* (What is Necessity and What is Contingency?), M., 1959.
Gumnickij, G. K.: 'Smysl žizni, sčast'e, moral'' (The Meaning of Life, Happiness, Morality), *VF* 1967, 5, pp. 102–105.
Hampsch, G.: *The Theory of Communism*, N.Y., 1965.
Hegel, G. F. W.: *Werke*, Jubiläumsausgabe, Stuttgart, 1927–1939.
Hook, S.: *Marx and the Marxists: the Ambiguous Legacy*, Princeton, N.J., 1955.
Il'enkov, E. V.: 'From a Marxist–Leninist Point of View'. in *Marx and the Western World*, pp. 391–408.
Iovčuk, M. T.: 'Problema duxovnoj svobody ličnosti' (The Problem of the Spiritual Freedom of the Person), in *Ličnost' pri socializme*, pp. 162–178.
Istorija filosofii (History of Philosophy), 6 Vols., M., 1957ff.
Jordan, Z. A.: *The Evolution of Dialectical Materialism*, N.Y., 1967.
Judin, E. G.: 'Filosofskij analiz struktury dejatel'nosti' (A Philosophical Analysis of the Structure of Activity), *VF* 1968, 2, pp. 161–165.
Kamenka, E.: 'Philosophers in Moscow', *Survey*, Jan., 1967.
Kazakevič, T. A.:
(1) 'Celesoobraznost'' (Purposefulness), in *Nekotorye voprosy dialektičeskogo materializma*, pp. 118–138.
(2) 'Cel' i svoboda' (Goal and Freedom), *V LGU* 1968, 23, pp. 50–59.
Kedrov, B. M.: 'O determinizme' (On Determinism), *FN* 1968, 1, pp. 41–48.
Kerimov, D. A.: 'Svoboda i pravo' (Freedom and Law), *FN* 1964, 3, pp. 14–24.
Kissel, M. A.: 'Ontologija Žan-Pol' Sartra. Kritičeskij analiz' (The Ontology of Jean Paul Sartre. Critical Analysis), *V LGU* 1966, 17, pp. 53–65.
Kniga V. I. Lenina 'Materializm i empiriokriticizm' (Lenin's 'Materialism and Empiriocriticism'), M., 1959.
Kodin, V. N.: 'K probleme opredelenija ponjatija "cel"' (On the Problem of the Definition of the Concept of "Goal"), *V MGU* 1968, 1, pp. 29–35.
Köhler, H.: *Das Menschenbild des dialektischen Materialismus*, München, 1957.
Kollektiv i ličnost' (The Collective and the Person), M., 1968.
Kommunizm i ličnost' (Communism and the Person), M., 1964.
Kon, I. S.: *Sociologija ličnosti* (Sociology of the Person), M., 1967.
Konstantinov, F. V.: 'Čelovek i obščestvo' (Man and Society), in *Čelovek i epoxa*.
Krasovskij, Ju. D.: 'Illjuzija svobody v ideologii baptizma' (The Illusion of Freedom in the Ideology of the Baptist Religion), *FN* 1967, 4, pp. 109–115.
Kratkij slovar' po etike (Concise Dictionary of Ethics), M., 1965.
Kratkij slovar' po filosofii (Concise Dictionary of Philosophy), M., 1966.

Kritika sovremennoj buržuaznoj filosofii i sociologii (Critique of Contemporary Bourgeois Philosophy and Sociology), M., 1963.

Kupcov, V. I., Terexov, M. P.: 'Ponjatie determinizma v marksistskoj filosofi' (The Concept of Determinism in Marxist Philosophy), *FN* 1970, 1, pp. 54–61.

Kuznecov, I. V.: *Problema pričinnosti v sovremennoj fizike* (The Problem of Causality in Contemporary Physics), M., 1960.

Lazarev, V. V.: 'Ekzistencialistskaja koncepcija čeloveka v SŠA' (The Existentialist Conception of Man in the U.S.A.), *VF* 1967, 3, pp. 160–169.

Lenin, V. I.:

    (1) *Polnoe sobranie sočinenij* (Collected Works), izdanie pjatoe, M., 1958ff.

    (2) *Collected Works*, M., 1961.

    (3) *Materialism and Empiriocriticism*, M., 1964.

    (4) *The Teachings of Karl Marx*, N.Y., 1964.

Leont'ev, A. N.: *Problemy razvitija psixiki* (Problems of the Development of the Psyche), M., 1965.

Ličnost' pri socializme (The Person in Socialism), M., 1968.

Lieber, H.-J.: *Individuum und Gesellschaft in der Sowjetunion*, Wolfenbüttel, 1964.

Ljubutin, K. N.: 'Starye idei v novoj odežde' (Old Ideas in New Dress), *VF* 1965, 7, pp. 126–136.

Lobkowicz, N.: 'Die Philosophie in der Sowjetforschung', *Moderne Welt*, 1966, 2.

Mabbot, J. D.: 'Free Will', in *Encyclopaedia Brittanica*, 1965, Vol. 9, pp. 853–857.

Makarov, M. G.:

    (1) 'Cel'' (Goal), in *Nekotorye voprosy dialektičeskogo materializma*, pp. 139–152.

    (2) 'Nekotorye aspekty kategorii celi v svjazi s razvitiem kibernetiki' (Several Aspects of the Category Goal in Connection with the Development of Cybernetics), in *Učennye zapiski*, Tartu GU, vypusk 165, Tartu, 1965.

Margolin, L. A.: 'Svoboda vybora professi' (The Free Choice of a Profession), in *Ličnost pri socializme*, pp. 179–187.

Marko, K.:

    (1) *Sic et non. Kritisches Wörterbuch des sowjetrussischen Marxismus–Leninismus der Gegenwart*, Wiesbaden, 1962.

    (2) 'Soviet Ideology and Sovietology', *Soviet Studies* XIX, Apr., 1968.

Markov, N. V.: 'Trud umstvennyj i fizičeskij' (Intellectual and Manual Labor), *VF* 1968, 11, pp. 37–46.

Marx, K.: *Grundrisse der Kritik der politischen Ökonomie, Rohentwurf*, Berlin, 1953.

Marx, K. Engels, F.:

    (1) *Marx–Engels Werke*, Berlin, 1958–1968.

    (2) *Ausgewählte Schriften*, Berlin, 1966.

Marx and the Western World, ed. by N. Lobkowicz, Notre Dame, 1967.

Marxistische Philosophie. Lehrbuch, ed. by A. Kosing, Berlin, 1967.

Materialy vtoroj mežvuzovskoj naučnoj konferencii po problemam psixologii voli (Materials of the Second Inter-University Scientific Conference on the Problems of the Psychology of the Will), Rjazan', 1967.

Mayer, G.: *Friedrich Engels: Eine Biographie*, 2 Vols., The Hague, 1934.

Meljuxin, S. T.: *Materija v ee edinstve, beskonečnosti i razvitii* (Matter in Its Unity, Infinity and Development), M., 1960.

Metodologičeskie i teoretičeskie problemy psixologii (Methodological and Theoretical Problems of Psychology), M., 1969.

Milerian, E. A.: 'Involuntary and Voluntary Attention', in *Psychology in the Soviet Union*, pp. 84–91.

Mitin, M. B.:
  (1) 'Nesostojatel'nost' ekzistencialistskogo ponimanie ličnosti' (The Untenability of the Existentialist Conception of the Person), *Kommunist* 1965, 8, pp. 101–111.
  (2) 'V. I. Lenin i problema čeloveka' (V. I. Lenin and the Problem of Man), *VF* 1967, 8, pp. 19–30.

Mixeev, V.: 'Kritik an der existentialistischen Auffassung der Freiheit', in *Das Problem der Freiheit im Lichte des wissenschaftlichen Sozialismus*, pp. 454–462.

Monnerot, J.: *Sociologie du communisme*, Paris, 1949.

Myslivčenko, A. G.:
  (1) 'Kritika ekzistencialistskogo ponimanija svobody' (Critique of the Existentialist Understanding of Freedom), *VF* 1963, 10, pp. 91–101.
  (2) 'O vnutrennej svobody čeloveka' (On the Inner Freedom of Man), in *Problema čeloveka v sovremennoj filosofii*, pp. 248–268.

Narskij, I. S.:
  (1) 'O probleme "čeloveceskoj prirody" v rannix trudax K. Marksa' (On the Problem of Human Nature in the Early Works of K. Marx), *V MGU* 1967, 6, pp. 11–20.
  (2) 'Istolkovanie kategorii "slučajnost"'' (The Interpretation of the Category 'Contingency'), *FN* 1970, 1, pp. 43–53.

Naučnye trudy, Gos. ped. inst., t. 2, vypusk z, Jaroslavl' 1963.

Nekotorye voprosy dialektičeskogo materializma (Problems of Dialectical Materialism), L., 1962.

Neubauer, F.: *Das Verhältnis von Karl Marx und Friedrich Engels dargestellt an der Bestimmung der menschlichen Freiheit in deren Schriften*, Meisenheim/Glan, 1960.

Nikolaeva, L. V.: *Svoboda – neobxodimyj produkt istoričeskogo razvitie* (Freedom – A Necessary Product of Historical Development), M., 1964.

Novik, I. B.: 'O kategorijax "vešč"' i "otnošenie"' (On the Categories 'Thing' and 'Relation'), *VF* 1957, 4.

Nuttin, J.: *Psychoanalysis and Personality*, N.Y., 1962.

Ojzerman, T. I.:
  (1) 'Marksistko–leninskoe rešenie problemy svobody i neobxodimosti' (The Marxist–Leninist Solution of the Problem of Freedom and Necessity) *VF* 1954, 3, pp. 16–33.
  (2) 'Nekotorye aspekty marksistsko–leninskogo ponimanija svobody' (Some Aspects of the Marxist–Leninist Understanding of Freedom).
  (3) *Formirovanie filosofii marksizma* (The Formation of Marxist Philosophy), M., 1962.
  (4) *Problemy istoriko–filosofskoj nauki* (Problems of Historico–Philosophical Science), M., 1969.

Osnovy marksistskoj filosofii (The Fundamentals of Marxist Philosophy), M., 1963.

Pancxava, I. D.: *Čelovek, ego žizn' i bessmertie* (Man: His Life and Immortality), M., 1967.

Parnjuk, M. A.: *Determinizm dialektičeskogo materializma* (The Determinism of Dialectical Materialism), Kiev, 1967.

Parnjuk, M. A., Jacenko, A.: 'Vozmožnost', dejstvitel'nost' i cel'' (Possibility, Actuality and Goal), in *Problema vozmožnosti i dejstvitel'nosti*, pp. 142–157.

Parygin, B. D.: *Social'naja psixologija kak nauka* (Social Psychology As a Science), L., 1965.

Payne, T. R.: *S. L. Rubenštejn and the Philosophical Foundations of Soviet Psychology*, Dordrecht, 1968.

Petrosjan, M. I.:
(1) *Gumanizm* (Humanism), M., 1964.
(2) *Essay über den Humanismus* (translation of *Gumanizm*), Berlin, 1966.
Petrovič, G.: *Marx in the Mid-Twentieth Century*, N.Y., 1967.
Pilipenko, N. V.: *Neobxodimost' i slučajnost'* (Necessity and Contingency), M., 1966.
Platonov, K. K.: 'Psixologija ličnosti' (The Psychology of the Person), in *Čelovek v socialis- tičeskom i buržuaznom obščestve*.
Plekhanov, G. V.:
(1) *Sočinenija* (Works), 2nd ed., M., 1924–1927.
(2) *Izbrannye filosofskie proizvedenija* (Selected Philosophical Works), M.
(3) *The Role of the Individual in History*, N.Y., 1940.
Pospelov, N. N.: 'V. I. Lenin o svobode i neobxodimosti' (V. I. Lenin On Freedom and Necessity), in *Kniga V. I. Lenina 'Materializm i Empriokriticizm'*, pp. 273–288.
Problema čeloveka v sovremennoj filosofii (The Problem of Man in Contemporary Philoso- phy), M., 1969.
Problema vozmožnosti i dejstvitel'nosti (The Problem of Possibility and Actuality), M.-L., 1964.
Problemy formirovanie ličnosti i volevoj process (Problems of the Formation of the Person and the Volitional Process), M., 1968.
Psychology in the Soviet Union, edited by B. Simon, Stanford, 1957.
Reshetar, J. S.: *The Soviet Polity*, N.Y., 1971.
Rapp, F.: *Gesetz und Determination in der Sowjetphilosophie*, Dordrecht, 1968.
Rodriges, S.: 'Problema čeloveka i kategorija "otčuždennyj trud" v "Ekonomičesko- filosofskix Rukopisjax 1844 Goda" K. Marska' (The Problem of Man and the Category of "Alienated Labor" in the "Economic-Philosophical Manuscripts of 1844"), *V MGU* 1969, 5, pp. 69–76.
Rossiter, C.: *Marxism: the View from America*, N.Y., 1960.
Rubinštejn, S. L.:
(1) *Bytie i soznanie* (Being and Consciousness), M., 1957.
(2) *Grundlagen der allgemeinen Psychologie* (translation of *Osnovy obščej psixologii*, M., 1946).
Rybakova, N. V.: *Očerki marksistsko–leninskoj etike* (Marxist–Leninist Ethics), L., 1963.
Sakarova, T. A.: 'Problema čeloveka v koncepcijax francuzkix ekzistencialistov' (The Problem of Man in the French Existentialists), in *Sovremennyj ekzistencializm*.
Samsonova, T. V.: 'K analizu problemy ličnosti v "Kapitale" K. Marska' (An Analysis of the Problem of the Person in Marx's *Capital*), in *Filosofskie problemy "Kapitale" K. Marska*, pp. 157–178.
Santalov, A. I.: 'Ugolovnaja otvetstvennost'' i "svoboda voli" (Criminal Responsibility and "Free Will"), *V LGU* 1968, 5, pp. 118–123.
Schaff, A.:
(1) *A Philosophy of Man*, N.Y., 1963.
(2) 'Die marxistische Auffassung vom Menschen', *Deutsche Zeitschrift für Philosophie*, 1965, 5.
Selivanov, V. I.:
(1) 'Problema voli v sovetskoj psixologii' (The Problem of the Will in Soviet Psychology), *Voprosy psixologii* 1964, 1, pp. 83–93.
(2) 'Ponjatie voli v psixologii' (The Concept of Will in Psychology), in *Materialy vtoroj mežvuzovskoj naučnoj konferencii po problemam psixologii voli*, pp. 3–5.
(3) 'K voprosu o ponjatii voli v psixologii' (On the Problem of the Concept of Will

in Psychology), in *Problemy formirovanija ličnosti i volevoj process,* pp. 96–110.

Simonov, P. V.: *Čto takoe emocija?* (What is Emotion?), M., 1966.

Šinkaruk, V. I.: Marksistkij gumanizm i problema smysla čelovečeskogo bytija' (Marxist Humanism and the Problem of the Meaning of Human Existence), *VF* 1969, 6, pp. 59–67.

Šiškin, A. F.:
(1) *Osnovy kommunističeskoj morali* (The Foundations of Communist Morality), M., 1955.
(2) *Osnovy marksistskoj etiki* (The Foundations of Marxist Ethics), M., 1961.
(3) 'Čelovek kak vysšaja cennost'' (Man as the Supreme Value), *VF* 1965, 1, pp. 3–15.
(4) 'Socializm i moral'nye cennosti čelovečestva' (Socialism and the Moral Values of Humanity), *VF* 1967, 10, pp. 64–75.

Smirnov, G. L.:
(1) *Formirovanie kommunističeskix obščestvennyx otnošenij* (The Formation of Communist Social Relations), M., 1962.
(2) 'Svoboda i otvetstvennost' ličnosti' (Freedom and the Responsibility of the Person), in *Kollektiv i ličnost',* pp. 128–148.

Šoroxova, E. V.: 'Princip determinizm v psixologii' (The Principle of Determinism in Psychology), in *Metodologičeskie i teoretičeskie problemy psixologii,* pp. 9–56.

Sovremennyj ekzistencializm (Contemporary Existentialism), M., 1966.

Spirkin, A.: *Kurs marksistskoj filosofii* (A Course in Marxist Philosophy), M., 1966.

Štraks, G. M.: 'O dialektike neobxodimosti i slučajnosti' (On the Dialectics of Necessity and Contingency), *V MGU* 1966, 3, pp. 84–86.

Šubnjakov, B. P.: 'Marksistsko–leninskoe ponimanie svobody voli' (The Marxist–Leninist Conception of Free Will), in *Naucnye trudy.*

Švarcman, K. A.: *Etika bez morali* (Ethics Without Morals) M., 1964.

Trubnikov, N. N.:
(1) 'Otnošenie celi, sredstva i rezul'tata dejatel'nosti čeloveka' (The Relation of the Goal, Means and Result of Human Activity), *VF* 1964, 6, pp. 59–68.
(2) *O kategorijax "cel'", "sredstvo", "rezultat"* (On the Categories "Goal", "Means", "Result"), M., 1968.

Tugarinov, V. P.:
(1) *Sootnošenie kategorij istoričeskogo materializma* (Correlation of the Categories of Historical Materialism), L., 1958.
(2) *O cennostjax žizni i kul'tury* (On the Values of Life and Culture), L., 1960.
(3) 'Kommunizm i ličnost'' (Communism and the Person), *VF* 1962, 6, pp. 14–23.
(4) *Ličnost' i obščestvo* (The Person and Society), M., 1965.
(5) *Kommunizm i ličnost'* (Communism and the Person), M., 1966.
(6) *Teorija cennostej v marksizme* (The Theory of Values in Marxism), L., 1968.

Tugarinov, V. P., Majstrov, L. A.: 'Gegen den Idealismus in der mathematischen Logik', in *Über formale Logik und Dialektik.*

Turovskij, M. B.: *Trud i myšlenie* (Work and Thought), M., 1963.

Über formale Logik und Dialektik, Berlin, 1952.

Učennye zapiski. Tartu GU (Scientific Reports of Tartu University), vypusk 165, Tartu, 1965.

Uemov, A. I.:
(1) *Vešči, svojstva i otnošenija* (Things, Properties and Relations), M., 1963.
(2) 'Ontologičeskie predposylki logiki' (Ontological Presuppositions of Logic), *VF* 1969, 1.

Ukraincev, B. S.: 'Processy samoupravlenija i pričinnost'' (Causality and Processes of Self-Regulation), *VF* 1968, 4, pp. 36–46.

Venable, V.: *Human Nature: the Marxian View*, N.Y., 1945.

Wetter, G. A.:
   (1) *Der dialektische Materialismus: Seine Geschichte und Sein System in der Sowjetunion*, Freiburg, 1960.
   (2) *Soviet Ideology Today*, London, 1966.

INDEX OF NAMES

INDEX OF SUBJECTS

SOVIETICA

Publications and Monographs of the Institute
of East-European Studies, University of Fribourg, Switzerland

1. BOCHEŃSKI, J. M. and BLAKELEY, TH. J. (eds.): *Bibliographie der sowjetischen Philosophie*. I: *Die 'Voprosy filosofii' 1947–1956*. 1959, VIII + 75 pp.
2. BOCHEŃSKI, J. M. and BLAKELEY, TH. J. (eds.): *Bibliographie der sowjetischen Philosophie*. II: *Bücher 1947–1956; Bücher und Aufsätze 1957–1958; Namenverzeichnis 1947–1958*. 1959, VIII + 109 pp.
3. BOCHEŃSKI, J. M.: *Die dogmatischen Grundlagen der sowjetischen Philosophie (Stand 1958)*. Zusammenfassung der *'Osnovy Marksistskoj Filosofii' mit Register*. 1959, XII + 84 pp.
4. LOBKOWICZ, NICOLAS (ed.): *Das Widerspruchsprinzip in der neueren sowjetischen Philosophie*. 1960, VI + 89 pp.
5. MÜLLER-MARKUS, SIEGFRIED: *Einstein und die Sowjetphilosophie. Krisis einer Lehre.* I: *Die Grundlagen. Die spezielle Relativitätstheorie*. 1960. (Out of print.)
6. BLAKELEY, TH. J.: *Soviet Scholasticism*. 1961, XIII + 176 pp.
7. BOCHEŃSKI, J. M. and BLAKELEY, TH. J. (eds.): *Studies in Soviet Thought*, I. 1961, IX + 141 pp.
8. LOBKOWICZ, NICOLAS: *Marxismus-Leninismus in der ČSR. Die tschechoslowakische Philosophie seit 1945*. 1962, XVI + 268 pp.
9. BOCHEŃSKI, J. M. and BLAKELEY, TH. J. (eds.): *Bibliographie der sowjetischen Philosophie*. III: *Bücher und Aufsätze 1959–1960*. 1962, X + 73 pp.
10. BOCHEŃSKI, J. M. and BLAKELEY, TH. J. (eds.): *Bibliographie der sowjetischen Philosophie*. IV: *Ergänzungen 1947–1960*. 1963, XII + 158 pp.
11. FLEISCHER, HELMUT: *Kleines Textbuch der kommunistischen Ideologie. Auszüge aus dem Lehrbuch 'Osnovy marksizma-leninizma' mit Register*. 1963, XIII + 116 pp.
12. JORDAN, ZBIGNIEW A.: *Philosophy and Ideology. The Development of Philosophy and Marxism-Leninism in Poland since the Second World War*. 1963, XII + 600 pp.
13. VRTAČIČ, LUDVIK: *Einführung in den jugoslawischen Marxismus-Leninismus. Organisation. Bibliographie*. 1963, X + 208 pp.
14. BOCHEŃSKI, J. M.: *The Dogmatic Principles of Soviet Philosophy (as of 1958). Synopsis of the 'Osnovy Marksistskoj Filosofii' with complete index*. 1963, XII + 78 pp.
15. BIRJUKOV, B. V.: *Two Soviet Studies on Frege*. Translated from the Russian and edited by Ignacio Angelelli. 1964, XXII + 101 pp.
16. BLAKELEY, TH. J.: *Soviet Theory of Knowledge*. 1964, VII + 203 pp.
17. BOCHEŃSKI, J. M. and BLAKELEY, TH. J. (eds.): *Bibliographie der sowjetischen Philosophie*. V: *Register 1947–1960*. 1964, VI + 143 pp.
18. BLAKELEY, THOMAS J.: *Soviet Philosophy. A General Introduction to Contemporary Soviet Thought*. 1964, VI + 81 pp.

19. BALLESTREM, KARL G.: *Russian Philosophical Terminology* (in Russian, English, German, and French). 1964, VIII + 116 pp.
20. FLEISCHER, HELMUT: *Short Handbook of Communist Ideology. Synopsis of the 'Osnovy marksizma-leninizma' with complete index*. 1965, XIII + 97 pp.
21. PLANTY-BONJOUR, G.: *Les catégories du matérialisme dialectique. L'ontologie soviétique contemporaine*. 1965, VI + 206 pp.
22. MÜLLER-MARKUS, SIEGFRIED: *Einstein und die Sowjetphilosophie. Krisis einer Lehre.* II: *Die allgemeine Relativitätstheorie*. 1966, X + 509 pp.
23. LASZLO, ERVIN: *The Communist Ideology in Hungary. Handbook for Basic Research*. 1966, VIII + 351 pp.
24. PLANTY-BONJOUR, G.: *The Categories of Dialectical Materialism. Contemporary Soviet Ontology*. 1967, VI + 182 pp.
25. LASZLO, ERVIN: *Philosophy in the Soviet Union. A Survey of the Mid-Sixties*. 1967, VIII + 208 pp.
26. RAPP, FRIEDRICH: *Gesetz und Determination in der Sowjetphilosophie. Zur Gesetzes-konzeption des dialektischen Materialismus unter besonderer Berücksichtigung der Diskussion über dynamische und statistische Gesetzmässigkeit in der zeitgenössischen Sowjetphilosophie*. 1968, XI + 174 pp.
27. BALLESTREM, KARL G.: *Die sowjetische Erkenntnismetaphysik und ihr Verhältnis zu Hegel*. 1968, IX + 189 pp.
28. BOCHEŃSKI, J. M. and BLAKELEY, TH. J. (eds.): *Bibliographie der sowjetischen Philosophie*. VI: *Bücher und Aufsätze 1961–1963*. 1968, XI + 195 pp.
29. BOCHEŃSKI, J. M. and BLAKELEY, TH. J. (eds.): *Bibliographie der sowjetischen Philosophie*. VII: *Bücher und Aufsätze 1964–1966. Register*. 1968, X + 311 pp.
30. PAYNE, T. R.: *S. L. Rubinštejn and the Philosophical Foundations of Soviet Psychology*. 1968, X + 184 pp.
31. KIRSCHENMANN, PETER PAUL: *Information and Reflection. On Some Problems of Cybernetics and How Contemporary Dialectical Materialism Copes with Them*. 1970, XV + 225 pp.